SO-CRS-046

PROBLEM SOLVING:

Toward a More Humanizing Curriculum

by

OTTO HOLLAWAY

Professor Emeritus,
Auburn University
School of Education

FRANKLIN PUBLISHING COMPANY

Philadelphia

Copyright © 1975 by Otto Hollaway
Library of Congress Catalog Card No.: 74-80139
ISBN No. 0-87133-006-7
All Rights Reserved
Manufactured in the United States of America

375.001
H719p
LB
1555
.H77
1206182

Preface

This book, *Problem Solving: Toward a More Humanizing Curriculum,* comes at an opportune time, when educators and the general public are searching for more purposeful and relevant educational programs that can educate *all* American children and youth in keeping with each individual's capacity and needs.

Much has happened in education during the past few decades. World War II took the spot-light off the serious shortcomings of American education and possibly checked the development of a nationalized system of education which has become an increasing threat each year since the late fifties. The movement toward national assessment programs and other restrictions can result in a national curriculum, destroying local autonomy, creativity, experimentation and democracy as a way of life.

Many leading educators endeavored to launch reforms after World War II aimed at making education more responsive to the needs of students and a democratic society. A large number of outstanding experimental programs were moving effectively forward but were challenged by critics of life-centered, problem-centered education like Bestor, Conant, Hutchins and Rickover. These critics and many others became more vocal following the launching of Sputnik in 1957. Such events created doubt in the minds of many Americans concerning the quality of American education and its leadership. Pressures demanded a return to the uniform college preparatory subject-centered curriculum. Such pressures resulted in millions of the taxpayers' dollars being poured into the National Science Foundation; the National Defense Education Act; the Elementary and Secondary Education Act; and many other acts which have supplied millions for research (on how to impart information more effectively); expanding state departments of education; new buildings; school libraries; visual aids; instructional equipment and supplies; state owned textbooks; programs for the disadvantaged and gifted. These efforts largely dictated the nature and quality of the learning experiences of pupils—a move toward a national curriculum which is too rarely questioned by the recipients.

Foundations have contributed many millions to promote program developments in television, programmed instruction and many other projects deemed important by the administrators of the foundations. School systems had to acquiesce to the objectives of the foundations before receiving the aid, seriously curbing local experimentation and creativity too frequently.

175095

Propaganda about the effectiveness of new devices and gadgets impress too many readers. I am willing to acknowledge *some* improvements in education are evident from the expenditure of many millions and the inertia created by the haloes and ballyhoos but soon the procedures, in the majority of classrooms, revert back to the old process of imparting information rather than helping students *learn how to learn* and cope with realistic life situations because the teachers have not experienced changes in philosophy, concepts of learning, uniqueness of individuals and etc.; therefore when the halo effect is over they demand uniform learning for all, with possibly some provision for learning the required content at a varied rate on the pretense—individual differences are being taken care of.

I have watched and studied these programs aimed at innovating educational practices and have been impressed again and again with the *lack* of understanding so many people in education have of the *change process.* To change an educational program all individuals involved and affected by the program *must change.* Each individual must change his perceptions of: the role of education, objectives, learning process, growth and development, guidance, nature of each unique individual, leadership, role playing, planning, group processes, individualized instruction, role and function of drill, and evaluation. People change through continuous democratic cooperative interaction involving all who are affected.

Problem Solving: Toward a More Humanizing Curriculum can meet these challenges. This guide to curriculum improvement will help all to feel more adequate, to develop more realistic goals, to seek alternative courses of action, to venture and experiment with new innovations, to project and test varied hypotheses, to draw generalizations and conclusions, to synthesize learning, to evaluate learning outcomes and processes, to apply learning to life situations and solve life problems resulting in adequate fully functioning individuals.

OTTO HOLLAWAY

Acknowledgments

The author is indebted to thousands of men and women who have made important contributions to this book: the teachers, administrators and supervisors who served as co-workers in the public schools during the author's twenty years as a teacher and administrator; the host of teachers, administrators and supervisors the author has been privileged to work with as a consultant during the past twenty-eight years; the thousands of graduate students in his classes in curriculum, supervision and administration over a span of twenty-seven years. They are too numerous to designate by name.

A group deserving special mention includes Dr. R. L. Johns, Dr. John Lovell, Dr. Paul Irvine, Dr. Kimble Wiles, Dr. Harold Alberty, Dr. Jack Frymier, Dr. Paul Chlore, Dr. Gordon Vars, Dr. Roland Faunce, Dr. Nelson Bossing, Dr. Louise Hock, Dr. Vernon Anderson, Dr. Louise Parrish, Dr. Rosland Zaph, Dr. Morrel Clute, Dr. Gertrude Noar—individuals with whom the author has served as a co-worker on national commissions who gave inspiration.

The author is indebted to a large group of colleagues in the School of Education of Auburn University who encouraged the writing of this book and reviewed and evaluated much of the manuscript.

The author is indebted to two guest writers: Dr. Morrel J. Clute who contributed the major portion of Chapter 8; and Dr. Wayne Jennings who contributed Chapter 9.

The author owes a debt of gratitude to Dr. Gertrude E. Mitchell who did extensive editing of the draft submitted to the publisher.

Many thanks are due Dean Truman Pierce who read and evaluated the work, recommended editorial assistance, and wrote the Foreword.

My wife deserves much credit for her sacrifices and encouragements.

Foreword

The expansion of educational purpose is an enlightening chapter in the evolution of the American public school system. Beginning with the limited, but important, objectives of making students literate in order that they might better serve their church and nation, schools today are charged with objectives covering almost the full range of human interests and aspirations. The seven cardinal principles of education developed by a special study commission and reported in 1918 embrace virtually every avenue of acceptable human activity.

The real programs of education, however, have not kept pace with expanding concepts of the role of the school in society. In fact, schools have never adequately achieved their goals with substantial numbers of their students, even in the era of limited objectives. The gap between what schools should do as defined by public expectations and what they actually accomplish is probably of more serious consequence today than at any other period in history.

Education does little about most of its stated goals. It continues to stress acquisition of information and command of the fundamental processes of learning to the neglect of other goals. While these two objectives are indispensable, their emphasis does not preclude consideration of other objectives to which the public has long been committed such as those concerned with health, economic adequacy, wise use of leisure time and competence as a citizen.

It seems, therefore, that the major problem of schools today is the development of curriculum and teaching programs which express adequately the purposes schools are to serve. This problem may be viewed as including two major dimensions: choosing the most appropriate content for study and utilizing this content to serve maximally the interests and needs of all students.

Dr. Hollaway eloquently identifies some of the weaknesses of present day schools in terms of both of these dimensions. He goes further by stating that for a distressingly large percentage of students, the net effect of school experience is opposite to that intended.

No being content with merely citing shortcomings, Dr. Hollaway proposes his own remedies. His remedies stem from three sources—philosophic commitment (purpose), needed social adequacy and psychological soundness. A fourth source of justification may be defined as humane consideration of the learner as an individual. The author interrelates these sources into an organismic whole upon which he bases needed curriculum and teaching programs.

Dr. Hollaway then takes on the task of describing a learning program which satisfies the need for educational reform as he defines it. The essence of his teaching and learning system is recognition of individual need, developing an educational program for the individual in terms of this need which takes into account the background of experience and uniqueness of each learner. The heart of his instructional methodology is problem solving in a way which takes into appropriate account the individuality of each student and his cultural environment. In short, his educational program is built on student needs and perceptions with the initiative of the student being central to his own learning.

This large package which Dr. Hollaway has put together is one greatly needed in most of the schools of today.

TRUMAN M. PIERCE, *Dean*
School of Education
Auburn University

Contents

problem solving curriculum can provide a growing process of hypotheses and tests which can enable students to develop a conceptual basis for experimentation.

Implementing curriculum reorganization through problem solving involves careful planning and democratic leadership at every level of the school program: central office, individual school, team, and team-pupil levels.

How teachers and students perceive their relationship with each other in a problem solving situation is central to what is taught and what is learned; the best learning environment stimulates the individual to reach constantly for new horizons, understanding, and experiences.

Five examples from schools are presented to show how problem solving can lead to innovative learning situations; the illustrations range from major application of a learning unit to briefer ones.

Problem solving focuses upon the learner's diverse interests,
needs, and abilities by its firm commitment to a concept of
caring about individual differences of all students who are
educable and who are in school—no matter in which social
strata they fall.
On the preservice level, future teachers, administrators, coun-

selors, supervisors, and curriculum workers who will work in problem solving learning environments will need an entirely different kind of philosophical, sociological, and psychological orientation from what has been given for the subject centered curriculum; at the in-service level, personnel will require careful retraining and those who have had preservice preparation will need to continue study through summer workshops.

Facilities and available materials can either complement or complicate educational processes; competent teachers can teach more effectively in well-ventilated, acoustically controlled, and well-lighted learning laboratories than in the confines of dimly lit, clamor-ridden, isolated cells.

Evaluation traditionally has been used as a means to eliminate the less capable students through standardized grading and testing; problem solving evaluation is ongoing from the initial planning sessions to the final discussion of learning outcomes by teachers and students.

PROBLEM SOLVING:

Toward a More Humanizing
Curriculum

Introduction: Reorganizing the Curriculum

Failure of the Subject Centered Curriculum

Each year this nation's children and youth are committed to an institution known as the public school. By law they are compelled to spend a large portion of their waking hours within its walls for a period up to, but not more than 12 years. Parents and children are assured that the school will develop and prepare individual students for adult life, though teachers and administrators in the schools have seldom thought clearly and concisely what they will do in terms of preparation and how.

It is hard to criticize public education without calling curriculum into question. Most recently, during the 1960's, students began to protest the lack of relevance and purpose of the traditional educational curriculum — particularly the lack of relationship between what they were taught and what they were experiencing in real life. Within that same decade, some leading pioneers in educational thinking also questioned the validity of what the school was doing to boys and girls. Critic John Holt has written:

> . . . I used to feel that I was guiding and helping my students on a journey that they wanted to take but could not take without my help. I knew the way looked hard, but I assumed they could see the goal almost as clearly as I and that they were almost eager to reach it. . . . I see now that most of my talk to this end was wasted breath. . . . Given their own way, they would have none of it.
>
> So the valiant and resolute bank of travelers I thought I was leading toward a much-hoped-for destination turned out instead to be more like convicts in a chain gang, forced under the threat of punishment to move along a rough path leading nobody knew where and down which they could see hardly more than a few steps ahead. . . .
>
> For children, the central business of school is not learning, whatever this vague word means; it is getting these daily tasks done, or at least out of the way, with a minimum of effort and unpleasantness. Each task is an end in itself. The children don't care how they dispose of it. . . .[1]

Critic Leslie Hart has severely criticized the subject centered academic school for its stereotyped pattern of organization, paralleling children

---

[1] John Holt, *How Children Fail* (New York: Pitman Publishing Corp., 1964), pp. 15-16.

in schools to animals in cages. He deplores this confining environment, citing the teacher's role:

> We may note that teachers not unnaturally deceive themselves enormously as a rule. It is the other teachers who are at fault! A teacher really must believe he or she is "teaching" the children, helping them, benefiting them, to retain mental health. The strict, blatantly directive teacher; the warm, gentle, persuasive teacher; and the cold, distant, authoritative teacher — all will insist on the validity of their approach. . . .
>
> The teacher desperately wants the right answer because it is cue and permission to proceed to the next material to be covered. The better and kinder teachers may lead; but few children are so stupid that they do not early realize they must suffer themselves to be led. . . . All of this stems from the effort to teach, to force certain predetermined "learning" upon the child — and worse, to force it upon a group of children in brash defiance of their differences and the variations of input materials they bring to the situation. . . .[2]

But criticism of the subject centered curriculum and the departmentalized school has persisted for many decades. John Dewey called the traditional subject centered school unsound and inadequate for a dynamic society.

> The main purpose or objective is to prepare the young for future responsibilities and for success in life, by means of acquisition of the organized bodies of information and prepared forms of skill which comprehend the material of instruction. Since the subject matter as well as standards of proper conduct are handed down from the past, the attitude of the pupils must, upon the whole, be one of docility, receptivity, and obedience. . . .
>
> Subject matter is taught as a finished product, with little regard to the ways in which it was originally built up or to changes that will surely occur in the future. It is to a large extent the cultural product of societies that assumed the future would be much like the past, and yet it is used as educational food in a society where change is the rule, not the exception. . . .[3]

Dewey insisted that an individual can live only in the present and that the present is not merely an extension or product of the past. Knowledge of the past and its heritage is of real significance, he contended, *only* when it enters into the present; the present generates the problems which lead one to search the past for meaning. Therefore, an individual does not turn his back upon the past, but uses it as a means for understanding and coping with the present.

---

[2] Leslie A. Hart, *The Classroom Disaster* (New York: Teachers College Press, 1969), pp. 293-295.

[3] John Dewey, *Experience and Education* (New York: Collier Books, 1938), pp. 18-23.

The inadequacies of the subject centered curriculum are long in number and serious in effect. What we call "the public school" has resulted in a structured program so divided that no unity or inter-relationship exists between what is learned in one class and what is learned in another. Its primary focus is upon collecting, assimilating, and transmitting a set of facts within a given discipline in order that the student may regurgitate them when examined. Whitehead said many years ago: "There is only one subject matter for education and that is life in all of its manifestations."

The best that can be said of the subject centered curriculum is that it is a rapid succession of recorded events that may be run over in the mind of an individual and which may have no impact upon his behavior or upon improvement of the society. It almost totally ignores and neglects the past experiences, aspirations, interests, needs, and uniqueness of the individual learner.

Directed toward the mastery of subject matter in a uniform manner, it demands the same learning of all individuals — without regard for their need for such learning or how they can apply it in solving individual problems. Proponents of the subject centered curriculum look upon an individual's ability to master contents within a text or manual as evidence that learning has taken place. Such simplistic reasoning is contrary to the newer learning concepts that:

1. Learning is resolving a tension, overcoming an obstacle standing in the way of the achievement of a goal the learner needs or wants to achieve;
2. Learning is an interacting process involving the total organism and the total life situation;
3. Learning is discovery of personal meaning resulting in changed behavior.

Many teachers and administrators in the subject centered curriculum situation are making efforts to care for individual differences through pacing, individualized instruction, and nongraded concepts using programmed materials; but they still expect uniform results from their students. While each learner may progress at his own rate, the content remains fixed, without regard for individual needs and abilities. Such approaches are relatively satisfactory when the major objectives are directed toward the mastery of skills within the lower levels of cognitive learning. On these levels, facts, patterns, trends, structures, principles, and settings can be recalled. The approaches also work in using intellectual abilities to organize materials for memorization and recall and on the lowest level of understanding for translating, interpreting, and summarizing.

But these approaches rarely help students to see the application of the outcome to unique and changing life situations, nor is there much opportunity to analyze relationships among interacting elements and parts or to check consistency of hypotheses. Such students, as a rule, are unable to synthesize and put together elements and parts to form a whole or to derive abstract relationships. They are unable to determine through evaluation if the materials and methods satisfy the quantitative and qualitative criteria of logic, accuracy, consistency, and high standards. The subject centered curriculum, in practice, largely ignores the higher levels of cognitive learning and gives little attention to the affective domain where the individual is receptive and open to new stimuli.

The traditional curriculum is ineffective in its arranging of subjects, drawing heavily on three orders:

1. The chronological approach which starts with the beginning of time and comes up as nearly as possible to the present;
2. The inductive approach which begins with the elementary or simple and moves toward abstract and generalized concepts;
3. The deductive approach which moves from the whole to its parts.

Chronology is used in history, economics, and political science. Induction occurs in mathematics (beginning with numerals, moving into addition, subtraction, multiplication, division, and then to higher processes) and in biology (starting with one-cell plants and animals, then to multi-cell ones). Deduction is found in geography, art, and music (after studying a total concept it is broken down into parts). Each of these approaches violates much of what is known about the psychological order of learning in which the learning situation is related to the child and his present background of experiences, interests, and needs so that each individual will be learning something uniquely different from the others.

In its reliance upon these three orders, the subject centered curriculum fails to develop effective methods reflective thinking or try out innovative ideas. Its ready-made answers rule out alternatives. It need not project hypotheses or collect and organize information to test them. It need not draw generalizations and conclusions or evaluate them. Worst of all, it need not apply solutions to everyday life.

The subject centered curriculum has been molded from the rigid materials of essentialism, authoritarianism, and materialism. Essentialism implies certain basic essentials that all people must know in the same order and to the same degree that other people possess such knowledge, if they are to be educated. Authoritarianism indicates that, in order to learn the essentials, there must be someone in authority — usually the teacher and school administrator — to see that each student masters said materials in a minimum way. Materialism points up the primary concern with materials to be covered, content to be memorized, and a cultural heritage to be transmitted. It dwells safely in the past, ignoring the contemporary or future world.

The storage concept of learning which it follows conceives of the school function as preparation for future living: The student stores information for later use. But we know this concept of learning is unsound and uneconomical because only when individuals frequently use information do they remember it. While it is true that the human organism can be conditioned just as can a rat or a guinea pig, this is none the less the lower level of education — a process of training rather than an experience of learning.

Leslie R. Perry has drawn together the objections to the traditional curriculum which were made by four of the best known writers and practitioners experimenting with reform early in this century: Bertrand Russell, A. S. Neill, Homer Lane, and W. H. Kilpatrick. Perry summarized their objections in these nine points:

1. Its (subject centered curriculum) aim was to see that a body of knowledge was learned and memorized.
2. Its method of testing was by recall of what had been taught.
3. The relationship of teacher and pupil was strictly formal, not personal.
4. Attitudes of the pupil to what was being learned were irrelevant.
5. The teacher dominated in subject matter, procedure of learning, and discipline; no responsibility was allowed for the pupils.
6. The pupil was assumed to know nothing and was expected to be basically passive.
7. If control were relaxed the pupil would behave wildly, like a young animal.
8. What went on in school, while preparatory to serious living, had no immediate connection with it.
9. Children were assumed the same at any age; therefore roughly the same manner of presentation would suffice for a school life.[4]

[4] Perry, Leslie R., ed., Bertrand Russell, A.S. Neill, Homer Lane, W.H. Kilpatrick, Four Progressive Educators (New York: Macmillan Co., 1967). pp. 15–16.

Today, many years after Russell, Neill, Lane, and Kilpatrick raised these objections to public school curriculum and despite criticisms of many others in the meantime, the traditional fare — disunified, inflexible, dehumanized, and artificial — continues to prevail in the 12-year institution.

Curriculum Reorganization through Problem Solving

But school curriculum need not be disunified, inflexible, dehumanized, and artificial. A school which would for the most part abandon the old curriculum for one using the problem solving approach could evolve a program which is inter-related, flexible, humanized, and individualized.

Problem solving is the process of overcoming difficulties or obstacles encountered in the attainment of a goal or objective which the learner needs or wants to achieve. He seeks to relieve his tension and restore his organism to a state of inner equilibrium and of equilibrium with his environment. Effective problem solving is a comprehensive process of receiving, blending, comparing, contrasting, projecting, generalizing, deriving, inferring, relating, synthesizing, and evaluating. It cuts across all subject areas as students attempt to solve a given problem. It is committed to the concept of educating a total child — intellectually, socially, emotionally, and physically. It is most effectively implemented with a large block of time consuming from one-third to two-thirds of the school day, enabling students and teachers to go out into the community and grapple with realistic problems in their natural setting. The teachers come to know each student as a distinct person. In its reliance on team teaching, the problem solving approach emphasizes the team rather than the individual teacher through cooperative planning, execution, and evaluation of the learning outcome. Each individual teacher plays the role in which he is most proficient while helping students work through the problem. Team teaching widens the range of human resources to facilitate the learning processes: efficient planners, expediters, discussion leaders, production helpers, record keepers, listeners and evaluators.

Reorganizing the curriculum through problem solving can help to dispel many myths held by educators and laymen about the function of education. It would overcome the fixed notion that the school exists to transmit the cultural heritage and to impart information. In problem solving the school is a place where people learn how to learn and become efficient, effective, and responsible citizens in their everyday affairs. It would strike at the misapprehension that there are thousands and thousands of students in our schools who are not interested in learning. In truth, they are not interested in what the subject centered school has insisted that they learn. Problem solving can also dispel the idea that thousands and thousands of students

6

from lower socioeconomic, ethnic, and racial groups who have suffered social deprivation are incapable of learning. It can help erase the notion that intelligence is almost totally determined at birth so that little can be done to overcome inadequacies allegedly demonstrated by an intelligence test. And it can counter the mistaken impression that changing the curriculum means developing another course of study, writing a new syllabus, or providing fresh textbook materials.

These reasons point up the value of the problem solving approach:

1. Identifying and using student problems enables teachers to take advantage of factors like interests, needs, past experiences.
2. Providing continuous practice in problem solving is preparing young people for active, responsible roles in community activities.
3. Working on actual problems is synonymous with critical thinking; educational psychologists today see thinking and problem solving as one and the same.
4. Problems of boys and girls are closely interwoven with activities, issues, problems and trends in their communities.
5. In identifying their own problems, boys and girls come to see value, use, and significance in special subject areas; these areas by their inter-relatedness often throw light on problems, suggest ideas, and provide new skills in the correlation of life situations.
6. Working together on common problems builds a sense of community pride, widening of interests, common purposes, common loyalties, common views, and improved citizenship.
7. Practice in problem solving gives young people confidence in their own abilities and those of their neighbors.
8. Young people learn the special research and critical thinking skills that enable groups to solve problems effectively.
9. They learn, too, that many social problems are never solved in any final sense; problems are juvenile delinquency, drug addiction, pollution, and war are apparently continuing ones, requiring study throughout their lives.
10. Pupils learn to respect differences in ability, background, viewpoints, philosophies, and values. Some differences can be resolved, they find, in dealing with common problems while others are respected as continuing variations in fundamental outlook.
11. Because problem solving learning is developed in terms of the actual problems of young people and society, the organized bodies of subject matter of many disciplines are employed as resource materials.

7

But, given these advantages, how is problem solving actually implemented? For its most effective use, problem solving needs a large block of time — perhaps one-third to two-thirds of the school day — so that teachers and students may go out into the field or community for research and investigation. It would incorporate teams of three to eight teachers responsible for 75 to 200 students.

By no means is problem solving a simplistic exercise of selecting the problem and then turning the students loose. Nor does it fall into the errors of progressive education by doing projects merely to please the students. Problem solving is hard work; the role of the teacher illustrates this fact. The team of teachers is constantly involved — and in turn involving countless other resource persons — in the early process of planning, an ongoing period of many discussions with student groups, and an aftermath of detailed evaluation of procedures and learning outcomes. Instead of a lecturer standing each day in front of the class, the team teacher becomes a facilitator of behavior change and of the learning process. He understands and is committed to the purposes and concepts of problem solving–team teaching, the problems and concerns of his students, the possibilities of large- and small-group processes and techniques, and the idea that he is a member of a team.

Problem solving also means hard work for the students. Instead of sitting quietly until called upon to recite the "correct" answer, the students must actively involve themselves in a search for possible answers. They are organized into large groups and small seminar subgroups for systematic study, discussion, and planning and which can be extended further into individual study and analysis. Flexible grouping is encouraged for the seminars, allowing students to shift from one group to another in terms of individual interests and needs.

There are no sequential arrangements or processes that necessarily need to be followed in all problem solving situations, although they will inevitably involve defining and delineating the problem and its subproblems, selecting information and projecting various hypotheses to determine the most valid, testing out the feasibility of these hypotheses, drawing various generalizations and conclusions, and evaluating not only the outcomes of the problem, but the processes used throughout the experience. Bingham has suggested the following processes as possibilities.

1. Identifying the problem and developing a feeling and motivation that will result in the pursuit of a solution;
2. Seeking to clarify and limit the problem and to understand its nature and subproblems;

3. Determining the various possible solutions in the light of knowledge presently available or projecting reasonable hypotheses;
4. Collecting data and information that may be pertinent to the problem;
5. Selecting, organizing, and systematically ordering the data which applies most pertinently to the crux of the problem;
6. Drawing generalizations and conclusions if the hypotheses are supported;
7. Putting the solution into action:
   a. Does the action satisfactorily reduce or overcome the difficulty encountered?
   b. Are the implications for action or use of procedures for solving the problem clearly recognized?
   c. Does the solution promote changes in feelings or attitudes which are helpful in implementing action?
   d. Is the solution one that will be lasting?
   e. Is the solution consistent within all aspects?
   f. Is the solution a positive one and will it be accepted by individuals affected?
   g. Is the solution carried with conviction and confidence?
   h. Is the solution in keeping with the capabilities, interests, and resources of the group?
   i. Are the limits of the solution defined?
   j. Is the solution such that it will help prevent subsequent similar problems?
8. Evaluating the problem solving process employed as well as the outcomes.[5]

The chapters which follow argue strongly for curriculum reorganization through problem solving–team teaching. The early chapters establish its pragmatic, humanistic, and democratic qualities as well as its social and psychological soundness within a dynamic society. Actual curricular reshaping, teaching and learning processes, and the uniqueness of the individual are then discussed. Examples of effective problem solving situations are offered. Two special needs — for trained personnel and for physical facilities — are presented by guest writers, Dr. Morrel J. Clute and Dr. Wayne Jennings. Finally, the use of evaluation in discovering the total learning process and outcome in problem solving is explained.

Perhaps the strongest argument for problem solving–team teaching is

---

[5] Alma Bingham, *Improving Children's Facility in Problem Solving* (New York: Teachers College, Columbia University, 1963) . pp. 13–21.

9

that it helps to create a learning situation through group inquiry which gives its participants an earned feeling of accomplishment. It can be seen in the examples appearing in Chapter 6. For the student problem solving is a challenge to think and learn rather than recite back the textbook's answers. Among the examples in Chapter 6 is this one: 123 tenth graders, four classroom teachers, an aide, and numerous resource persons worked four hours each school day for eight weeks on a problem: "Improving the Quality of Living Through the Wise Use and Protection of the Resources and Environment." During the eight weeks, they:

1. Wrote news articles, booklets, and letters;
2. Consulted resource personnel from government and private agencies;
3. Made field trips to observe the problem first-hand to water filtration plants, farms, fields, forests, streams, wildlife reservations, fish hatcheries, tree nurseries, and energy plants;
4. Collected documented materials;
5. Developed a list of special vocabulary words relating to the subject;
6. Did soil borings to test erosion;
7. Built a balanced aquarium and a balanced terrarium;
8. Set up controlled experiments of plant and animal food and nutrition;
9. Landscaped the schoolgrounds and resodded parts;
10. Conducted soil tests to determine how soil and water can be saved;
11. Studied and tested out local car pollution;
12. Prepared model farm and city homes for community and fair display;
13. Depicted the problem through posters and other art media;
14. Studied in depth the world's natural resources depletion;
15. Constructed graphs and charts to show use of natural resources;
16. Wrote and acted out a dramatic skit summarizing the group's efforts;
17. Produced a movie on how to use and conserve environmental and natural resources.

BIBLIOGRAPHY

Aiken, Wilford, *The Story of the Eight-Year Study*. New York: Harper and Brothers, 1942.

Alexander, William M., ed., *The High School of the Future: A Memorial to Kimball Wiles*. Columbus, Ohio: Charles E. Merrill Publishing Co., 1969.

Beggs, David W., III, ed., *Team Teaching — Bold New Venture*. Indianapolis: Unified College Press, 1964.

Berman, Louise M., *New Priorities in the Curriculum*. Columbus, Ohio: Charles E. Merrill Publishing Co., 1968.

Bingham, Alma, *Improving Children's Facility in Problem Solving*. New York: Teachers College, Columbia University, 1963.

Blair, Medill and Richard G. Woodware, *Team Teaching in Action*. Boston: Houghton Mifflin Co., 1964.

Brubaker, Dale L., *The Teacher as a Decision-Maker*. Dubuque, Iowa: Wm. C. Brown Co., 1970.

Combs, Arthur W., ed., *Perceiving, Behaving, Becoming*. Washington, D.C.: Association for Supervision and Curriculum Development, 1962.

—————, *Educational Accountability*. Washington, D.C.: Association for Supervision and Curriculum Development, 1972.

Dewey, John, *The Child and the Curriculum — The School and Society*. Chicago: University of Chicago Press, 1943.

—————, *Democracy and Education*. New York: The Macmillan Company, 1967.

—————, *Experience and Education*. New York: Collier Books, 1938.

Doll, Ronald E. and Robert S. Fleming, eds., *Children Under Pressure*. Columbus, Ohio: Charles E. Merrill Books, Inc., 1966.

Doll, Ronald E., ed., *Individualizing Instruction*. Washington, D.C.: Association for Supervision and Curriculum Development, 1964.

Educational Policies Commission, *Education for All American Youth*. Washington, D.C.: 1945.

—————, *The Purposes of Education in American Democracy*. Washington, D.C.: 1938.

Eichhorn, Donald J., *The Middle School*. New York: The Center for Applied Research in Education, 1966.

Fenton, Edwin, *Teaching the New Social Studies in Secondary Schools: An Inductive Approach*. New York: Holt, Rinehart and Winston, 1966.

Grooms, M. Ann, *Perspectives on the Middle School*. Columbus, Ohio: Charles E. Merrill Books, 1967.

Hanna, Lavone A., Gladys L. Potter, and Neva Hagaman, *Unit Teaching in the Elementary School*. New York: Holt, Rinehart and Winston, 1963.

Hanslovsky, Glenda, Sue Moyer, and Helen Wagner, *Why Team Teaching?* Columbus, Ohio: Charles E. Merrill Publishing Co., 1969.

Hart, Leslie A., *The Classroom Disaster*. New York: Teachers College, Columbia University, 1969.

Haubrich, Vernon F., *Freedom, Bureaucracy and Schooling*. Washington, D.C.: Association for Supervision and Curriculum Development, 1971.

Henderson, George, *Education for Peace*. Washington, D.C.: Association for Supervision and Curriculum Development, 1973.

Hock, Louise E. and Thomas J. Hill, *The General Education Class in the Secondary School*. New York: Holt, Rinehart and Winston, 1960.

Holt, John, *How Children Fail*. New York: Pitman Publishing Corp., 1965.

Leeper, Robert R., *Curriculum Change: Direction and Process*. Washington, D.C.: Association for Supervision and Curriculum Development, 1966.

Marchak, John P., "Does Team Teaching Pay Off?" *Everyweek*, January 1968.

Neagley, Ross L. and N. Dean Evans, *Handbook for Effective Curriculum Development*. Englewood Cliffs, N.J.: Prentice-Hall, 1967.

Peterson, Carl H., *Effective Team Teaching: The Easton Area High School Program*. West Nyack, N.Y.: Parker Publishing Co., 1966.

Poles, Nicholas, *The Dynamics of Team Teaching*. Dubuque, Iowa: W.O. Brown Co., 1965.

Ratner, Joseph, ed., *Intelligence in the Modern World — John Dewey's Philosophy*. New York: Random House, 1939.

Shaplin, Judson T. and Henry F. Olds, Jr., *Team Teaching*. New York: Harper and Row, 1964.

Waskin, Yvonne and Louise Parrish, *Teacher–Pupil Planning for Better Classroom Learning*. New York: Pitman Publishing Corp., 1967.

Yamamots, Kaoru, ed., *The Child and His Image: Self-Concept*. Boston: Houghton Mifflin Co., 1972.

Chapter 1.   Philosophical Bases: Pragmatism, Humanism and Democracy

Curriculum reorganization through problem solving reflects the pragmatic, humanistic, and democratic philosophies of American education. In a democracy where the people participate in decisions affecting the welfare of their society, the school assumes a wider and more important role than in a dictatorship — where its main function is to teach official truth and to discourage independent thinking and action. In a democracy the schools must try not only to educate children and youth, but also adults. It must assume as well leadership in education for community living. The problem solving–team teaching concept particularly fulfills these responsibilities by its emphasis on individual and group cooperation in order to think through a specific problem.

The subject-centered curriculum is currently losing approximately thirty-five to fifty percent of youth through dropouts prior to the completion of high school. In addition to those who are dropping out or being pushed out, there are thousands upon thousands of additional youth who are merely occupying space, warming seats, and holding on because of external pressures from home, peers, and the community, with the hope that they may eventually receive a high school diploma which is essential for current employment. Even though they are staying on in school, they are receiving relatively little benefit since the school program is almost totally inappropriate and inadequate for their unique needs, interests, abilities, and future endeavors. If the present rate of dropouts and pushouts continues through the 1970's, we will be confronted with unemployment for approximately twenty-five percent of the adult population, a situation which would soon spell the doom to democracy in the United States. The educators and the general public must find a solution to the problem of caring for individual differences so that each and every American boy and girl will be educated to the fullest extent of his or her potential capacity in terms of interest, needs, abilities, and aptitudes. It is the contention of this writer that this problem can be solved successfully in a good problem-solving teaching school. There individual pupils are permitted to work at a large array and variety of learning experiences of varied difficulties which permit each individual to succeed which is so basic, to an adequate self-concept.

An individual who thinks well of himself and believes in himself has a feeling of can-ness. He thinks well of others, and sees himself in relationship to others and values his stake in others and realizes that he cannot fully succeed if he is selfish in his endeavors. He will see himself as a part of the world in movement and in a process of becoming, capable of coping with life's situations and life demands. Many individuals in the schools today have encountered repeated failures in practically all educational experiences. Such individuals will drop out of school and will fill our jails, reformatories, and mental institutions. They will be continuous burdens on society.

The transmission of the cultural heritage that once dominated education is now not only impractical but utterly impossible. It is generally agreed that today's high school and college graduates will have to retrain or be re-educated from four to six times during a life of normal expectancy. Therefore, it becomes the responsibility of the school to help boys and girls develop the efficiency to learn continuously after they have finished formal schooling.

In order for the student to discover personal meaning in the learning situation, he must see direct benefits to himself, colleagues, family, and society. Thus, the major function and responsibility of education must shift from the old concept of transmitting information and the cultural heritage to a more meaningful, realistic, and dynamic concept of critical thinking, problem-solving, and scientific discovery of knowledge needed to cope with life situations. The only sure preparation we can give them which will enable them to be effective tomorrow is to help them live successfully today. In the process of living successfully today, they learn how to discover and use information in the solution of problems. They are learning how to learn and will continue to learn long after they leave the schools and universities.

Pragmatism, a philosophy which has its origin in American thought and American traditions, reflects the principle of scientific problem solving; it further asserts that problem solving is best accomplished through a team or group effort and that problems should emerge from a social context. Childs in American *Pragmatism and Education* reinforces these principles:

> A variety of factors account for the pre-eminence of pragmatism in American thought and education. One is the fact that pragmatism is more than a philosopher's philosophy. Its emphasis on experience, on experimental activity, on the creative role of intelligence, and on the values and procedures of democracy brought these elements in the life of the American people into fuller consciousness and thereby

enhanced their influence in public affairs, including the enterprise of education.

The pragmatic movement also evoked general interest because it centered its attention on problems of common concern. . . .

The founders of pragmatism also preceived that the method of experimental science made necessary and at the same time provided the basis for a new interpretation of the nature and the pattern of reflective thought. . . .

Naturally, a philosophy which holds that experience can rest on its own bottom, and which proclaims the autonomy and the self-correcting character of experimental procedures, is responsive to the values implicit in political and social democracy. . . . As the pragmatists have emphasized, there is an intrinsic connection between freedom of thought and inquiry and the maintenance of a society cooperative controlled in the interest of the good life of all its members. . . .[1]

The schools are committed to implementing democracy as a way of life. This commitment has been articulated by the faculty of the College of Education at Ohio State University:

The fact that the public schools of America are free schools places upon them distinctive responsibilities. They were created by determined people experienced in the ways of freedom. Such people know that the battle for freedom is a continuing one. They know that freedom, difficult to gain, is easily lost. . . .

The public schools of America belong not to the boards of education, nor to teachers, nor to groups of influential citizens, but to all the people. No public school can withdraw from or neglect this relationship to the people who support it. . . .

An educational program that emphasizes these purposes has no place for an authoritarian blueprint, even though this be formulated by wise individuals or well-intentioned groups. . . . The distinctive characteristic of a free world is the encouragement given to all to participate in the planning of the common life. This is not less true of educational planning than it is of all other planning that free men do.[2]

Commitment of democracy means that the school program must be uniquely different from what it is in other types of social orders. George Counts puts this idea very succinctly:

We in America, in my judgment, have never given adequate thought to the development of an education that is suited to our

---

[1] John L. Childs, *American Pragmatism and Education* (New York: Henry Holt and Co., 1956), pp. IV and V of Preface.

[2] "A Statement by the Faculty, College of Education, The Ohio State University," *Educational Research Bulletin* 30 (December 12, 1951) : 225–226.

democracy, particularly in the present industrial age. If we ever do, the result will be something new in the history of education. It will express at the same time both the emphasis upon knowledge, understanding and enlightenment and the cultivation of the basic ethical values of democracy — devotion to equality, individual worth, intellectual freedom, political liberty, democratic processes, general welfare, and the mastery of relevant knowledge.[3]

A statement by John Dewey further emphasizes this commitment:

> A society which makes provision for participation in its goals of all its members on equal terms and which secures flexible readjustment of its institutions through interaction of the different forms of associated life is so far democratic. Such a society must have a type of education which gives individuals a personal interest in social relationships and control, and the habits of mind which secure social changes without introducing disorder.[4]

The four founders of pragmatism — Charles Sanders Pierce, John Dewey, William James, and George Herbert — were involved in a massive experiment. Part of this experiment involved the establishment of pragmatism as a viable philosophic base for democracy. Dewey devoted his entire professional career to an attempt to assure that the democracy envisioned by the pragmatist would be reflected extensively in educational practice throughout America. In many — if not most — American educational institutions past and present, the democracy of the pragmatists failed to achieve the intended goal.

A careful observation over the past decades will indicate that the concepts of pragmatism have had impact in law, government, industry, agriculture, literature, art, and religion more extensively than in education. A fundamental concept of the pragmatism which underlies these fields reflects that man must have a participatory function in establishing what is most beneficial to all. American education — since the turn of the twentieth century — has held the position that the principle of participatory function should be reflected in classroom procedures. Yet, today's schools as social institutions are being repeatedly criticized as authoritarian strongholds in which discipline and regulation have become the tematic emphasis. Through problem solving–team teaching schools, the pragmatic concepts of democracy can be realized to a degree never before attained. *But* we must stop overemphasizing the materialistic, mechanistic, and

---

[3] George S. Counts, "Education for Democracy," *The Phi Delta Kappan* 30 (February 1949) : 223.

[4] John Dewey, *Democracy and Education* (New York: The Macmillan Co., 1916), pp. 85 and 89.

lower cognitive learnings and turn our attention and energies toward humanizing education — helping learners discover personal meaning in each learning situation.

Problem solving–team teaching embodies the humanistic concept of education in that it is built around individual needs, interests, aptitudes, and abilities. A large percentage of the educational practices in this nation reflect an essentialist–authoritarian–materialistic philosophy, demanding basically the same learning of everyone — emphasizing preparation for the next higher rung of the educational ladder, future living, and mastery of content; transmitting the cultural heritage through uniform instructional materials; and evaluating in terms of rigid, predetermined standards. Such an educational program threatens rather than challenges American children and youths. And far too many of them are being severely injured by authoritarian environmental forces they are encountering in the home, schools, church, and community.

It is time education be humanized — making the learning situations in each classroom so meaningful and realistic that each student will daily discover personal meaning and changed behavior will result. Each learning situation should be so designed that boys and girls will employ critical thinking, thereby resolving tensions and overcoming obstacles standing in the way of the achievement of a goal *which the learner individually and collectively needs or wants to achieve.* Each student must have a reasonable degree of success each day of his school life if he is to gain acceptance, recognition, and status as a distinct personality. This success is necessary for the student's development of a positive and realistic attitude toward self, other people, and — in general — life. Such individuals develop a feeling of "can-ness," becoming willing to apply themselves in an effort toward self-realization. Such individuals will remain in school. They will be open to new experiences, willing to accept *increasing responsibilities* as they mature into *civically and socially responsible youths and adult citizens.*

Unfortunately, most boys and girls are biologically mature before they have their first opportunities to engage in meaningful problem solving situations. They cannot identify and select problems; project hypotheses; collect, organize, and use information; test hypotheses and draw conclusions; find viable solutions; evaluate outcomes and processes; and assume accountability for outcomes.

Humanism means much more than just subject matter or content. It is *an approach, a point of view, a set of purposes, a concept of the individual's worth, a philosophy.* Its content cannot be the same for any two learners.

16

Areas of learning like music, art, and literature are slightly more oriented toward humanizing education than the social sciences, physical sciences, behavioral sciences, and vocational offerings. But all areas have a humanizing impact upon the learner by helping him to commit himself to cherished goals, ideals, and values. Such learning does more than merely stretch the intellect; it also awakens emotions, ideals, appreciations, feelings, and commitment.

The subject centered curriculum, grounded in essentialism–authoritarianism–materialism, has multiplied the problems of humanizing education. According to Arthur W. Combs:

> Since people are human at birth, it would seem the problem of humanization ought to be no more difficult than strengthening and encouraging the tendencies with which people are born. Unfortunately, it is not that simple. . . . Instead of helping people to become more humane, we have created an incredible number of barriers in all our institutions, including education, that make the growth and development of humaneness a difficult task for students.
>
> Some of the forces which contribute to the processes of dehumanization and alienation are: technological revolution, the problems of urbanization, the explosion of information and the fetish of objectivity, which possesses us everywhere. . . .
>
> What makes people human are matters of feeling, belief, values, attitudes, understandings. Without these things a man is nothing. These are the qualities which make people human. They are also the qualities which make the education of people human. They are also the qualities which, in our zeal to be objective, we have carefully eliminated from much of what goes on in our public schools. . . .
>
> Everyone starts life with the capacity to become a good human being. People are not born bad or inhuman. The qualities we describe as human are "warm" qualities of compassion, understanding, fulfillment, love, caring, justice, and the like, while the qualities we describe as inhuman, on the other hand, are "cold" ones, generally the reverse of these. We speak of a man as "a good human being." By that we refer to his uniqueness and value as a person, his sensitivity and compassion for others, and his capacity to interact effectively in his world. . . .
>
> What kind of person an individual becomes is dependent in very large measure upon the kind of world we create for him to grow up in. As Earl Kelley tells us, "Whenever we get to worrying about the younger generation we need to remind ourselves that they were all right when we got them." After birth everyone becomes more or less human as a consequence of his experience. We learn who we are and what we are from the nature of our interactions, especially those with the significant people in our lives.[5]

[5] Mary Margaret Scobey, ed., *To Nurture Humaneness,* 1970 Association for Supervision and Curriculum Development Yearbook, pp. 173–174.

17

Rationalizations for Current Practices

Much of the curricular practice stems from imitation. There is safety in numbers. If a school has achieved wide publicity for the development of a certain curricular practice, many other schools attempt to install a similar program. But imitation is valuable *only* if the model we choose reflects sound principles.

Some individuals make curricular choices on the basis of emotional appeal. If the individual feels good about a particular activity because it gives emotional satisfaction, many people are inclined to continue these practices. On the other hand, when practices fail to give personal satisfaction, they are usually discarded. Emotional reactions can be very deceptive and misleading; if the curriculum is determined solely by this criterion, educational systems will suffer from resulting chaotic conditions.

Another justification for following certain curricular practices is that they seem to work. Having successfully tried something, many are convinced that the results are superior to what had been formerly done. Consequently, they continue to use similar practices in many other diverse situations, failing to realize that what works in one situation may not necessarily work in others.

A Better Basis: Sound Assumptions

Certain guides can be used philosophically to determine the soundness of assumptions. The first deals with its reliability: Does the assumption result regularly in the same or reasonably similar outcomes? If not, it is probably illogical. Many people base behavior on unreliable assumptions without having tested them.

A second criterion for judging the philosophical soundness of what we do is validity; a valid belief conforms to knowledge and experience upon subjection to various situations. For example, the law of gravity will work not only in terms of validity, but also reliability.

The final criterion is consistency. An assumption is consistent when it supports other beliefs. For example, many teachers express a belief in the dignity and worth of each individual pupil, and yet they frequently engage in ridicule and scorn, indicating an inconsistent philosophy. Problem solving's philosophical bases are reliable, valid, and consistent in terms of the *learner,* what is *taught and learned,* the *learning process,* and how we perceive the *role of the teacher.*

Problem solving–team teaching operates on the assumption that the individual is neither good nor bad, but by and large a product of his environment — an aspiring person endeavoring to gain self-fulfillment and feelings of adequacy and worth. A curriculum which reflects this philoso-

18

phy will support the theory that it is the business of the school to help make possible the optimal development of each individual. The aim of education is the development of the *unique* capabilities and potentialities of each individual to the greatest degree he is capable of developing and adjusting to a continually changing environment.

The problem solving curriculum would be built around the real problems which people meet in day-to-day living. It stresses that the individual can not only adjust to a changing environment, but also improve the environment and make life more tolerable. Such a concept places relatively little importance upon learning facts, imparting information, or transmitting those parts of the cultural heritage which do not relate to everyday problems. It is concerned instead with the importance of the individual learning how to learn.

The pragmatic, humanistic, and democratic philosophies undergirding problem solving–team teaching holds to the theory that knowledge can be constructed only in terms of the consequences of acting upon it. If an hypothesis works and gives desirable results, then a fact or principle is established. If it fails to work, it is discarded.

Problem solving relies primarily on the perceptual-field theories of learning. These theories hold that the ultimate in learning is to be achieved through solving a problem.

The problem solving concept is particularly democratic in its insistence that the school provide an opportunity for individuals to participate in important decisions affecting their well being. It provides many opportunities like cooperative formulation of policies for use in student self-government in the classroom, cafeteria, auditorium, gymnasium, or playground. Students have a participating role in deciding upon the criteria for the selection of problems; they help to identify instructional materials; they do various independent and group research. In these roles, the students have many opportunities to do independent thinking.

All too often American youths are expected to acquire a sense of responsibility through the lecture and preachment approach, without engaging in real decision-making. But democracy is a concept that is rarely — if ever — effectively taught; it can, though, be easily and consistently caught by repeated exposure through the human interactions among students, teachers, administrators, and adult citizens of the community. Many adult citizens are perplexed over increasing amounts of student freedom. Freedom is sometimes assumed to mean license to do as one pleases. However, the freedom provided in problem solving–team teaching is disciplined and guided so that the individual is able to make choices.

19

Freedom must be associated with responsibility; the two cannot be separated. It offers opportunities for individuals to live interdependently and collectively. The concept of sharing experiences is central to problem solving–team teaching; it assures freedom when individuals are living in groups and when they are working, discussing, expressing, and interacting continuously. Dr. Arthur W. Combs has written of the importance of experience through interaction for youths:

> If schools are going to be more human it is clear that they must become more relevant to the needs and experience of students and must find more effective ways to induce students to take a major responsibility for their own learning. . . .
>
> To meet the needs of students it will be necessary to involve them deeply. . . . Feelings of belonging and responsibility come about only as a consequence of feeling a part of and being given responsibility for other people.
>
> Responsibility and self-direction, we need to remind ourselves, are not learned from having these things withheld. It is hard, however, to give young people responsibility and independence because we are so afraid they might not be able to handle it. We are literally frightened to death that students might make mistakes. . . .
>
> Our whole school structure is built upon a fabric of right answers, and preoccupation with being right can get in the way of creativity, independence, self-direction, responsibility, and autonomy. A person afraid to make mistakes will be afraid to try. People afraid to try must live forever with the status quo. The production of self-directing, responsible people calls for teachers and administrators with courage enough to let young people make mistakes. . . .
>
> Let us not be diverted from the goal of independence, either, by the cries of the young people themselves as we give them greater responsibility. In the beginning they will no doubt reject it because they do not feel able to handle it. This, however, should not discourage us from giving them more. . . . The principle of pacing that applies to everything else we know in education applies to learning about responsibility as well. Opportunities have to be congruent with capacities. Capacity, however, is achieved from experience. You cannot expect a child to read if you never let him try and you cannot expect him to be responsible without success experience. It is a basic principle of democracy that "when men are free, they can find their own best ways." Although most of us piously subscribe to this fundamental doctrine, it is amazing how few of us are really willing to put it to the test. We do not really believe people can find their own best ways. They certainly cannot if they are never given an opportunity.[6]

[6] Arthur W. Combs, *To Nurture Humaneness* (Washington, D.C.: Association for Supervision and Curriculum Development, 1970), pp. 185–186.

Focus on the Learner

Each individual learner is a product of the accumulated experiences growing out of his interactions with other people. No individual comes into this world stupid or inadequate in the sense that we normally think of these conditions. Instead, these conditions develop as a result of the individual's interactions and inter-relationships with other people. No human being can thrive without having relationships with people who bear sense of concern and a respect for that individual. The relationship, in other words, must be a loving one because no one can become an adequate person if he has been deprived of a loving relationship during the infant years. Otherwise, he will have an inadequate concept of self and a negative concept of others. Self and others are not separate identities; they are inter-related. Self-concept is molded largely through social experience.

Everyone is born with a relatively high degree of creativity. Conformity in school tends to destroy this creativity by forcing a person to do what other people wish him to do. A person is constantly reminded of the wrong results from a gamble or an experiment. A child comes to school already manipulated by parents, other adults, and peers; many teachers capitalize on such manipulations. The student, with further manipulation, becomes docile and indifferent. Too many teachers characterize a good child as one who is sufficiently afraid of the figure at the front of a classroom to do what he is told.

Consequently, by the age of 9 or 10, most students have stopped asking questions and have slipped into the safe pattern of response which they perceive a teacher wants. They begin to live daily with the disconnected bundles of subject matter which have relatively little bearing on the world outside the classroom. They passively accept a day filled with dull, repetitious tasks.

Dr. Earl Kelly remarked at a Core Curriculum Conference several years ago that, when students are confronted with such punitive teachers, then the tasks of reading, writing, and speaking become near impossible ones. There are high school students who have a deadly fear of speaking and of writing. He cited a group of his own graduate students who would not enter into a discussion; when they did, their words were prefaced with phrases like "I don't want to stick my neck out, but. . . ." This reticence indicates a self-concept of a turtle; when the person is threatened, he draws into a shell of silence for protection. The self-concept was not present at birth; it was learned. What happens to students when educators attempt

21

to teach speaking, reading, and writing — the very means for human communication — is a grim subject.

Problem solving–team teaching offers the possibility of an individual nurturing a wholesome relationship with others, encouraging the personality to open up rather than retreat into a shell. By developing a feeling of "can-ness," the student can develop a positive and realistic view of self, others, the school, and life in general. He is willing to tackle new problems and try alternative solutions. He expects success and behaves in ways to assure it. He trusts himself and has less doubt about confronting new ideas and problems; he does not have to be selfishly striving for self-actualization. And he can accept occasional failure in stride because he is able to objectively assess mistakes and then remarshal his forces and energies for new creative ventures.

Unfortunately, in some schools where the curriculum is subject centered, only the academically talented students are fortunate to experience such development. Those learners who do not excel experience meaninglessness, humiliation, rejection, despair, inadequacy, frustration, and failure. Caught in the treadmill of repeated failure, they are unable to make valid contributions to group endeavors recognized as important by teachers, other students, or adults. They develop a negative attitude toward themselves, other people, and life. They cannot look objectively at new problems because their self-fulfillment is at stake. The problem solving–team teaching school can help salvage such individuals.

Dispelling Myths

Present educational practices and points of view must change. Modern research and experimentation conclusively demonstrates that all individuals are, in some way or another, gifted and potentially creative — if educators would only bother to discover and develop these possibilities. Rarely — if ever — will a person be found who is not capable of excelling others in some endeavor. Teachers need to learn where the less gifted can excel and give recognition; the learner will then begin to become an adequate person with a feeling of "can-ness."

Research further bears out the fact that individuals are unable to learn not because they lack the potential, but because they *perceive* they cannot learn. After having been told many times over — usually indirectly — that they are unable to learn, they finally accept the judgment. Once teachers and other school personnel become thoroughly convinced that all students in their school can learn and improve if opportunities are provided, then it is their responsibility to convince each child that he is important as a person with worth and dignity and that he is capable of learning. The problem solving–team teaching class can present opportunities for these goals of achievement to be realized.

Many children and youths are rejected by teachers and other school personnel because they do not meet these educators' preconceived and packaged notion of the perfect student. These students often come from socially deprived homes and from an environmental setting unlike that of the teacher's setting. Other students are rejected because they are not as clean and tidy as teachers would like them to be, and still others because of the color of their skin, their cultural background, or their national origin. Teachers cannot help or work with an individual until they have demonstrated to him that a person is completely and uncompromisingly accepted for what he *is*. When he has been thoroughly convinced that he is genuinely accepted and recognized as a person of worth and dignity, then it is possible for the teacher to start working toward his improvement.

Dr. Arthur W. Combs, in addressing the Alabama Elementary Principals, said about the learner:

> There was a time when young people were useful and helpful but now we are embarrassed by them. You can't bury them in caves in Kentucky like we do with excess butter and you can't ship the surplus to Russia like we do wheat. We are embarrassed by these young and we don't quite know what to do with them; and they are having a hard time finding anything worth living for. . . .
>
> Somehow you and I are going to have to find ways of helping these young people to find commitments. . . . Take the dropout; the dropout is a child who hasn't discovered that the school has any meaning for him and he has no commitment to it. We told him what he needs to know. The problem was that he never discovered what we told him had any value, so he dropped out. . . .

The learner and his needs have often been lost in the professional gamesmanship of "new curriculum" or "innovation" because such gimmicks have a way of becoming the end, not the means. The learner and his relatioships to culture and society should be at the center of what we consider to be effective education. According to the late Kurt Lewin, this is the sound approach:

> A teacher will never succeed in giving proper guidance to a learner if he does not learn to understand the psychological world in which that individual lives. To describe a situation "objectively" in psychology actually means to describe the situation as a totality of those facts and only those facts which make up the field of that individual. To substitute for that world of the individual the world of the teacher, the physicist, or of anybody else is to be not objective but wrong.[7]

_____
[7] Kurt Lewin, *Field Theory in Social Science* (New York: Harper and Brothers, 1951) , p. 62.

In problem solving–team teaching, systematic experiences can make it possible for students — under the leadership of qualified personnel — to study their own situations and behavioral patterns to identify and examine values which they understand and therefore accept as adequate guides to more intelligent and productive behavior. Students can then:

1. Participate responsibly, on the basis of careful study and discussion of issues, in determining policies and establishing procedures for regulating student behavior and relationships in the school and community;
2. Identify significant problems which are common;
3. Study the problems and develop plans of action.

Teaching the Student to Self-Govern

Ask teachers what they teach and why, and many reply that they are teaching what is in the textbook, the stated course of study, or the syllabus which has been prepared as a guide. They usually insist that the authors of a textbook, course of study, or syllabus are experts in the field who know a great deal more about the subject matter and are more aware of the research. Therefore, the classroom teacher has the benefit of such expertise. These teachers are using the criterion of authoritative opinion.

Others tend to teach what they feel the students enjoy, long ago learning for themselves that pupils are not very attentive and do not learn effectively if uninterested or bored. They are using the criterion of felt need.

Some teachers insist that they must offer that which prepares the individual for adult life, as exemplified in spelling skills or vocational courses. They are relying on the criterion of adult need.

Still others select certain learning experiences because these are instrumental in helping students pursue future learning. For example, reading is taught not for the sake of knowing how to read, but for its importance in acquiring facts, concepts, and generalizations. Elementary algebra, possibly of limited value within itself, helps in terms of calculus or other higher mathematics. This is the criterion of mastery of content for future use.

These criteria — authoritative opinion, felt need, adult need, and mastery for future use — all have value, but they fail to satisfy the basic philosophical question: How do we decide what shall be taught? To cope with this problem we must ask further questions: What is of the greatest value and what is most nearly and uniformly true at all times? These are hard questions, but they must be considered from the standpoint of the philosophies of pragmatism, humanism, and democracy which support the problem solving–team teaching approach.

24

Truth and value are relative to human experience. The individual's ability to control and govern his own experiences is the criterion by which truth and value are to be evaluated. In problem solving the teacher is charged with responsibility for helping the student learn in order to cope with both present and future problems.

Dr. A. D. Albright, vice president of the University of Kentucky, spoke about what we teach in a September 1970 speech at Auburn University:

"The more innovative institutions today sense that rather than seeking to produce finished practitioners, they must now prepare students for continuing to learn, following their departure from their respective institutions. For if the graduate knows how to identify a problem, a significant problem ('and by significant I mean one related to social issues or problems of difficulty'), and to research the knowledge related to it and to make decisions about solutions, he will be better able to keep abreast of new ideas and techniques and to master those novel cases with which he is confronted. This is hard to accept for many of us whose thinking developed in a different world. . . .

The problem of liberalizing a professional curriculum has really not been resolved. . . . The objective of producing a problem-solving graduate carries fresh implications. Problems are used to teach thinking, that is analysis and synthesis, which are basic to the search for knowledge. They are a means of gaining confidence in decision-making. . . . Systematic inquiries into knowledge are also necessary as means of introducing the student to existing information. And even if the forms of presentation resemble those of the past, educators must take into account the fact that the psychology of the students today is quite different than it was a few years ago. He becomes an active participant in his learning rather than a passive recipient of knowledge. . . . The curriculum is becoming more innovative and possesses a high degree of flexibility, producing a versatility in the student's attitude toward future careers. The aim of this flexibility is two-fold: to permit the development of a concentration of study around the student's interpretation and potential and to permit the student a considerable range of choices in his program. The latter phase of a problem solving emphasis includes the pursuit of research of his own planning subject to faculty acquiescence at least, if not approval. Until recently students in professsional schools have been so heavily loaded with courses that they have virtually been deprived of practically all choices. The faculties and some of the schools are beginning . . . to reverse this all too typical situation. . . .

Various philosophers have advocated this problem solving aspect as a very strong educational tool. It seems it is also an excellent way to motivate students, which is, I am told, a highly important element in learning. Inter-disciplinary trends are now beginning to affect the curricula of the schools. . . . There must be interdisciplinary exchanges and interprofessional collaboration, if schools are to

25

shift from concrete courses, isolated courses, toward the broader experience that stimulates imagination, induces comprehension, and requires the student to provide a synthesis. Thus the student is engaged consciously in conceptionalizing, designing and model building, criticism, systems analysis, behavioral operation, information-processing, and utilization. Too much teaching has emphasized rote-learning: note-taking, memorization, and doing experiments in which the answers are already known. The more innovative schools now believe there is a better learning theory than this and are discarding the stereotype patterns of the past. . . . Many of these schools rely heavily on problem solving, not the little problems, but purposeful problems that will help change behavior and improve the quality of living.

An important consideration in the education of which I speak is to ensure some transferability of learning. The study of a problem is not merely to find a solution; solutions are transitory. The follow-through is a most important element of the process. One learns the most from a problem by developing generalizations that somehow have application in other cases or instances. The problems will not always have preconceived answers, certainly not in the coming 10 years; instead the class or people in a class seem to evalute the alternative solutions to a problem. When utilizing this approach in helping to educate people, the moral dogma is no longer applicable, accepting only one solution to a problem, since many problems have several solutions. This prepares the student to reason and to find solutions to novel situations, and to become skilled in decision-making. . . ."

The Learning Process in Problem Solving

The outmoded and discredited concepts of learning which have dominated education for the past century are still haunting us. For example, the theories of mental discipline, discredited decades ago, refused to be buried. A second die-hard is the storage theory of learning which assumes that the mind is like a reservoir into which knowledge is poured for future use. Such theories gain most of their support from the essentialist-authoritarian-materialistic philosophers of education and their commitment to the idea that all individuals must be subjected to rigorous, painful, distasteful, and unenjoyable experiences in order to become strong in character and perseverance. These theories rely heavily on extrinsic motivational forces such as threat, punishment, ridicule, sarcasm, promotions, grades, bribes, and banners.

In place of the theories should go these more positive ones:

1. Learning is the discovery of personal meaning for each individual learner, resulting in his changed behavior. For students to discover personal meaning in a learning situation, the circumstances must bear directly on their daily lives.

26

2. Learning is the overcoming of obstacles that stand in the way of achieving a goal that the learner needs or wants to achieve. Learning situations must be of such a nature that the students can see immediate as well as long-term benefits.
3. Learning is the restoration of an organism to a stage of equilibrium with the environment. This implies that the individual is disturbed over the problem and has a genuine interest in finding some solution.
4. The individual learns as a total organism and in terms of total life situations since the whole is far greater than the sum of the parts.

These and other perceptual-field concepts used in problem solving-team teaching indicate that learning is most beneficial and most highly applicable when it stems from internal drives and forces, and that learning itself is a real reward to the individual because he is accomplishing needed goals.

The subject centered curriculum is psychologically unsound by its reliance primarily on conditioning, mental disciplining, and storage concepts of learning. It is further sociologically unrealistic in its leaning on the past, ignoring contemporary needs and interests. It seldom treats individual differences within the classroom. Problem solving, on the other hand, deals with current problems. Within its framework groups identify and select particular problems pertinent and important in terms of valid criteria which have been cooperatively developed. The group's members work to define, subdivide, and hypothesize about the problems. A problem could be wise use of natural resources, curbing delinquency, clearing slums, curing dreaded diseases, regulating aviation, using drugs wisely, adjusting to more leisure time, or living with social pressures.

Pragmatically, humanistically, and democratically, the school is a natural laboratory for problem solving. Curriculum reorganized for the implementation of problem solving offers the experiences of individual growth and learning and the opportunity for a student's positive involvement in social situations. It is an education suitable to our democracy.

BIBLIOGRAPHY

Albirty, Harold B. and Albirty, Elsie Jo, *Reorganizing the High School Curriculum.* New York: The Macmillan Co., 1962.

Arnstine, Donald, *Philosophy of Education.* New York: Harper and Row, 1967.

Bayles, Ernest E., *Pragmatism in Education.* New York: Harper and Row, 1966.

Brameld, Theodore, *Philosophies of Education.* New York: Holt, Rinehart and Winston, 1955.

Childs, John L., *American Pragmatism and Education.* New York: Henry Holt and Co., 1956.

Dewey, John, *Democracy and Education.* New York: The Free Press, 1944.

————, *Experience and Education.* New York: Collier Books, 1913; Kappa Delta Pi, 1938.

————, *The Child and the Curriculum.* Chicago: The University of Chicago Press, 1902.

Dupuis, Adrian M., *Philosophy of Education in Historical Perspective.* Chicago: Rand McNally and Co., 1966.

Gribble, James, *Introduction to Philosophy of Education.* Boston: Allyn and Bacon, Inc., 1969.

Henderson, George, *Education For Peace.* Washington, D.C.: Association for Supervision and Curriculum Development, 1973.

Kelley, Earl C. and Rasey, Marie J., *Education and the Nature of Man.* Harper and Brothers, 1952.

Kelley, Earl C., *In Defense of Youth.* Englewood Cliffs, N.J.: Prentice-Hall, 1962.

Leeper, Robert R., ed., *Humanizing Education: The Person in the Process.* Washington, D.C.: Association for Supervision and Curriculum Development and the National Education Association, 1967.

————, *Curriculum Concerns in a Revolutionary Era.* Washington, D.C.: Association for Supervision and Curriculum Development, 1972.

Martin, Hane R., *Readings in the Philosophy of Education.* Boston: Allyn and Bacon, Inc., 1970.

Neagley, Ross L. and N. Dean Evans, *Handbook for Effective Curriculum Development.* Englewood Cliffs, N.J.: Prentice-Hall, 1967.

Rathborn, Charles H., *Open Education: The Informal Classroom.* New York: Citation Press, 1971.

Ratner, Joseph, *Intelligence in the Modern World — John Dewey's Philosophy.* New York: Random House, 1939.

Scobey, Mary M. and Grace Graham, eds., *To Nurture Humaneness.* Washington, D.C.: Association for Supervision and Curriculum Development, 1970.

Smith, B. Othanel, William O. Stanley, and J. Harlan Shores, *Fundamentals of Curriculum Development.* New York: Harcourt, Brace, and World, Inc., 1957.

Tanner, Danial, *Secondary Education: Perspectives and Prospects.* New York: Macmillan Co., 1972.

Venable, Tom C., *Philosophical Foundations of the Curriculum.* Chicago: Rand McNally and Co., 1967.

Weber, Christian O., *Basic Philosophies of Education.* New York: Rinehart and Co., 1960.

Wirth, Arthur G., *John Dewey as Educator.* New York: John Wiley and Sons, 1966.

Chapter 2. Social Adequacy Within a Changing World

Our society has become highly complex and segmented: technological, scientific, industrialized, and urbanized. Ironically, as this development has made our society more interdependent, it has also led to a social fragmentation. A person highly dependent upon physical services in, say, an urban setting can also be socially isolated and even alienated. Within such complexities, education has come to play a central role in helping the individual attain social adequacy or adjustment. As used here, social adequacy includes both an individual's own feelings of worth within the society and his ability to cope with social pressures, including changing occupational roles.

A problem solving curriculum—by its attention to individual needs and abilities—offers a promising approach for meeting this social adequacy role of the schools. The academic, book-centered schools have failed to help students adapt to changing social conditions. As a consequence of poor preparation by these schools, individuals have found themselves unemployed and unemployable because they lack the ability or know-how to cope with life situations and pressures.

What kinds of social conditions and pressures exist in the American society which argue for an education that is socially adequate? This chapter will identify some major influences: social stratification, living environments, changing values, and basic concepts now threatened by such change. Of central importance is how these influences relate to the social role of education. Within the traditional subject centered curriculum, an individual student has little opportunity to confront and handle social realities. If he is fortunate, instead, to attend a school in which problem solving is part of the curriculum, then he has the chance to develop according to his own unique capabilities because the school curriculum has tried to prepare him for social adequacy. The problems he has been asked to help solve within the learning situation have helped to pave the way for positive coping with life situations.

The concept of social adequacy—an individual's ability to cope effectively within a complex social order—is closely related to basic philosophical beliefs pertaining to curriculum construction and reorganization. It is also closely related to the psychological factors (discussed in Chapter 3) which

29

promote the most effective development of the learner in the modern day society.

Some educational philosophers would deny the centrality of the school's social role. The perennialists, for example, do not concur in the idea that the schools must be continuously changing in order to adapt to the needs of a changing society. Such men as Robert Hutchins and Mortimer Adler allege certain unchangeable, absolute principles and universal truths to which all men should adjust—regardless of the present realities of their contemporary and changing world.

The essentialist view, held by men like Arthur Bester and Mortimer Smith, sees education contained in essential subject matter—including high school literature, grammar, rhetoric, logic and mathematics. They exclude vocational and practical studies as irrelevant and inappropriate for modern man's education. These "essential subjects" are prescribed for the universal importance of disciplining the mental faculties of man so that he can adjust to an "external reality."

Both essentialism and perennialism, in terms of curriculum theory, emphasize forces and truths beyond man's control and to which each is obligated to conform without regard of the nature of society itself. A problem solving curriculum, on the other hand, is designed along these lines: *That human intelligence can learn how to create new knowledge in the form of solutions to human problems.* Under this design, man can direct future experiences and reconstruct social realities. Since man is interacting with his social environment rather than independent of nature and change, he must learn how to solve contemporary perplexities rather than acquiesce and adjust to existing forces of external truth. Evidence abounds in sociology of the interrelationships of man with his external environment; such a changing context is *not* to be interpreted as a curriculum to be defined and influenced solely by the internal desires and interests of the individual learner. This mistake was made by misinformed interpreters of the early progressive movement in their emphasis on child-centered and activity curriculum and in their over-reactions to the traditionalists' external truth and essential subject matter. The problem solving curriculum, in denying the dualism of the subjective and objective, seeks an integration of and interaction between the internal self and the external social reality. Thus, problem solving teaching is not forced to choose between educating citizens for social adjustment and responsibility and, on the other hand, educating the individual for self-realization or fulfillment.

Reorganization through problem solving avoids both extremes of the traditional school and of the child-centered school by teaching the learner how to direct his own development through the public process of social problem solving. The only true education, John Dewey contended, comes through the stimulation of the child's power by the demands of the social situation in which he finds himself. This educational process has two sides: psychological and sociological. One cannot be subordinated to the other or otherwise neglected without disastrous results.

Kinds of Social Stratification

As the American society has become highly stratified, the social environment in which a child develops is heavily influenced by four distinct forms of stratification. The first is social stratification, and it involves two roles: the person's family role such as mother, father, son, or daughter and his status or function with the society. Social stratification—present since the earliest nomadic tribes some seven or eight thousand years ago—is found in every existing human society. Many individuals have insisted that its functioning is necessary as a continuation of society and of human existence. But modern sociologists often disagree that social stratification is necessary; they insist instead that man can reconstruct society in such a way as to reduce much of the social stratification which is so oppressing to millions of individuals who are unfortunate enough to be at the lower levels of the strata.

Plato was one of the first individuals to acknowledge the realtiy of social stratification. He pointed out three social classes in his ideal republic: physical, spiritual or patriotic, and one of the ruling philosopher king in whom wisdom resided. He insisted that the selection of people to fit into the proper class was done primarily through the educational system. Education, according to the Platonic view, was relatively simple. At each level of increased abstraction in the curriculum, those who were incapable of understanding things at that level would simply drop off and join their proper classes. Environmental effect were ignored in Plato's educational scheme. It is important to keep in mind that, during this Greek philosopher's time, his country's democratic process affecting a select few was supported by thousands and thousands of slaves who were considered by the citizens to be subhuman animals. According to the system, it was the upper-class responsibility to keep these subhumans in a state of slavish ignorance so they could not rebuke the ruler.

As ruler-upper class-slave structure began to break down, there was an increase in the desire of people to explore the world and to seek a better place for themselves. A split between rulers and slaves developed, breaking perhaps for the first time the bonds that held people in complete slavery.

31

With the example of Martin Luther, men began to insist on the right to know and understand the Bible for themselves—creating a break in the social control of ignorance particularly in relation to the printed page. This probably reduced the gap between rulers and slaves, driving a wedge which signalled the end of the states' system and the beginning of a real urban pattern of social classes—a pattern present today in American life.

These conditions are necessary to the operation of a social class system; (1) a consciousness on the part of the individuals within a given class that they are different in significant ways from the rest and (2) some differential behavior not shared—at least to the same extent—with the rest of the society. For example, the Negro-white distinction would yield both class consciousness and differentiated behavior by the types of occupations, earned in one, voting rights, and geographic spread.

Class should be distinguished from caste. In human society, the caste system which has endured for 3,000 years or more persists to this day. A caste is distinguished by the fact that its members are in it for life; outside of transmigration of soul, no chance exists for mobility from one caste to another. Furthermore, the caste, by its total exclusiveness, defines and controls the social interactions of its members. Many have argued that the American Negro is involved in a system of caste structure; until two decades ago, this was largely true. Sociologist Michael Harrington has pointed out through his research the sharp distinction between the poor and the rest of our population. Some 50 million "poor" in America, he has reported, are increasingly invisible.

Migrants to a new America were told that each individual was at liberty to grow, develop, and mature to the full extent of his capabilities—no matter what his past servitude or social conditions. This concept was in large part realized during the earlier colonial period when there was relatively little social distinction between individuals of various occupational abilities or cultural origins. The situation changed drastically with the introduction of Negro slaves who lived in a complete state of servitude at the mercy of their masters—almost as completely as the slaves of the old world. The condition prevailed even long after the Civil War. Alongside this social condition arose the national myth that every individual could climb the rungs of the success ladder—economically, educationally, and socially—irrespective of former status. We took pride in boasting that Abraham Lincoln, born in a modest log cabin and self-educated before he became a lawyer, rose to be President of the United States. Any realistic student of sociology will readily recognize that there was only one Abraham Lincoln and few could duplicate his rise above the undesirable conditions that prevailed in his childhood.

One thing we fail to realize is that this opportunity has never existed and does not exist today to the same degree for the American black man, the American-Mexican, the American Indian, or even the American oriental. While we have made considerable progress in overcoming some of the class structures which prevailed in our earlier history among some individuals, we still have a long way to go before it can be said that a quality of opportunity is possible for all individuals in accordance with their unique capabilities.

A second kind of classification prevalent in American society and in some ways related to the class structure has largely occured since the Industrial Revolution: occupational stratification. It is exceedingly difficult to have interaction and intercommunication in many communities between people of varied occupational pursuits due to the high degree of specialization and division of labor which has taken place in the scientific, technological development of this nation. Individuals in one occupation have relatively few if any contacts with people in other occupations unless they are able to cross the line through some other route such as the economic one. Occupational stratification presents a barrier to confronting the more realistic problems of American society; we need to learn ways and means of overcoming these handicaps if we are to succeed in solving some of the problems.

A third form of classification has also largely contributed to the conditions which have developed since the dawn of the Industrial Revolution: economic stratification. In many ways it parallels occupational stratification. In any given American community the economic conditions and occupational endeavors of its families are noticeably reflected in the kinds of houses in which they live, the schools their children attend, the home conveniences they have, the kinds of automobiles they own, and the particular social services they can or cannot afford to support. In most every community of any size in America, there is relatively little interaction or communication among groups of different incomes. This lack is even more pronounced in other parts of the world.

More recent than social, occupational, or economic classifications is a fourth form: age stratification. It has become so acute that individuals of more than a few years in age-span rarely associate voluntarily or frequently with each other in terms of their own values and experiences. Therefore, people of one age-group do not communicate with or have impact upon those of other age groups. Under such conditions, children have few opportunities to learn values and ideals from people who are appreciably older or younger than they are.

Curriculum reorganization through problem solving can, in many ways, overcome the adverse and harmful effects of social, occupational, economic, and age stratifications. In learning through problem solving the team of teachers and the students must go out into their community as they confront various problems. The approach involves people of every age group, social stratum, occupational endeavor, and economic income-level. In interacting while working toward the solution of common problems, people learn to respect and admire other individuals. The school is the only setting for such wide, first-hand contact with many individuals of a community area.

Six Kinds of Communities

Walt Whitman once said that children tend to become like the objects around them, and the first objects they see will probably be the most influential in shaping what they become. The school is one of the most powerful interacting forces operating to shape the life and behavior of boys and girls. The objects which pupils see in school are selected, arranged, and used in order to encourage learning. Within a curriculum reorganized for problem solving learning, these objects are selected and planned carefully to have a wholesome influence upon their lives. The kind of environment that surrounds the problem solving teaching and learning process differs distinctly from that of the subject centered traditional curriculum in terms of facilities, buildings, classrooms, desks, libraries, laboratories, and instructional resources — including the curriculum itself or the sum total of formal and informal student learning experiences under the school's supervision. There are equally important components of the student's school environment in the problem solving situation which are outside: the people with whom they associate, their parents, and other citizens. These components — though not parts of the classroom itself — have a most meaningful and influential effect upon student learning and how the student will react to future life situations.

Teachers constitute a key element in this environment: in large part they set the tone and provide the conducive learning setting. Students also influence other students. Research demonstrates that the achievement most strongly related to educational background and aspiration might well be tied to the students in the school and how they feel toward learning. In fact, many educators argue that the student-to-student influence probably outweighs all other environmental factors. As an example, children from a given family background when put into schools of different social composition will achieve at quite a different level than previously, although the effect is less noticeable for a privileged than an underprivileged student. If a student from a home strongly and effectively supporting education goes into a school where most pupils do not come from such homes, his achievement will not be drastically hampered. On the other hand, when a disadvantaged student from a home without such educational support is put with classmates having strong educational backgrounds, he usually has a remarkable improvement in his own achievement.

The most important influences upon students, then, are *other people* — and particularly teachers and fellow students.

Within socially, economically, and occupationally stratified subcultures, the child coming into school will in large part join other children from his community from similar backgrounds and with similar experiences. While it is true that they come from somewhat different homes economically and socially, they still hold in common certain elements which tend to determine their levels of aspiration and achievement.

For their part, teachers will bring their own aspiration to the children in the form of personally held values, attitudes, and feelings. These intangibles will have impact on the students. However, these teachers often reflect the same subculture as the children's. This blandness of similarity argues for the need to break down barriers of social, economic, and occupational stratification so that different peoples can mingle and interact within the problem solving process — enabling them to gain new insights into the possibilities of education and life itself.

The kind of society in which boys and girls grow up has a most profound impact upon their learning, goals, and future. While good physical facilities and sound curriculum are indisputably valuable, there are other determinants of student progress in school, among them the home and neighborhood. We shall look at six different home/community situations to see how each has impact upon its children. The first situation is the typical American suburban area primarily inhabited by people who have relatively good positions or skilled occupations, command a relatively high income, and support their families at a high level of existence. A large number of the parents are college graduates and they want the same level of education for their children. Such communities provide a very stable life for boys and girls as they grow toward maturity in well-kept houses, surrounded with beautiful lawns and landscape and clean streets. Community pride in homes, streets, and other facilities is evident. The homes, usually spacious and well-planned, have adequate room for all children to live comfortably in their relationships with the rest of the family. Students often have their own private bedroom with comfortable beds, desks, chairs, wall-to-wall carpeting, attractive drapes, and beautiful lighting. They may even have built-in shelves for storage of various items in which students are interested; a large collection of books, magazines, papers; and a radio, phonograph, high-fi set, or their own private television set.

These children interact with people of similar social, economic, and occupational levels. They have frequent access to music and have an opportunity to become highly proficient in some musical or art skill if they have an interest in this direction. They will also likely have shop and craft facilities. Such boys and girls frequently have opportunities to attend scout meetings and other social events which make life quite tolerable and lovable. The parents of such children usually drive modern, well-equipped automobiles; they also have home conveniences. In the neighborhood, churches, health services, welfare services (where needed), and recreational facilities are well supported. Spacious play-areas are provided for children to have first-hand contact with others of similar backgrounds and interests. Such students are usually interested vitally in their own school work and will take an active role in seeing that the school is made more enjoyable.

Suburban children will have many conveniences of their own such as bicycles for the smaller children, motor scooters for the larger ones, and even private automobiles for high schoolers to use in recreational endeavors, social life, and travels. Families in these areas generally take an annual vacation, including the children as an integral part of the family group that enjoys living, eating, and working together.

Children from these homes have many of the incentives that encourage continuous learning, and the home provides many opportunities for learning through first-hand experiences.

Under a problem solving curriculum these suburban homes and schools can be supportive of learning far above the national average. Such a learning situation can provide maximum opportunities for boys and girls to develop and fully function as adequate, self-realizing individuals who are able to take their positions in American society and carry out varied responsibilities as they grow to maturity. The curriculum which uses problem solving offers more diversity as the students go into the larger community and have chances they might not otherwise have to interact with people of different backgrounds and interests.

The second situation is a large-city slum area. For the children here, the outlook is bleak: Constant frustration, anxiety, and irregularity crowd their lives. They are continuously being rejected by the rest of society; they are unable to feel that they are people of worth and dignity who have

36

a worthwhile stake in life. Such individuals start school with many strikes against their chances for possible success and satisfaction in life.

Students from slum areas of our large cities, by and large, live in inadequate facilities which are overcrowded and have poor lighting and ventilation. Frequently, "home" is a small apartment within a crowded tenement where living is barely at the subsistence level. Many come from broken homes caused by addiction to alcohol, narcotics, and other drugs. They have few contacts with their parents; even if the parents are still living together, odds are that both will be working and away from home for most of the waking hours of the student. Often they have left when the students awake, leaving responsibility for preparing breakfast to the oldest child. In many instances students find it easier to skip breakfast. They go to school hungry as well as poorly clothed and groomed. Some of these students may dream of a better life, but many have already given up in despair — seeing the situation as hopeless within a continuous pattern of failure and rejection.

The small apartments are usually poorly equipped, having few modern conveniences to make life a little more enjoyable and entertaining. There are relatively few recreational activities in the home, nor are there books, magazines, or even a newspaper. If they have a radio or television set, it is likely to be an old model in need of repair.

Occasionally, in the classroom, the student who lives in such drab reality may draw a dream picture of a beautiful home, surrounded by a spacious green lawn on which children are playing. Teachers who encourage this kind of fantasy may be providing a little heaven for the student at that immediate moment, but the escape is short of duration. If the tenement-bound students find any consolation, satisfaction, or enjoyment in school work, it is frequently only a brief escape from boredom, hunger, or frustration. He may visit a grandparent or relative where life is somewhat easier. But this escape, too, is brief. He must return to the tenement flat where curtains are ragged, beds are poorly made, floors are unsanitary, walls are grimy, plumbing is faulty, electric lighting is inadequate, and much is in need of repair.

Schools in a tenement area, as a general rule, are poorly maintained and staffed with too many incompetent teachers. The buildings, frequently among the oldest in the city, have poor library and laboratory facilities and mediocre instructional materials.

For such students, a subject centered curriculum provides a limited, if not dismal learning experience. The class may occasionally plant a few bean seeds in a school window box and watch them grow; they may even get a little insight into science experiences, but such insight is rare. They must rely almost solely on the printed page as a learning resource, usually reading and studying materials far beyond their comprehension. The classroom probably has few maps or globes. Audiovisual aids are meager. The few contacts with the outside world come through television programs piped into the school. A school drama might give the students a chance to play an imaginary role. Their parents might be invited to see the play, and some will even come. The performance gives the students a real lift for the moment, but the moment cannot counter-balance the endless hours of "being lectured to" as they sit passively in a classroom.

Student learning is all too often interrupted by the red flickering light of a police car announcing a search for some individual who has violated some law. It is sometimes easier for students to identify with the violator than with the authorities.

Schools in slum areas serve an entirely different kind of function than schools in other areas do. Simply "modernizing" the curriculum does not go very far toward grappling with the real problems that affect the student's own well being or the welfare of his community. Urban projects are unlikely to gain community support because its residents have already, for the most part, given up in despair — concluding that life is nothing but drudgery and that little hope exists for them or their children.

The emphasis of a problem solving curriculum upon direct involvement of the student in a group learning situation under the skilled team of teachers and resource persons would offer more than momentary relief from a pattern of failure. It could take him past the tenement and schoolhouse walls into the community and even beyond. In pursuing a problem with his group, the student encounters people who can provide a positive force in terms of human achievement. He will be dealing with subject material related to social realities rather than merely reciting back what is in the textbook.

In situation three there is another living environment for children: a small town surrounded by a rural community where most of the people own their homes, farms, businesses, and small industries. The town is a small county seat within a prosperous American rural community. Its people are neither wealthy nor poor. Though there are no rich families in the community, many individuals can afford to drive a Buick or Chrysler which is bought every two or three years. Others can afford slightly less expensive cars and may not exchange them as often. Most of the wives and older daughters wear fashionable clothes; the children are well-dressed, clean, and orderly. Many of the families have the means for a yearly vacation. They live relatively close to a college or university which the children can attend. Many parents are college graduates themselves.

Boys and girls in such a community usually have adequate home facilities. There are home conveniences to make life easier. Most of the homes are large enough so that no more than two children will have to occupy the same bedroom. Such bedrooms have desks, chairs, adequate lighting fixtures, curtains on the windows, and rugs on the floor. Relatives live nearby, especially grandparents whom the children will frequently visit and in the process be exposed to the values of older people — a valuable contact for growing minds. Most of the families' ancestors had lived in this area of the country.

The children are usually treated by their parents in a friendly and orderly manner, with encouragement to do constructive things and to attend school on a regular basis. Students from such homes usually have bicycles. There are particular areas in the community for outings, fishing, and sports or games. Most homes have refrigerators, stoves, freezers, and television sets.

At the town's center is the courthouse square where some of the parents work. Around the courthouse square are a number of small businesses owned by other parents. The courthouse square boasts of grass, flowers, and shrubs growing on the lawns where students often play after school hours. The school grounds, also attractively kept, offer a place where students can get together. The school itself has many of the modern conveniences that induce effective learning. In the rest of the community are several well-kept churches, a recreational facility, and a small library where both children and adults spend leisure hours.

Many of the teachers were born and reared in this part of the country; consequently they understand the boys and girls and the background of their experiences because they have had similar experiences. Many of the teachers are also wives of business and professional people: doctors, lawyers, county officials, and some of the merchants. They will have a distinct interest in the well-being of the students, instilling in them the general belief that they have faith in the children's abilities to grow, develop, and mature. The school is attractively structured: Teachers have adequate desks; students have work areas where they can meet in small or large groups or for individual study.

Such schools will frequently have problem solving–team teaching as a part of the curriculum because their planners and educators have learned to live close to nature and because they are familiar with the problems that affect the well-being of students and of the community itself. These

175095

students, in some respects, might not have all the advantages accorded students from the suburban areas, but they have opportunities and environmental surroundings far superior to those in the slum areas. In some instances they may even be able to profit from life, liberty, and schooling *more* than suburban students from large areas because they live close to nature and feel a kinship to each other and to the entire community which builds wholesome living, effective cooperative planning, and corporate implementation of school and other community affairs. The majority of these students will grow into respectable, capable individuals who need not depend upon menial tasks for a livelihood. Many will go on to higher education so that they can learn a profession, skill, or trade for earning a decent and respectable livelihood.

Situation four deals with students from a predominantly rural community which is relatively poor — without adequate living, educational, civic, social, and church facilities. The community depends almost entirely upon agriculture, and there are many tenant farmers who barely eke out an existence. The tenant farmers do not have much to which they can look forward, nor do their children. There are a few large landowners who have many tenants cultivating their lands. There are some small landowners who operate their own farms, but they are having a difficult time because of unfertile and nonproductive land.

Even though a rather wide margin separates the landowner from the tenant farmer, in many instances a fairly close relationship exists — with a concern on the part of the landowner for the welfare of the tenant farmer and his children. This is especially true if the tenants are of the same racial and ethnic group as the landowner. Rather than a marked social barrier between the different groups, there is instead a frequent though impersonal association and interaction. They will attend the same churches and some of the same community functions.

The community's minority members do not fare as well. Since the schools have been desegregated for a relatively short time, these individuals are not accepted in the social circle of the whites. They are not privileged to attend many of the same community functions where they could participate and interchange ideas with others. But this situation is gradually improving and, in the not too distant future, these situations will be largely erased so that people can live in a more wholesome relationship with each other — giving, sharing, and communicating more extensively.

The students in this predominantly poor rural community attend schools that are not of a high order, but which do provide limited opportunities for them to grow, develop, and mature. In more recent years, students from minority families are attending the same schools as those from the major ethnic group; in a few instances, they are also attending the same churches and may be participating in the same recreational facilities of the community. They may all go to the old swimming hole down on the creek; they occasionally have a picnic attended by people of various racial and ethnic groups; they might hold a community barbecue to which all are invited. Such opportunities for interaction and communication go far beyond those of only a few years past.

The students from minority homes are not privileged to attend the most modern schools which are supported by a high level of living. These modern schools are far superior to the schools in slum areas which were described earlier. Some of these modern schools are actively involved in a curriculum reorganization program that involves problem centered learning; they are becoming more and more committed to this kind of experience by grappling with the real social, economic, and civic affairs of the community.

Many of the students from the wealthier and landowning families will attend college. Some of the students from tenant farms will go on to trade schools, learning at least a semi-skill which will enable them to earn a living above the bare subsistence level. More and more of the minority children are also attending trade schools and some students from tenant homes will attend a college or university. The teachers in the community's schools tend to be reasonably well prepared and have some of the modern outlooks conducive to problem solving learning that cares for individual differences and enables the student to move out from under continuous failure and frustration. This is the greatest hope for such a community.

Students from these poorer homes in the rural community do not have the most desirable environmental surroundings found in suburban, small-town, or village schools, but their conditions are far superior to those in the slum areas of America. They should be helped in moving ahead and in entering the mainstream of American life. More schools in the community than just the most modern ones need curriculum reorganization through problem solving; the less fortunate students under a problem solving situation, would gain a positive feeling of social adequacy as they would be learning within the group structure — a structure which takes in individual differences and needs.

The final situation involves a community in a foreign country: a Pakistani peasant village. Its people live in a culture strikingly different from our own. But the families and children in this simple village have a better chance in life than families and children in our large city slums, even though the villagers are a long way from reaching self-realization.

Social and economic forces in this rural Moslem society have a tremendous impact on the development and socialization of its young people.

Homes are primarily made of mud-wall construction, with an open court in front where much of the family living takes place. The courtyards are usually protected from the hot sun and drenching rain by the overhead branches of large trees. Students in these homes are made aware of the importance of religion as perceived by the Pakistani people. They observe villagers going to and from prayer four and five times daily. Also, parents insist that the government-owned schools teach religion and reinforce the teachings of the Moslem home.

Families are usually large and closely knit; it is not uncommon for three or four different family groups to live under the domination of a grandfather, who is head of household. The children have great difficulty distinguishing themselves and their brothers and sisters from their cousins. Family ties are extremely strong and behavior is rigid; proper human relationships are emphasized throughout their lives. Many of the families will own land outside the village wall and they will often work cooperatively and visit one another. But those who do not own land are not privileged to be associated with those who do.

The children learn social-class structure within the village in a meaningful and realistic way. The village is poor, depending almost entirely upon agriculture; for this reason, there are more boys outside of school because most families need them in the fields. The boys not attending school will be compelled to take up menial tasks for a living; they will probably remain poor throughout their lives. The boys privileged to attend school will have a chance to get jobs. Many of the parents send their boys to school precisely to improve their economic condition.

The village and the country as a whole are badly overpopulated and underdeveloped. Food, clothing, and other goods are scarce and expensive. Each working day, the people leave the mud-wall clusters and walk over narrow footpaths to the fields, returning at night to the crowded village — center for social and family life.

Mass media are almost nonexistent. Newspapers, movie houses, and radios are relatively few; what radios there are seldom work effectively. Landowners have access to the language paper of their native land; a few may have an English paper which they are privileged to read. When the one radio station located in the village breaks down, there is seldom anyone to repair it immediately. Science and technology, also largely nonexistent in village life, have small impact upon its inhabitants.

When the student leaves for school each morning he joins his peers along the way. The peer group wields some social influence; however, a stronger influence is parental rule — strict though usually kind. Upon entering school the students are confronted with a second strong influence: a teacher who demands unquestionable obedience. Between school and home the students are free to romp and play and perhaps indulge in a free piece of sugarcane. But in school or at home, discipline is very strict.

The school, usually located near a narrow, winding stream, has one mud-wall and a weather-beaten door leading into an open court. Upon entering the court, the students drop their books and shed their shoes which they place in neat rows inside the base of the wall. They look around at the rustic beauty and natural classroom of the spacious courtyard: A winding stream ambles through its middle and a great spreading tree gives protection from sun and rain.

These students are living in a culture quite different from an American one. They come from homes that are unlike those we have. They attend schools and religious services which contrast our own. They share with us the cultural quality of being socialized by the influences of their particular environment. They, too, are working toward improving their own lot in life.

Each of these five environments — American suburban, large-city slum, small-town, rural and a Pakistani village — points up the striking differences in the kinds of teaching each of these communities needs in their schools. Teachers, if they are to be effective in coping with the unique needs of each individual student, must be very skillful and resourceful. Also, the five situations underline the differences among students as they begin to learn their social roles. One point is painfully obvious: The American slum and the Pakistani village schools have far less opportunities to develop their pupils into wholesome individuals.

School and Social Adequacy

Anthropologist Margaret Mead has consistently held throughout her research and writings that the schools can and must determine the quality and scope of human culture if they are to play their role of cultural reconstruction. Schools cannot be content, she maintains, with the limited role of transmitting what adults know to children. Instead, the school must teach adaptive capacities that adults do not have. The whole teaching and learning continuum attempted by American schools has focused upon the passing on of bland generalities and the growth of a child into a man.

This focus — particularly inadequate in light of our accelerated, technological society — is now exploding in the faces of the school people and the community in general. Schools must learn how to close the gap they have so effectively perpetuated through an outmoded curriculum which is unrealistic and meaningless to the majority of youths. Unfortunately, many thousands of school people remain unaware that our school system is badly outmoded. Relatively little attention is being paid to the more basic issues in education. If anything, we seem to want more of what we already have — more children in our schools, more hours to study, more required work, more science and math, more time in school. Lost in the rush are the unique needs of boys and girls.

Curriculum reorganization through problem solving, if properly implemented and developed, can make a significant breakthrough in overcoming this major lag between present curriculum and urgent needs which is prevalent in today's educational institution. Through problem solving education in the latter 70's and early 80's we can better prepare students to cope with life in a world of automation, of global communication, of space explorations, and of the haunting spectre of nuclear oblivion.

The problem of education obsolescence goes far beyond such issues as methods of teaching reading or math, science vs. humanities, how much teachers should be payed, length of summer holidays, or the number of years to be spent in college. We must face up to the realization that our present system of education — both past and present — is outdated: *It is dangerously unrelated to the changing society of which we are very much a part.* An adjustment is in order *if* the next generation is to survive.

Dr. Mead was quite disturbed over how poorly the present educational program was meeting the demands of a dynamic society.

> Is it not possible that an educational system that was designed to teach what was known to little children and to a select few young men may not fit a world in which the most important factor in everyday life are those things that are not yet but soon will be known?
>
> Is it not equally possible that our present definition of a pupil or a student is out of date when we define the learner as a child or at best an immature person, who is entitled to moral protection and subsistence in a dependency position, and who is denied the moral autonomy that is accorded to an adult?
>
> Look at our educational system today. We can see that in various ways it combines the different functions: (1) the protection of the child against exploitation, and the protection of society against the precocity and inexperience, (2) the maintenance of learners in a state of moral and economic dependency, (3) giving to all children the special wider education once received by those of the privileged group, in an attempt to form the citizen of a democracy as once the son of the noble house was formed, (4) the teaching of complex and specialized skills which under our complex system of division of labor is too difficult and time-consuming for each set of parents to master or to hand on to their own children, (5) the transmission of some-

thing which the parents' generation does not know in the case of immigrations with varied cultures and linguistic backgrounds to children whom the authorities or the parents wish to have educated.[1]

We need to educate children and youths for rapid and self-conscious adaptation to a complex and changing world. So far, we have failed to recognize the ever-changing needs of education demanded by our dynamic society. Despite the fact that subjects taught to college freshmen may be basically altered by the time these students become seniors, it is still alleged that colleges are able to give students a good education — finished, wrapped, and sealed with a degree. Many individuals, when receiving a degree, will continue on for a higher one because they feel that their education has not been complete. But, a student who returns to school perhaps after a year's lapse is not continuing his education, but "going back" to school. We are avoiding the most vital truth of a new age: No one will live all his life in the world into which he was born and no one will die in the world in which he worked. Nor do students learn all that is to be learned under the tutelage of a teacher or a school.

The new school must recognize that its primary responsibility is not the outpouring of knowledge from the "wise old teacher" into the unformed minds of young people. *Its primary responsibility is the sharing of knowledge by the informed with the uninformed — whatever their areas — and the primary requisite for the learner is the desire to know.* It is not simply a matter of keeping children and young adults, whom we treat like children, in school longer. We need to create an educational environment which is sensitive to *individual differences* at the elementary, secondary, and higher educational levels. Within such an environment, students can continue to learn when they have left school.

Basic Concepts and Changing Values

At one time the American home played a dominant role in the education of children and youths. In the home students learned a sense of responsibility and the importance of doing an honest day's work for an honest day's pay. There, in large part, children learned that they had a responsibility for the welfare of the rest of the family and that this sense of welfare extended to the community level. It was not uncommon in the earlier part of this century to find children throughout many American communities involved in an important productive role, helping to produce the goods and services which sustained the life of individual family members. Nor was it uncommon for boys and girls to participate actively in many

---

[1] Margaret Mead, *Children in Contemporary Culture* (Chicago: University of Chicago Press, 1955), p. 24.

45

community-wide efforts: clearing and caring for school grounds, church-yards, cemeteries, and other tasks. In participating, they felt a social sense of gratitude.

The situation has drastically altered in the present accelerated, indus-trialized, urbanized, interdependent, and scientifically-oriented social system. As the society has changed, so has the individual's social role. Chil-dren and youths no longer help to produce goods and services; like their parents, they are passive consumers in most situations. They no longer feel a sense of responsibility for the welfare of the family or the community. In the wake of such a loss, the school must assume an increasingly central role in helping to impart these concepts to students by providing work experiences and service projects to involve them in community situations and to help them interact with adults in the community while solving these problems.

In the late 1800's and early 1900's the American community also played a major role in educating boys and girls and in developing their value concepts. Citizens in these communities, though closely knit, nonetheless had a high degree of independence together with a respect for the well being of *all* community participants. If an individual living in a typical rural community or small town had an accident and was incapacitated for a period of time, then his neighbors would offer consolation and assistance. If crops needed planting or harvesting, the community would pitch in so that the individual would not be seriously hampered, financially or occu-pationally, by his mishap. If he was in a small business or industry, the neighbors would carry on his responsibilities as though he were doing the job himself. This community situation no longer prevails.

Today, people are on a more impersonal relationship with one another. It is common for people not to know the name of those who live across the street. Even in a rural community, it is no longer improbable for people living a short distance from one another to know relatively little about each other. This social estrangement is a relatively recent phe-nomenon and it is affecting the earlier value systems which developed out of a largely agrarian culture. The value systems which have undergirded American democracy and other democracies throughout the world were based upon five concepts: The Hebraic–Christian code of ethics, the humanistic spirit, a democratic faith, rule by law, and the scientific method. These have had a profound impact upon the thinking and actions of our people, governing and tempering their relationships with each other.

The Hebraic–Christian code of ethics has been a major source for American values. When the founding fathers laid down a moral founda-tion for democracy, they proclaimed — without qualifications — the supreme worth and dignity of the individual. Every man is unique *because* he is a man. Such recognition leads inevitably to the principle of equality among the members of a society. Jesus himself was a carpenter and he proclaimed in a most celebrated way through his sermons that the meek would inherit the earth. The great Hebraic–Christian ethics establishes the moral foundation for peace and good will among nations: "God is made of one blood," the prophet declared, "all nations of men." There are no chosen races or nations commissioned by God; none is entitled by its own nature to rule over and enslave its fellow man.

The code of ethics condemns war for the evil it is. Jesus himself was a prince of peace. The concept conceives man, of all creatures, as living in a moral order. Man is admonished to do justice, be generous, help the unfortunate, show mercy toward the weak, comfort the heavy-laden, serve his fellow man, be honest and truthful, cultivate a humane and general spirit, and love his neighbor as himself. Lincoln's phrase "with malice toward none and charity toward all" speaks to the tradition of the great Hebraic–Christian ethics. Today, the code is threatened by contemporary and totalitarian movements. It is also threatened by an industrialized civilization which is tearing us apart. In an atmosphere of social estrangement, the code of ethics is easily forgotten.

Throughout man's history, *the humanistic spirit* has been one of the great liberating forces. The spirit first appeared in real strength in ancient Greece. It is the force which has been used on both sides of the Atlantic to break the shackles of feudal authority and has aroused men to engage in bold political speculation to help free men. It is reflected in the nation's great state papers: the Declaration of Independence, the Federal Constitution, the Bill of Rights; it abounds in the writings of Washington, Jefferson, Pierce, Lincoln, and other American leaders. The humanistic spirit proclaims man to be the architect of his own destiny for good or evil. It endows man with a capacity for choice. He is challenged to act, think, and triumph over his surroundings. The spirit seeks to help man live a more secure and abundant life by filling it with things worthy and of good repute. It was given expression more than 2,300 years ago through the life and death of Socrates, who is reputed to have asked: "Are you not ashamed of settling your heart on wealth and honor while you have no care for the wisdom and truth and the making of your soul better?" The humanistic spirit sees man as an aesthetic creature, capable of creating and responding to the true and beautiful. It challenges man, in the words of the man of ancient Greece, "to know thyself." It proclaims the doctrine of respectability of man in society.

While the humanistic spirit has never been secure in man's historical development, it is in its greatest peril today — threatened by contemporary ideologies of totalitarianism under which free minds lapse into silence, go into exile, or suffer imprisonment, torture, or death. Ironically, at the same time in history that it is threatened, the humanistic spirit is today facing an unprecedented opportunity: With a firm resolution, men should be able to build a world without material poverty and misery, disease, or frustration. They might even be able to build a world of great beauty and grandeur in which there could be people of strong body, mind, and character — heirs of all which is best in the human legacy.

The democratic faith is the American social faith and its foundation. The Constitution was shaped by values of a democratic society. In almost 200 years our society has evolved, continuously developing and growing; it has applied the concept of democratic faith in that growth. Democracy confirms the worth and dignity of the individual by its declaration that all men are created equal. Democracy regards political and social liberty as the only dependable guardian of individual worth and equality. It declares that, in the long run, the masses of people remain the best judges of their interests and that they alone can be trusted with both liberty and power in managing their common affairs. In short, *they can and should rule themselves.*

Democracy rests upon the due process of law, placing faith in methods of enlightenment, persuasion, and peace to adjust the differences among men. It advocates basic morality in that men must be guided by the canons of simple honesty, truthfulness, and intellectual integrity; in the exercise of power, men must be just, humane, and merciful. Democracy further rests upon individual opportunity. Only in a democracy which is mobile and progressive can man make his own way according to his own beliefs, energies, and talents. The concept can survive only in a society where security is guaranteed through opportunity. Equally important, democracy rests upon individual responsibility. In a free society, responsibility is equated with freedom: All men must be disciplined by a sense of common brotherhood, a love of truth and justice, and a devotion to the general welfare.

Today, the fundamental change in the distribution of power as marked by the rise of our industrial civilization is challenging the concept of democratic faith. If some small class in our industrial society should succeed in gaining control of the new engines of death, such a group could destroy our free institutions in but a few hours. A similar challenge exists in the sphere of economic power. At the present time, little of the productive potential is concentrated in the masses and the majority is concentrated within a small class of wealthy individuals so that the instability of our

48

economy poses a serious threat to our democracy. Most economists agree that, unless preventive measures are taken, we shall experience sooner or later a crisis. Our democracy is challenged by the very complexity of our industrial society. One must wonder whether the ordinary citizen can achieve the level of understanding necessary for fulfilling his civic and social responsibilities.

Our democracy is also challenged by the rise and spread of totalitarian doctrines and systems — both abroad and at home. It is threatened by war and the fear of war. It is imperiled by its own failures such as the doctrine of white supremacy. If democracy loses in its present worldwide struggle, it will lose primarily because it has been false to itself.

One supreme achievement of western man has been rule by law. Only when the law is interrupted or destroyed by some great social convulsion and people are confronted on all sides by the rule of unrestrained force, do men fully sense its meaning and value. Without law there is no order and without order men are lost. The establishment of the principles of law in the western world was a product of centuries of struggle, suffering, invention, and faith. Rule by law, too, stands challenged today. First expressed in the Greek and Roman governments, it has developed into the highest form under constitutional sovereignty — that is, the laws by which laws are made and judged and the laws which govern the governors. It was the English-speaking people who were mainly responsible for the growth of constitutionalism. But even under the best constitutions there are times of crises when raw power in the hands of a few becomes sufficient to destroy the law. For the system to survive against such danger, it must be supported by appropriate and adequate education of all its people. Jefferson once warned that he who expects the ignorant to rule themselves expects what never was or ever will be.

Rule by law is being challenged today by the emergence of new conditions and forces: domestically by the rise of great power groups within our society and internationally by the rise of totalitarian movements which have enslaved more than 500,000,000 people since the end of World War II. The people of democracies must not be unmindful of the concept of communism as voiced by Lenin when he declared that freedom is a bourgeois prejudice, and it does not matter if three-fourths of mankind may be destroyed if, in the process, the remaining quarter becomes communist.

Scientific Method

Science, including both method and application, is the greatest single force moving and shaping the modern age. It has become deeply rooted in American life. Science offers a means for prediction and control. It procures food and shelter, wards off and cures diseases, and makes life more secure, pleasing, and meaningful. Man's lengthy struggles to emancipate himself from the forces of nature have been largely achieved. Science is much more than a body of knowledge: in essence, it is a method for obtaining knowledge and therefore a molder and bearer of values. It has both broadened and deepened man's conception of his relationship to the universe.

Science, art, and philosophy satisfy a deep craving in the human heart: the simple desire to know and understand, look beneath events, explore unknown regions, vanish the veil of ignorance, and fathom the mysteries of life. Science has developed its own moral tradition. The scientist must practice intellectual virtues of accuracy, precision, integrity, and openmindedness. Science holds a potential for greater future knowledge. Although it is often said we live in an age of science, there are many spheres and interests where science is unwelcome. In human relations, economics, politics, and moral dogma there exist strong opposition to the induction of the scientific method.

Science — along with the other concepts we have cited — stands endangered today. The greatest threat to the scientific spirit is found in the totalitarian state. It is here that control is carried to the point of compelling scientists not only to hold findings in secret, but also to fabricate data which support the doctrines and policies of the dictator. The threat was very evident during the reign of Hitler when he compelled his biologists and anthropologists to make fabricated statements in support of his own doctrine and belief that the Nazi people, as the most powerful and capable on earth, should rule all mankind.

Science is particularly threatened in democratic America. We see scientists working to betray their own country, selling and giving closely guarded results of research to agents of the communist world. It remains to be seen whether men will use science as their servant of savage appetites and passions. Even though science may have its own moral tradition, it does not embrace the whole of human experiences. Science alone is not enough. Albert Einstein remarked:

> It is true that convictions can best be supported with experience and clear thinking. These convictions which are necessary to the permanence of our conduct and judgment cannot be found solely along the solid scientific path. Yet, it is clear that knowledge of what is, does not open the doors directly for what should be.[2]

---

[2] Albert Einstein, *Profile of Man* (New York: Dodd, Mead and Co., Inc., 1962), p. 10.

It is essential that the scientist and those who implement the scientific method rely upon the Hebraic–Christian code of ethics, the democratic faith, humanistic spirit and rule by law to provide the foundations for scientific findings.

In this chapter a potpourri of subjects has been examined: social stresses due to stratification, five home/community environments, changing values in the roles of the American home and community, and the basic concepts which have shaped our nation. How do these diverse subjects relate to the American school's role of preparing the individual student for social adequacy? In essence, the school has become a central force in coping with social stresses and changing values and in reinforcing the basic concepts as the American home and community have grown more fragmented.

A child born into this push-button world is, first of all, isolated according to the social, economic, and occupational strata of his parents. Most slum children will never cross the ghetto line, much less make it to the comfortable small town or affluent suburbs unless the school he attends helps him to achieve a socially adequate role. None of the children — whether from slum, farm, small town, or suburban setting — can look to the home or the community for a sense of personal and community pride as did those living in the earlier American agrarian culture where the home and community played dominant roles. Home and community are too segmented today. By default, the school must assume what was formerly the educative function of the family and community: to develop a sense of social adequacy.

Ours is a society which has advocated education for everyone. Ours is also a society in which education is the key for many to escape poverty and despair. The times are anxiety-ridden. Ideological differences divide international conference tables. National conflicts — mainly class and racial — tear at our unity. High juvenile and adult crime rates eat into our security. We pollute the air, water, and food supplies to an alarming degree. Our relationships and attitudes toward other people — not only in the nation, but throughout the world — are growing increasingly inhumane.

Under these stresses, it is absolutely necessary that we revitalize education and reinforce our commitment to a democratic way of life through educational experiences which prepare a student to cope with the society in which they will live rather than prepare them for a society which has long since passed. The problem solving curriculum rather than the subject centered one can do this.

BIBLIOGRAPHY

Auer, Bernard M., *The Environment of Change*. New York: Time, Inc., 1965.
Bantock, G. H., *Culture Industrialization and Education*. New York: Humanities Press, 1968.

51

Bremback, Cole S., *Social Foundations of Education.* New York: John Wiley and Sons, Inc., 1971.

Brown, George, *Human Teaching for Human Learning.* New York: The Viking Press, 1971.

Bryner, James R., *The Schools in American Society.* Riverside, N.J.: The Macmillan Co., 1973.

Charnofsky, Stanley, *Educating the Powerless.* Belmont, Calif.: Wadsworth Publishing Co., Inc., 1971.

Combs, Arthur W., *Educational Accountability.* Washington, D.C.: Association for Supervision and Curriculum Development — National Education Association, 1973.

Dewey, John, *My Pedagogic Creed.* New York: Teachers College, 1959.

Doll, Ronald C., *Curriculum Improvement.* Atlanta: Allyn and Bacon, 1970.

Elkin, Frederick, *The Child and Society: The Process of Socialization.* New York: Random House, 1965.

Full, Harold, ed., *Controversy in American Education.* New York: The Macmillan Co., 1972.

Gibson, Dorothy, *Education in a Dynamic Society.* Reading, Mass.: Addison-Wesley Publishing Co., Inc., 1972.

Havighurst, Robert J., *Society and Education.* Boston: Allyn and Bacon, 1967.

Henderson, George, ed., *Education for Peace.* Washington, D.C.: Association for Supervision and Curriculum Development — National Education Association, 1973.

Landes, Ruth, *Culture in American Education.* New York: John Wiley and Sons, Inc., 1965.

Karier, Violos and Spring Karier, *Roots of Crisis.* Chicago: Rand McNally and Co., 1973.

Leeper, Robert R., ed. *Supervision: Emerging Profession.* Washington, D.C.: Association for Supervision and Curriculum Development — National Education Association, 1972.

Mead, Margaret, *Childhood in Contemporary Culture.* Chicago: University of Chicago Press, 1955.

Rosen, B. C. and others, *Achievement in American Society.* Cambridge: Schenkman Publications, Inc., 1969.

Van Til, William, *Curriculum — Quest for Relevance.* Boston: Houghton Mifflin Co., 1971.

Weber, Christian O., *Basic Philosophies of Education.* New York: Holt, Rinehart and Winston, 1960.

Weinberg, Carl, *Social Foundations of Educational Guidance.* New York: The Free Press, 1969.

Chapter 3.   Psychological Soundness

Few students who feel inadequate, are continually frustrated, and remain for the most part unmotivated can grow into confident and productive individuals who have learned to cope with situations in life. Chances are they will spend 12 years in a school which has a subject centered curriculum where they will learn to give the "right" answers, do most of the assigned homework after reading the assigned texts, and avoid upsetting confrontations. But the individual inside of them will remain bottled up. They will not have learned, above all, *how to learn*.

Much educational practice in the subject centered curriculum revolves around the notion that man has to be prodded or moved into action by an external force or stimulus. Such thinking has led to a system of education which seeks to provide the forces necessary to move students from inertia to prescribed activity. The organism has been seen as a sort of inert mass of protoplasm to be molded into "something." Under this kind of approach to student motivation, teachers cannot afford to trust the organism; indeed, they need to be constantly on guard against a reversion on the organism's part to some base animal character. And if students cannot be trusted to decide what is good for them, the thinking continues, then someone (curriculum makers) must choose what is "good for them" and still others can be kept moving through this "good experience." Children are regarded as a kind of adverse force within the schools, and they are certain to go wrong if educators do not keep them straight.

Unfortunately, those assigned the task of forcing students through this assembly line of education make the discovery that some students have ideas of their own. Somehow these students have managed to wiggle out of line to find their own ways for self-fulfillment. They have learned that the only way to escape the dies designed to cast them into conformity is through rebellion or escape. Rebellion, however, does not always take a creative, constructive direction; nor does escape or turning away develop productive or creative people. Such students often make problems for schools and society.

This fixed notion of human motivation has been with us for a long time. It tends to see the human organism as basically untrustworthy and certain to move in the "wrong" direction unless carefully supervised. Motivation, within this view, is a matter of controlling the external events to assure that students will arrive at the prior and "proper" determined ends. It involves force, coercion, control, management, direction — aimed at molding the child "the way he should go."

Motivation in Problem Solving

A more hopeful view of motivation and of man's potential is provided by problem solving–team teaching: Everyone has a basic internal need to grow. This view of man and of learning offers a challenging idea about children's motives. Man has a built-in thrust or need to become fully functioning or adequate — a psychologically healthy person. Through expression and need gratification, he is able to mature into a self-actualizing or fully functioning personality. But this inner core or nature of his may be thwarted or perverted unless it is given the right environment for expression; growth emerging out of expression and need gratification rather than through repression or inhibition.

Generations of teachers have been indoctrinated through the subject centered curriculum with the concept that children must somehow be "made" good. Motivation, according to the concept, is seen as a matter of stimulus/response and direction/control. On the other hand, problem solving–team teaching assumes that people are always motivated; in fact, they are never unmotivated. They may not be motivated to do what those in charge would prefer, but it can never be stated truthfully that they are unmotivated. The direction of this motivation within the framework of good problem solving learning is toward health. Students want the same things for themselves that teachers want for them: to be adequate, fully functioning, and self-actualizing persons. Here is an optimism about humanity that is reassuring in this age of gloom. Its promise is that education can be of more account than the prophets of doom believe and that it can assist mankind toward a path of fulfillment rather than one of destruction.

Education does not have to convert the beast or tame him; the task does not call for directing, controlling, remaking, and remolding an innately antagonistic organism. Learning in the problem solving class becomes a matter of working *with*, not against the organism. Teaching becomes facilitating, helping, assisting, aiding, and encouraging an organism which seeks the same eventual goals as teachers themselves seek. It makes a great deal of difference, therefore, *how* we go about dealing with children: whether we believe they are fundamentally opposed to us or if we believe that they are basically seeking the same ends as we are. A teacher who respects a student's ability behaves quite differently from one who believes a pupil is obstinate and unable. The teacher who disapproves of or distrusts the fundamental motives of his students cannot permit them the freedom to seek what they need. His view of himself as a responsible teacher requires that he use coercive methods of control and even, if necessary, force. He will see pupil–teacher planning, group decisions, spontaneity, and self-determination as puzzling, fuzzy-minded, or threatening. Problem solving, by its very basis of a different view of man, is a suspicious procedure. He may even view his colleagues who support a problem solving curriculum as irresponsible. In his anxiety the teacher is unwilling to see that trust in each individual's motivation toward health helps teachers to become more human and schools more effective models in terms of the society beyond the school walls.

The natural thrust of motivation can be clearly seen in first-grade students. There is an almost limitless desire to "know" and find out about things. But something happens as students move through the subject centered school. Teachers tend to assume more and more responsibility for deciding what is to be learned, how the child will be motivated for that learning, and the way he shall learn. C. W. Hunnicutt once remarked that, as students progress through school and become increasingly able to make choices, they are given ever-decreasing opportunities to make decisions. Man is essentially dependable and trustworthy; his innate impulses must propel him toward actualization — *if* he is free to move. He has an inherent need to use his capabilities in a constructive manner and a built-in thrust toward actualizing his abilities to "become." Ill health, conversely, is falling short of growth.

A student who has been unsuccessful at school-oriented tasks or has found himself condemned for his errors may develop many self-defenses. It is easier for the student to take punishment imposed for not trying than it is for him to be ridiculed because he is wrong. The task of school people is to create conditions which are conducive to actualizing the inner core or nature of students and which minimize situations inhibiting growth. Problem solving learning can help in the task. If students are motivated toward health, teachers will not feel bound to impose the defensive idea that they know what is best for their charges. Tensions, conflicts, and frustrations experienced by both teachers and students because of differences in goals will be largely absent. In a problem solving situation the teacher is not dictator or coercer, but provider of alternates. He is a friendly representative of society, skilled equally in understanding people and in creating situations which set them free to become the best they can. Rather than manipulators of children, teachers should be people who can enter into meaningful and productive relationships with students. Teachers are themselves people.

55

Problem-oriented teachers develop a faith in the student's ability to make wise decisions and to direct his own life; they are able to develop an atmosphere of mutual confidence. Within this atmosphere, mistakes have their value. A student is not made to feel that he has failed *because* he made a mistake. To the contrary, a student can gain new insights and derive more realistic directions from his mistakes. Within a supportive problem solving classroom environment, the student can afford to make mistakes. The main point is that he is involved in a process of becoming. As his abilities are given an opportunity for expression, he moves toward total self-actualization.

The self concept is one of the most important factors affecting the way in which an individual will behave. A healthy self concept is one that is achieved—developed from relations an individual has with others. It is influenced by the quality of these relationships: first with family, then with peers in unstructured situations, then with teachers and peers in more structured situations. If the climate is unwholesome and unkind, growth is stunted or arrested and illness occurs. The inclusion of honest concern about human meanings, feelings, and understandings prevalent in the problem solving curriculum is not an easy matter because our schools are representatives of the society in which we live and much of that society has made a fetish of objectivity. It is natural, therefore, to jump to the conclusion that those principles governing the control and production of the "things" in our world apply also in our dealings with people.

If a positive view of the self is important in developing creative, productive people, then the self must be admitted into the classroom and provision be made for its development. The teacher who brings the self of students into his classroom must be a facilitating person. He must develop situations in which he shows each child that—to teachers and fellow students—he matters and that the child is accepted as he is. Permissiveness is often taken to mean freedom to create physical chaos, to upset or destroy property and the classroom decorum. But, when used in the problem solving-team teaching situation, permissiveness means the freedom for a student to have ideas, beliefs, and values as well as permission for him to be himself while pursuing interests and challenges in his search for a meaning in life.

People become adequate; they are not born that way. Society's—and education's—problem is not to find and coddle adequate personalities. Rather, it needs to produce them as reasonably as fast as it can. What people need to learn, they can be taught. Adequate personalities are not a gift: They are the crowning achievement of problem solving-team teaching. Within such a curriculum, the student has alternative choices, enabling him to weigh varied conditions and circumstances through projecting hypotheses and testing them for generalizations and conclusions. The process helps him to build a conceptual basis for experimentation. This experimental concept—basic to problem solving—has been shaped by sound psychological principles derived from the field, organismic, and perceptual concepts of learning.

Field Theory: Person and Environment

Field theory[1] has a wide latitude and variety of psychological and sociological implications for education. Its proponents see its potential value in many areas: child behavior, adolescent development, problems of the feebleminded, anxieties of minority groups, national differences, and educational group processes. These areas contribute to the principal domain of problem solving-team teaching at its highest innovative application. Field theory—no ivy tower set of concepts—embodies the broad humanitarian and democratic value system which enables man to understand the types of investigation frequently called "action research." Action research has the same focus as problem solving: changing social conditions.

The field theory of learning deals with the life span of the whole of psychological realities—containing a totality of possible facts which are capable of determining and guiding the behavior of individuals. Its concepts—comparable to those of problem solving—are broad enough to apply to all possible kinds of human behavior, but specific enough to enable a person to deal with concrete everyday situations. Field theory has these qualities:

1. Behavior is a function of the field which exists at the time the behavior occurs.
2. Analysis begins with the situation as a whole; from this whole the component parts are differentiated.
3. The concrete person in the concrete life situation can be represented collectively or mathematically.

Proponents of the field theory of learning and of problem solving-team teaching insist that the psychological environment can produce change in the physical world because there is a two-way communication between an individual and the space surrounding him in the outer world. They also contend that there is no permanent boundary separating the individual from his environmental surroundings, but there is a membering or a screen—though not a barrier—separating the two so that the transition is a

1 The German scientist and psychologist Kurt Lewing can possibly be credited with being the most outstanding proponent and contributor to the field theory.

permeable one. Environmental forces surrounding an individual can have impact upon him; that person, in turn, can influence the environment. The structure of the individual, according to field theory and problem solving proponents, is heterogeneous rather than homogeneous. But the individual is subdivided into separate, yet intercommunicative and interdependent pods. The fact that there is a permeable boundary between life as the individual lives it and the physical world in which he resides has far-reaching significance; facts in the nonpsychological world can rapidly change the whole course of events in an individual's life. The possibility always exists that a fact from the environmental surroundings might penetrate the boundaries of an individual's life, turning everything topsy-turvy in his psychological environment. An unexpected telephone call or a serious automobile accident involving a member of one's family, for example, can easily change the course of a person's life.

Behind the field theory supporting problem solving-team teaching is the assumption that it is far more purposeful for the psychologist or the educator to understand the momentary concrete, psychological situation by describing and explaining it in the theoretical field than it is to attempt a prediction on how a person will behave at a future time. In reaching such an understanding, field theory draws upon these dynamic principles: energy, tension, need, valence, and force or vector. An effective problem solving-team teaching situation uses all of these concepts.

Psychological *energy* is released when an equilibrium is out of a state of balance; the energy is spent to return the system to a state of equilibrium with its environment. The disequilibrium continues to disrupt the life of the individual until the tension throughout the system becomes equalized again, returning to a state of equilibrium.

Tension, when used in the field theory concept, can be manifested in several ways. One common use of tension is through a system or portion of an individual's being as it works toward equalization and harmony with the surrounding system. This kind of tension is released through processes like thinking, remembering, feeling, perceiving, or acting. For example, as a person faces the solving of a problem, he becomes tense in one of his systems. To solve the problem and therefore reduce the tension, he engages in the process of thinking until some satisfactory solution is found in order to return to a state of equilibrium.

Another application of tension can be seen in the idea that the human organism is made up of several component parts or adjacent systems. When a tension is created in one of these systems, the boundaries may be either weak or rigid; but there is a tendency for a diffusion of the tension into adjacent systems. The weaker the boundaries, the more readily tension will flow from one system into another. Or, if the system is bound with several different systems—some of which may be weaker than others—the tension tends to flow from the system where the tension exists into a system where boundaries are weak. In doing this, the human organism is able to reach a state of equilibrium. Such equilibrium is relatively stable throughout the total organism and equal in all of the different systems.

Need, a third dynamic concept envisioned by the field theory psychologist, constitutes one of the most dynamic and forceful conditions operating within an individual's body. Need can be psychological, physiological, or sociological. For example, an individual may have a need for food, water, or sex; he may want a job or power or friendship; he may wish acceptance and recognition from his co-workers. These needs have a dynamic impact upon the life of the individual, causing him to exert energy. Need, one of the most powerful motivating forces in the life of a dynamic individual, is drawn upon extensively in problem solving-team teaching. It constitutes a central nucleus around which all the other dynamic forces cluster.

Valence, an additional conceptual property of psychological environment, may be positive or negative. Positive valence tends to attract whereas negative tends to repel. For example, a positive valence might be an urge for food, forcing an individual to seek some source to satisfy hunger. But he might move away from the source because of a negative force, perhaps the presence of a bear.

The last dynamic concept seen by the field theory psychologist and used in problem solving teaching is *force* or *vector.* Whereas tension is a property of the inner personal system, a force exists in the psychological environment of an individual. While force is closely associated with need, it does not produce the same tension as a need.

Field theory views behavioral change as a constant developmental process, growing more noticeable and pronounced as the individual matures. A person's activities, emotions, needs, information, and social relationships with others tend to increase up to a given point of his maturation. After this point diversity and development of his behavior tend to level off and even decline.

As an individual grows older, his behavior increases in complexity. A small child usually has a close relationship with one other child; an older child usually has close relationships with a number of children. Behavior also becomes more hierarchial in structure and it may become more complex in the sense that the older child will engage in many activities simultaneously. The young child is, by and large, a creature of the present; only as he grows older does he begin to think about the past, see the present within a larger perspective, and make plans for the future. This developmental-hierarchial process has an integrating impact upon an individual, helping him to become increasingly interdependent and consistent in his integration and in the separation of needs and activities into larger parts. He starts analyzing life situations in terms of their totality. For example, learning to play basketball, building a motor, or writing a story calls upon a larger scope of separate activities than in the past.

As an individual grows, he begins to use differentiation — a tool important to the field theory of learning and problem solving situations. Differentiation is an increase in the number of parts of a whole with the whole being far greater than the sum of its parts. An adult who becomes increasingly capable of differentiating his tension system can cope with the psychological environment more meaningfully and realistically. Not only does he distinguish between concepts like reality/unreality, good/bad, and true/false; he further recognizes the varying shades of possibility and probability. He is able to differentiate between the individual organism and psychological environment. When he is at this point in his development, his complicated network of hierarchies and selected relationships has become highly organized.

In stressing that the educator understand the psychological situation of a given moment through the means of energy, tension, need, valence, and force or vector, the field theory of learning underlines the interrelationship of individual and the space surrounding him in the outside world. Problem solving learning—in drawing upon this theory and its concepts—helps to develop a psychological soundness in the student by engaging him actively in the effective resolution of tensions and conflicts.

Organismic Theory: Comprehensiveness

A second theory of learning and psychology giving substantial support to problem solving team teaching—the organismic—has borrowed many concepts from the Gestalt view. In essence, the Gestalt psychologists start with the perceptual field as a whole, differentiating it into figures and backgrounds. Then they study the properties of each of these components in terms of its mutual influence and relationship to the whole. The concept of learning undergirding both the Gestalt and organismic views replaces doctoring of association with insight. It also proclaims that a person learns a task as a meaningful whole rather than breaking it down in piecemeal fashion, as is usually done in subject centered, departmentalized schools. Though borrowing much from the Gestalt people, the organismic psychologists moved a little further by extending the Gestalt principles to the organism as a whole — incorporating the biological as well as the psychological and sociological. Organismic psychology has these qualities:

60

1. Emphasizes the unity, integration, consistency, and coherence of a normal personality;
2. Starts with the organism as an organizing system and analyzes it by differentiating the whole from its constituent parts because the whole, not the isolated parts, must be studied;
3. Assumes that the individual is motivated primarily by one sovereign drive rather than by a plurality of drives and that this sovereign drive or motive will work continually toward the goal of self-actualization or self-realization, with the individual taking whatever avenue is open to him in achieving full potential;
4. Does not regard the individual as a closed system but tends to minimize the primary and directive influences of the external environment in normal behavior—stressing the inherent potentialities of the organism for growth;
5. Incorporates, within its scope, all that the organism is and does;
6. Contends that there is more to be learned from a comprehensive study of one person than from an extensive investigation of an isolated psychological function of many individuals.

Therefore, organismic theory is frequently considered more applicable to clinical psychology than to education in general; however, it has many potential possibilities for enhancing the learning in sound problem solving-team teaching endeavors.

Proponents of organismic theory contend that the organism consists of differentiated members which are articulated together. These members do not become detached or isolated from one another except under abnormal or artificial conditions; generally they work in support of the other members. If an individual is hungry, for example, he will exert all of his energies in an effort to secure food through the various processes that he has used in the past. However, the organism could be disrupted: If the hungry person suddenly becomes frightened, a new process will emerge, placing the original effort in the background and conceivably changing the organism.

Organismic psychology has three primary concepts: (1) the equalization process, (2) the self-actualization process, and (3) adjustment with the environment. The equalization process involves keeping the available energy supply fairly constant and uniformly distributed throughout the organism. This average distribution of energy represents the condition that an organism tries at all times to maintain. When disruption occurs, the organism is constantly endeavoring to return to this state of equalization. As an example, if the individual is hungry, he will tend to eat. If he is tired, he will rest. If he is sleepy, he will sleep. These are ordinary examples of the equalization process operating within an organism—provided that environment is adequate. The organism, for its part, maintains a balance. As the individual matures and grows older, he develops preferred ways of behaving so that interference and conflicts are kept at a minimum. He also becomes more adept at preserving the balance in the organism.

Self-actualization is a master motive of organismic psychology and learning. Many organismic psychologists would even insist that it is the *only* motive an organism possesses. Other motives like hunger, sex, power, achievement, and curiosity, in their view, are merely manifestations of the sovereign purpose of achieving self-actualization. They command attention because they make immediate demands on the individual and because they are prerequisites to the organism's self-actualization. This creative concept of self-actualization is one of the basic ingredients of problem solving learning. A person who has achieved self-actualization has developed more fully and completely.

Both organismic psychology and problem solving operate on the assumption that each individual is uniquely different from other individuals. Therefore, each person will achieve self-actualization through a wholly different approach. There is much discussion at this time over how teachers, school administrators, and psychologists can effectively determine the potentialities of each individual in the problem solving-team teaching situation. Proponents of organismic psychology would insist that we find out what a person prefers and what he can do most effectively since his preferences frequently parallel his potentiality.

With self-fulfillment and self-actualization as the goals, we must not only discover an individual's potential, but also help to determine what steps he can take to develop that potential. In problem solving learning situations, the conscious motivation of an individual has great impact and force over and beyond his unconscious ones. The unconscious tends to remain in the background, coming to the fore only when the conscious motivation recedes. An unconscious motivation is useful in the self-realization process, but not nearly as applicable as a conscious one.

Perceptual Psychology: The Adequate Self

Problem solving-team teaching is permeated with the perceptual view that every individual is constantly in the process of working toward becoming an adequate personality. If conditions are favorable, an increasing number of persons can be helped to achieve a more satisfying life. The self-actualization process which lies at the heart of perceptual psychology is partly built upon helping a person develop a self view that is positive. When he begins to see himself in a positive sense, then he can view other people and life in general in this same manner. Reverting to a biblical concept, as an individual thinketh, so can he become. In a problem solving-team teaching situation, perceptual psychologists perceive the self-actualized person as one who is able, liked, wanted, and accepted. He is a person of worth and integrity because he has worth and integrity in his self-view and in the views of others. The well-adjusted self-actualizing individual has a tremendous advantage in dealing with life and in providing the basis for greater personal strength. Such a person can cope by meeting life with some expectation of success and by behaving in a way that tends to bring about the actual act of accomplishment. A self-actualizing individual's personal self-view permits effectiveness without worrying about conformity or nonconformity.

The concept of self is shaped from the ways in which a person has been treated by those around him during his growth process. Problem solving-team teaching holds out the hope that each individual will be assured of a reasonable degree of success each and every day he attends school. The strongest assurance for individual future success is success in current life situations. Problem solving-team teaching—undergirded with perceptual psychology—develops a feeling of unity, oneness, and togetherness within the groups as participants share a common faith and work toward common goals. The self is extended to include one's fellow man. In an actual problem solving situation, the individual develops a feeling of respect and responsibility toward fellow participants. Such a person will behave responsibly because he has identified with others, learning through the cooperative experiences that what is good for himself is also good for his fellow man.

Problem solving-team teaching provides maximum opportunity for each individual to be open to new experiences and to accept others without resorting to a defensive behavior. This attitude is possible because he is relatively free from threat and failure. He need not be overly disturbed by the errors he makes or the transgressions of fellow students. This concept of openness and acceptance is by no means innate, but learned from a person's relationships with other people. Clinical evidence points to a child's capability for accepting most formidable handicaps *if* he is surrounded by understanding people. The acceptance concept can be continually experienced in problem solving learning where students regularly interact with peers and teachers.

Perceptual psychologists tell us that the inadequate concept of the self, on the other hand, is both common in our culture and seriously crippling. The psychological self—though not as visible as the physical—is nonetheless subject to the danger of being crippled through the ways an individual has been treated during his life. Unfortunately, most Americans today have grown up in an authoritarian home, were educated in authoritarian schools, have attended an authoritarian church, and live surrounded by an authoritarian culture. Our nation is far from achieving realistic and true democracy; the gap between what is and what could be takes its toll upon the psychological self by preventing the individual from developing into a self-actualizing individual. Situations are regularly reoccurring in the traditional subject centered, lock-step school and in the broader authoritarian culture which cause people to look at themselves and find that what they see is inadequate. It is not enough to perform a task; the performer, upon self-inspection, must know that what he has done is sufficient. Without this positive feeling, the individual is left with inadequate concepts of life. Day by day he is filled with unreasonable fears and plagued by self-doubt. He is trapped in a spiral of negative feelings.

The perceptual psychologist sees the mere speck of protoplasm which is present at the time of human conception as constantly and dynamically involved in becoming a fully functioning human being. As the individual's body and mind grow and develop, he is fed by the environmental conditions which surround him. It is true that physical growth stops around the age of 20, but psychological growth continues indefinitely—when properly fed. Problem solving-team teaching—using perceptual theories of learning and growth—provides an environmental background in which the student can interact and grow. It is well known that the quality of the perceptual process determines in large part the quality of an individual's behavior. The individual grows into unified organisms by his actions and interactions. There is no such thing as the body apart from the personality or the psychological self separate from the biological self. What affects one affects all.

Research and experimentation have shown that perception is a highly selective process. A person does not see all that surrounds him, nor does he hear all that may happen within his environmental surroundings. This act of selecting from among experiences is what makes an individual distinct. Problem solving-team teaching is particularly concerned with purpose because each person tends to perceive that which suits his purpose and fits comfortably among his past experiences without threatening him. In the problem solving process the student has opportunities to select facilitating factors and block out damaging ones.

64

The psychological self feeds upon ideas which come from other people. If, through problem solving, the school provides an enhancing relationship between its students, it can break some of the barriers separating individuals and help them be more receptive to new experiences. By such a process, the individual develops into a fully functioning and adequate personality—dependent not primarily upon material things, but the quality of people around the learner.

Few individuals in our society have been able to overcome adverse impact from the home, church, school, or community and develop into fully functioning, adequate people. But a sound problem solving-team teaching situation, guided by facilitating people, can provide such opportunities for full development. Perceptual psychologists tell us that each person has an essential core of latent capacity and potentiality which must be nourished if he is to grow into a fully functioning citizen. If the growth does not take place, sickness results and the person becomes frustrated, denied, or suppressed. It is the school's role to encourage an individual's inner nature, not suppress it. The student in a problem solving classroom can experience basic need gratification resulting in health and self-fulfillment rather than in frustration.

A child who has free choice during his normal development, according to perceptual psychologists, will select what is good for his growth because it tastes good, feels good, and gives pleasure or delight. The observation implies that the individual probably knows better than anyone else what is good for him. In a problem solving learning situation the student learns his strengths and limits by overcoming obstacles and by working to meet challenges — even if he, at times, fails. Failure which is frequent can be overpowering and destructive. Each step in problem solving-team teaching involves the unfamiliar and a possibly dangerous situation. Adopting the approach often means giving up a simpler method in exchange for one that is more difficult and demanding. Growth amid such circumstances requires courage and strength as well as protection, permission, and encouragement from peers, teachers, and the learning environment itself.

But the reward is considerable: Problem solving students can develop a framework of values, philosophy of life, or religion by which to live. Each is needed as much as sunlight, food, and love. The self-actualizing person can learn, in such situations, to fuse selfishness and unselfishness into a higher unity. Work tends to become much the same as play. Vocation and avocation blend together. This kind of learning can encourage healthy people to dip into the unconscious and preconscious to use their primary processes instead of fearing them and to accept their impulses instead of suppressing them. They feel free of many of the traumatic and current human problems common to our society. Conflict, anxiety, frustration, sadness, hurt, and guilt are not absent from the healthy personality, but such a person learns to cope with them rather than be enslaved.

Sound problem solving learning creates a miniature society which fosters rather than inhibits growth. The better culture and its schools will gratify all of these basic human needs and will help achieve self-realization; the poorer culture and its schools will inhibit them. Problem solving-team teaching capitalizes on the theory of human motivation which assumes that needs are arranged along a hierarchy of priorities. When needs of the greatest priority have been satisfied, the next needs in the hierarchy emerge and press for satisfaction. The concept provides no place for antisocial behavior resulting when society has denied fulfillment of a man's inborn needs.

The problem solving curriculum borrows heavily from perceptual psychology in its insistence that the primary responsibility is to help people develop into fully functioning individuals. Accordingly, the goals of education should be not only what is desirable for the individual, but for the whole of society. The curriculum is centered around purpose, helping the student to inquire: "Who am I and what am I striving to become?" Only when an individual has asked such questions and arrived at satisfactory answers can he move towards becoming a fully functioning personality. He cannot ask these questions until he is convinced that he is an individual of worth and dignity, he is fully accepted as a person, his experiences are important in the eyes of those around him, and he can make a contribution.

In such learning situations, rather than translating or twisting experiences to fit a preconceived self-structure, the self and its personality are allowed to emerge from experiences. An individual is able to live at the present moment and exclude the rigid organization frequently imposed by a formal school program. It means that a person is becoming increasingly adaptable in his ability to change the organization of self in order to discover the processes important to his living and being.

Problem solving learning will enable an individual to move through the process of becoming increasingly trustworthy of his own organisms as a means of arriving at a satisfactory behavior. Such an individual feels right about the situation at hand, confident, and trustworthy. He is continuously guiding his behavior by means of discovering the immediate feeling process. He wants to feel close to any source of information rather than be closed to it. And he has a feeling of direction toward something concrete and worthwhile for himself and for society. In short, he is in the process of becoming a fully functioning person.

Concepts of Human Growth and Development

Writers in the fields of education and psychology and those with a special interest in curriculum are giving increased emphasis to the physical, emotional, social, and intellectual parts of child growth and development. Through such insights teachers can determine which experiences are most suitable for pupils at specific ages. The insights include a rather comprehensive investigation of what psychological, social, and biological needs boys and girls should have at the various stages of their maturation process. They further provide clues to the worries, needs, interests, anxieties, and problems constantly confronted in curriculum development. Without such concepts a curriculum can turn into sterile soil, incapable of fostering growth and learning.

While these concepts of human growth and development have become increasingly important, it is ironic that they are largely ignored by many teachers who are increasingly concerned with mere academic achievement—particularly since the sputnik impact on American education in the late 1950's. Growth and development form a unifying process involving the total organism. No individual can operate effectively without interrelating and synthesizing his mental, physical, social, and emotional organisms. When disunity in total growth and development occurs, the child or youth tends to develop acute adjustment problems. The rich environment tends to select what a person needs to achieve growth and developmental patterns. It is crucial that the pupil be dealt with as a whole human being rather than treated in terms of separate parts. An individual may become physically ill because of an emotional disturbance and, in turn, his physical growth can have great impact upon his emotional stability. An extremely overweight person, for example, might develop behavior which makes him less effective as an individual.

It is generally accepted that intellectually healthy children, on the whole, will be well developed physically and have good emotional adjustment. Dealing only with a student's intellectual growth is totally unrealistic. How an individual relates to his family, peers, and associates has a tremendous impact upon how he perceived himself and how far he is able to achieve.

Growth, while very irregular, is a continuous and gradual process. The environment has a great deal to do with orderly and sequential development of an individual. At times mental growth will occur and physical growth may be somewhat arrested. On other occasions physical spurts in growth may absorb all the metabolisms of energy a person can develop, leaving little chance for effective intellectual involvement. The environment further influences an individual's progression from a self-centered person to a socially conscious being. But, whatever the circumstances and influences, any severe setback in growth over a long period will result in difficulties.

Certain stages of growth from childhood to adulthood play a significant part in an individual's life. As a person goes through these stages, he becomes increasingly capable of coping with problems. The 10-year-old with a good motor control, for example, is likely to be well adjusted and not overly anxious about any specific demands made by family or friends. Understanding the characteristics of growth and development helps not only in planning intellectual, but also physical activities for boys and girls. It must be recognized, of course, that children do not go through these stages simultaneously. Growth—as a continous and unifying process—cannot be pushed beyond the limits or pattern of maturation. Each child must live in the present; to do this, the school must help him develop the skills, concepts, and attitudes necessary to a successful living experience.

Meeting Developmental Tasks and Needs

During a certain period of an individual's development a situation or problem—that is, a developmental task or need—will arise. Performing these tasks successfully will lead to the individual's happiness, acceptance by society, and confidence in handling future tasks or needs. They must be done with a reasonable degree of success at the proper time or they will never be achieved well. Failure in these tasks will in turn result in partial or complete failure in achieving later tasks or needs. To quote Havighurst, "the organ which misses its time of ascendancy is doomed, not only as an individual; it endangers at the same time the whole hierarchy or organs."[2]

Some developmental tasks and needs are biological or physiological in origin. Others are primarily sociological or psychological. As an example, the physical maturation process enables an individual to walk when his bone structure has adequately developed. But a person denied human companionship in his early years may never learn to talk well or effectively. The human personality or self is a psychological process emerging from the inner actions of the organism and environmental forces which act upon the individual. Havighurst has said that "when the body is right and society requires and the self is ready to achieve a certain task, the teachable moment has come. Efforts at teaching which would have been largely

---

[2] Robert J. Havighurst, *Developmental Task and Education* (New York: David McKay Co., 1952) , p. 3.

wasted if they came earlier give gratifying results when they come at the teachable moment."[3]

These developmental tasks and needs are common to all individuals:

1. Achieving a new and more mature relationship with age-mates of both sexes as a person grows older;
2. Achieving and accepting a masculine or feminine biosocial role;
3. Accepting one's physique and using the body effectively so the individual can realize that he is not necessarily abnormal;
4. Achieving more and wider emotional independence of parents and other adults as the individual matures biologically;
5. Achieving a degree of economic independence, starting from mere use of an allowance to earning a livelihood;
6. Selecting and preparing for an occupation;
7. Developing an appropriate give-and-receive affection pattern with parents, siblings, and others as a basis for effective preparation for marriage and family life;
8. Developing intellectual skills and concepts necessary for effective civic involvement;
9. Desiring and achieving socially responsible behavior;
10. Acquiring a set of values and an ethical system as guides to behavior.

Each of these 10 common tasks and needs plays a critical role in human growth and development. A few call for specific comments. The child, at an early age, has a very immature relationship with age-mates of both sexes. But if he is to develop into a fully functioning individual, capable of coping with situations and human interactions, he must become increasingly more mature and more tolerant in his relationships with people as he grows older. He must progress in his development from a self-centered person to a more socially responsible one.

Achieving a masculine or feminine biosocial role is one that society in the past has emphasized. It remains to be seen if the hippie movement upsets these expectations. Many individuals, at least in part, resent the biosocial role expected of the two sexes. The female in particular frequently feels cheated and resents the fact that she is compelled to play a role somewhat uniquely different—both economically and socially—from the male, especially in rearing children.

Accepting one's physique and using the body effectively are very acute needs confronting the adolescent boy and girl. During this period it is

_____
[3] *Ibid.*, p. 5.

69

not unusual to have young people question, "Am I normal?" Such doubts can be found in the girl who matures early or the slow-to-mature boy who bears the nickname of Pee Wee or Runt. Teachers need to be sympathetic and understanding of these self-doubts.

Achieving emotional independence of parents and other adults begins in early childhood. The small child who is merely able to sit alone in a highchair learns that he can feed himself, though inaccurately; he will soon develop a resentment of outside help. The child who has been committed to make choices between alternatives like wearing apparel, selecting playmates, or dating resents having parents impose restrictions depriving him of this emotional independence. Such resentment may well account in part for the marches and demonstrations prevalent in the America of the 1960's.

Selection and preparation for an occupation should start at a very early age. In the primary grades, children should have a chance to understand the significance of various occupations which help them to live more comfortably—for example, garbage collection and street sweeping—so they can learn early to respect work which is performed competently. During the middle years girls and boys should be exposed to numerous exploratory occupational opportunities so that they can identify with certain types at the senior high and college levels that they may wish to pursue more intensively.

Preparation for marriage and family life starts at the cradle. A child soon senses whether there is a give-and-take affection pattern prevailing between parents, siblings, and himself. Without this assurance, individuals begin to develop adverse attitudes toward marriage and family life.

A problem solving-team teaching situation—more interested in developing adequate personalities than walking encyclopedias—can provide opportunities to implement these 10 developmental tasks and needs. The emphasis by no means downgrades cognitive learning as unimportant; rather, the focus falls on supplementing it fully with affective and psychomotor learnings.

Basic Learning Concepts

Problem solving-team teaching consists of purposeful, realistic life situations. It capitalizes on the basic principles and concepts of learning which have been developed through research and experimentation in organismic and perceptual psychology. It not only emphasizes the gathering and disseminating of information, but also the important problem of helping people to behave differently as a result of the information they have received. Human misbehavior is rarely due to a person not knowing how to behave. Everyone knows much more about how he should behave than he reflects in daily living. In a problem solving classroom the learner is looked upon as an active agent who is constantly organizing the world around him by labeling and grouping, noting and establishing relationships, hypothesizing, and predicting possible outcomes. The pupils, in creating somewhat their own world, are not dependent upon the world about them to mold their personalities.

To create a problem solving environment conducive to learning, growth, and development, the school must give due consideration to student productive learning which is both qualitatively and quantitatively rich. What a student has learned must be supported by others so that he has a chance to meditate his experiences through interactions with various groups. Of central importance is the learning *how to learn* or learning how to do critical, analytical thinking. It goes beyond the stage of helping a student to collect and evaluate a wide range of information by having him apply the information to some actual solution of everyday problems.

He must also choose problems or areas of learning which have personal meaning to assure motivation. From a wide range of possibilities and alternatives, he must choose one approach. In doing so, he will learn how to think flexibly and creatively. He will do a great deal of brainstorming in free-group discussions, going far beyond the limits of a typical subject centered curriculum. Through the wide range of conversational dialect, he has many opportunities for exchanging ideas and paraphrasing, leading to enriched symbolic skills. Such teaching in the problem solving situation is supported by flexible materials and scheduling.

In solving the problems, the student learns. He generalizes from data and groups ideas into meaningful clusters. He searches out and asks questions as he is learning to cope with important issues and their numerous possible solutions. In a critical thinking classroom that is warm and accepting, a student is not only accepted, but challenged. He can form ideas and images of what might be while he is generating models and theories to explain the phenomena he is studying. He can make critical judgments based upon logic and reasoning; he is free to make decisions and to take important stands which make a difference— not only in his own life—but in the well-being of the community.

In problem solving learning is perceived in terms of these fundamental principles:

1. *Learning is the discovery of personal meaning resulting in changed behavior.* What constitutes "personal meaning" varies, naturally, from student to student and even from teacher to teacher. Also, personal

meaning varies in terms of intensity and importance. When a student listens to the radio or television, he may hear a stock market report which has relatively little personal meaning for him. It is merely something that passes through his conscious memory and then quickly forgotten because it bears no relationship to his well-being or the welfare of those he knows. On the other hand, if a student learns that a favorite classmate has been injured in an automobile accident and is in critical condition in the hospital, needing blood transfusions, then he is personally moved. He may even offer his blood. There are many common problems which concern the well-being of students; if students were allowed to grapple with these problems, they could bring a high degree of personal meaning into the learning situation.

2. *Learning is resolving a tension or overcoming an obstacle which stands in the way of achieving a goal the learner needs or wants to achieve.* For example, a fourth-grade boy, vitally interested in building electric motors, discovers that instructions to construct a particular model in which he is interested are at the eighth-grade level. If his motivation is strong enough and the need to build a motor urgent, he can overcome obstacles like complicated sentence structure or advanced vocabulary. He can succeed in building the motor. But how often do we provide opportunities for students to overcome obstacles to a meaningful goal they want to achieve?

3. *Learning is the restoration of the total organism to a state of equilibrium—not only the internal equilibrium of the organism, but that between the organism and its environment.* We have known for many years that the kidney is one of the major organs, helping to purify the blood and discharge waste material that will permit the organism to maintain a state of internal equilibrium. When the kidney stops functioning properly, a person becomes seriously ill; unless the equilibrium is restored, the organism perishes. In a similar way students are confronted with social, economic, and cultural stresses which upset both the internal organismic structure and their relationships with other people. But how frequently do we use these stresses in learning situations in order to develop a high degree of motivation?

4. *Learning is multiple or one learns many things simultaneously and learns as a total organism.* Too many individuals in the traditional classrooms have been saddled with the memorization of content which is of little importance to them. In the process they learn to dislike the subject area under consideration, the school work itself, the teachers who present it, and the subject of education in general. It is important to keep in mind that, as they learn these negative responses, they react as a total organism—intellectually, socially, emotionally, and physically. Of course

72

they are also learning much more than the teachers had planned, and these negative learning experiences are frequently reflected at a later date when the same individuals vote against bond issues or oppose legislation designed to give adequate support for education.

5. *The individual learns in terms of past experiences by extending, reorganizing, and restructuring these past experiences into new situations.* As the person uses past experiences in learning, he is able to make transfers which have meaning and purpose for his own life. But it is important that the use of past experiences must be planned and developed to incorporate some of the principles cited earlier.

6. Individuals learn within the context of total life situations rather than by fragmentary, non-interrelated parts. An individual, for example, can learn a poem in entirety more readily once he comprehends the running theme and subthemes instead of merely plowing through a line-by-line memorization. The same principle applies equally to other areas of the school program. If a student is to understand the Industrial Revolution's impact upon world civilization and upon his own life, he must see not only the historical aspects; he must see these aspects in relation to others such as economic and social problems. In short, he must examine the Industrial Revolution as it relates to industrialization, urbanization, specialization, mass communication, and mass transportation. He must understand how the Revolution relates to government and international relations. Otherwise, his perception of its impact would be inadequate, the "tunnel-vision" problem inherent the subject centered curriculum keeps various subjects in almost total isolation from each other. Students do not have the opportunity to see relationships and to tie together facts and ideas. Such parts of the learning process, however, are important to problem solving-team teaching.

7. *Learning is developmental, involving readiness, maturation, past experiences, needs, interests, transferabilities, and generalization and synthesis.* Whereas the subject centered curriculum is largely unmindful of these relationships, the problem solving curriculum makes full use of them.

8. *Learning is determined by the perception of self, a feeling of adequacy or can-ness vs. a feeling of inadequacy or failure, the perception one has of others, and the perception one has of life in general.* All three theories of learning—field, organismic, and perceptual—undergird this key principle on which problem solving learning is based.

9. *Learning is uniquely different for each individual learner.*

10. *Learning is improved by good dynamic group relationships, by a rich environmental surrounding, and by a prevailing atmosphere of acceptance within the learning environment.*

73

11. *Learning is an active or interactive process involving the learner in a meaningful, realistic way.* It cannot be passive. As a learner becomes more involved in the planning and developing of experiences, his commitment increases.

12. *Learning is adding to or meeting a felt need satisfaction or it is avoiding a decrease or withdrawal of a felt need satisfaction.*

13. *Learning, to be meaningful, must be challenging to the individual, but it should not be unduly threatening.* A challenging situation is one where an individual has a reasonable degree of opportunity to succeed if he applies himself diligently. An undue threat, on the other hand, presents a situation in which the individual is bound to fail, no matter how extensively or persistently he applies himself.

14. *Learning is most effective when the learner is motivated by goals which are intrinsic to the learning activity.* The boy who overcomes obstacles like complicated sentence structure and advanced scientific vocabulary in order to read complex instructions and then successfully build a sailboat is intrinsically motivated. His strong motivation led to success in a difficult task. This type of motivation is drastically different from extrinsic ones of rewards, banners, praise, ridicule, sarcasm, threats, punishment, and failure—which coerce students to learn what the teacher or group of teachers have decided they should learn.

15. *Learning is most effective when there is freedom to make mistakes and when a child can see the classroom as a safe place for experimentation.*

16. *Learning is most effective when there is freedom to make mistakes and select, plan, develop, and evaluate the learning outcome.*

17. *Learning is most effective in an environment where the teacher guides, arouses new interests, creates a positive environment, and challenges a student into clarifying his own insights and ideas.*

A curriculum structured around the solving of problems recognizes these 17 qualities of learning. In a problem solving process in which these qualities are used, no student need feel inadequate, frustrated, or unmotivated; instead, he will be actively involved in the building of his confidence and productivity. Such a curriculum is psychologically sound for him.

BIBLIOGRAPHY

Association for Supervision and Curriculum Development, *Preceiving, Behaving, Becoming.* Washington, D.C.: National Education Association, 1962.

———, *Learning and Mental Health in the Schools.* Washington, D.C., National Education Association, 1966.

———, *Individualizing Instruction.* Washington, D.C.: National Education Association, 1964.

————, *To Nurture Humaneness*. Washington, D.C.: National Education Association, 1970.

————, *New Dimensions in Learning*. Washington, D.C.: National Education Association, 1962.

————, *Human Variability and Learning*. Washington, D.C.: National Education Association, 1961.

————, *Freeing Capacity to Learn*. Washington, D.C.: National Education Association, 1960.

————, *Learning More About Learning*. Washington, D.C.: National Education Association, 1959.

Bingham, Alma, *Improving Children's Facility in Problem Solving*. New York, Teachers College, 1958.

Friedberg, Margorie, *The Child and His Image*. Boston: Houghton Mifflin Co., 1972.

Garrett, James L., *The Humanities and Humanistic Education*. Reading, Mass.: Addison-Wesley Publishing Co., Inc., 1973.

Gordon, Ira J., *The Modifibility of Human Potential*. Washington, D.C.: Association for Supervision and Curriculum Development — National Education Association, 1972.

Haubrich, Vernon F., ed., *Freedom, Bureaucracy and Schooling*. Washington, D.C.: Association for Supervision and Curriculum Development — National Education Association, 1972.

Leeper, Robert R., ed., *Curriculum Concerns in a Revolutionary Era*. Washington, D.C.: Association for Supervision and Curriculum Development — National Education Association, 1973.

Martin, J. and C. Harrison, *Free to Learn: Unlocking and Upgrading American Education*. Englewood Cliffs, N.J.: Prentice-Hall, 1972.

Morine, Harold and Greta Morine, *Discovery: A Challenge to Teachers*. Englewood Cliffs, N.J.: Prentice-Hall, 1973.

Neagley, Ross L. and N. Dean Evans, *Handbook for Effective Curriculum Development*. Englewood Cliffs, N.J.: Prentice-Hall, 1967.

Rogers, Carl R., *Freedom to Learn*. Columbus, Ohio: Charles E. Merrill Publishing Co., 1969.

Shulma, Lee S. and Evans R. Keislar, *Learning by Discovery*. Chicago: Rand McNally Co., 1969.

Schmuck, Richard and others, *Problem Solving to Improve Classroom Learning*. Chicago: Science Research Associates, 1966.

Strom, Robert and E. Paul Torrance, *Education for Affective Achievement*. Chicago: Rand McNally and Co., 1973.

Van Til, William, ed., *Curriculum: Quest for Relevance*. Boston: Houghton Mifflin Co., 1971.

Waskin, Yvonne and Louise Parrish, *Teacher-Pupil Planning*. New York: Pitman Publishing Co., 1967.

Chapter 4. Curricular Reshaping for Teamwork

Implementing a problem solving-team teaching curriculum is a process which demands careful and cooperative planning in the earliest stages.

When the city of Decatur, Ala. voted for a bond issue during the 1968-69 school year, it began construction of two middle schools—each with a 1500-student capacity—to relieve its crowded elementary and senior high schools. Both schools were carefully planned and designed to provide a sound transition between predominantly problem solving elementary classes and senior high courses featuring some interdepartmental teaching.

Within each middle school were three sub-schools staffed by teachers who were committed to the concept of individualized instruction and team teaching. The two staffs received special training from summer in-service workshops. Each teacher on the team worked with approximately 140 students at a given time. These 140 students—one of three pods making up the sub-schools—were sixth, seventh, and eighth graders.

When the two middle schools opened in 1971-72, plans had been carefully worked out. Each pod worked four hours a day on a problem solving unit—assisted by the team of four teachers, a teacher's aide, the principal, assistant principal, and a guidance worker. The remaining two hours of the school day were spent on unified arts, music, industrial arts, fine arts, home economics, physical education, and broad exploratory subjects. Each school's well-rounded physical education program which included intramural sports was emphasized. Basic skills like reading, language arts, vocabulary, spelling, and math were continually reinforced, through the work of the problem solving process and, when necessary, through special diagnostic remedial and developmental teaching approaches.

Within the two middle schools, students of all capabilities were grouped together: the gifted, the average, the slow-learners, and even the handicapped. Everyone worked cooperatively and congenially in the same classroom on the same problem. Each was encouraged to contribute according to his own capabilities.

The traditional report card became less important as the schools developed new ways—mainly through parent conferences and other evaluative techniques—to state student progress.

Physical facilities underlined the sound curriculum approach. Buildings had been constructed to emphasize group interaction and inquiry. The pod formations enabled students to move about freely. Noise was minimized through acoustical tile ceilings and wall-to-wall carpeting. Buildings were air-conditioned and even had emergency lighting and ventilating systems in case power should fail.

Parents had free access to the schools; they were encouraged to visit and particularly attend special open house programs during which many of the problem solving experiences were summarized dramatically.

Decatur's experience in adding these two middle schools to its system illustrates the deliberate planning necessary at many levels: the school administration central office, the school itself, the team of teachers, the pupils, and the community.

Democratic Leadership: Key Implementation Factor

A problem solving curriculum also demands democratic leadership to put the concept into operation. It is a particularly dynamic kind of leadership which is constantly shifting from individual to individual regardless of the level at which curriculum planning takes place because, under democratic rules, leadership is a function belonging to the group. If group goals are to be attained and evaluated, the leadership must be *cooperatively* implemented.

Such a process involves an essentially democratic approach. An individual becomes a leader when his contributions are more noticeable at a given level of discussion than those of the other members of the group. While he is the leader he is the person who at that particular moment can most effectively contribute to the attainment of the group's goals. Since leadership is generally widespread and diffused throughout the group, a person might well be a leader on one occasion and then yield the role to another individual. Thus, leadership and followership are interchangeable concepts. Various learning situations unfold as types of evaluative responsibilities emerge and as roles among the group members are varied in terms of responsibilities for evaluating outcomes. At the same time the group itself is constantly evaluating its members for potential leadership at a given time—particularly in terms of an individual's perception, his motives, and his abilities in effecting group interaction and collaboration.

A group—while cooperatively planning the problem solving experience— must keep in mind the norms by which it will attempt to operate. Only the person who can operate within these norms should be viewed as a potential leader; the individual who would violate such critical norms does not serve the group usefully.

Some of the qualities necessary to group leadership at a given time are:

1. a willingness to cooperate,
2. an ability to communicate freely and effectively,

77

3. a sympathetic attitude toward the group,
4. an ability to lead toward solution of the immediate problem,
5. the willingness to serve others as well as himself, and
6. an emotional stability displayed in implementing these endeavors.

This type of leadership can be exerted by individuals with or without official group status. But, during the time when a person is interacting with the group, he must not try to use such official status or position to bring about any consensus which he might personally feel should be formulated.

An individual who has high prestige among the group members, who is more spontaneous, who makes more direct attempts to influence the interaction processes, and who is more open to interactions among others is the most likely to be a leader in a given situation. His high regard and concern for the feelings of others and his fair use of these feelings help to move the group toward a common solution. Such a leader tends to have a realistic concept of himself and of others. He is constantly accepting others as individuals of worth and dignity who can make valid contributions to the group.

The kind of democratic leadership which is being described here must meet three criteria:

1. Adequate recognition of each person's importance and the contributions he might make,
2. Effectiveness in actual accomplishment of the task, and
3. Realization of individual contributions through group activities and interactions.

Within this leadership situation, each member of the group possesses skills, ideas, and contributions which may at one time or another serve as a positive resource upon which the group will want to draw as it confronts the problem. No individual's contribution can be used unless he is willing and unless he assumes some of the responsibilities involved in group interaction.

Gibbs has stated: "A group member may gain the status of a group leader for a short period of time. The length of time that he retains this position is in direct relationship to his ability to participate in the group activity and to contribute more toward the achievement of the group goals than any other members.[1] Further, he emphasized, a group changes as its

---

[1] Gardner Lindzey, ed., *Handbook of Social Psychology* (Boston: Addison Wesley Publishing Co., Inc., 1954) , p. 8.

membership changes. Since each member contributes to the group in some way, the group itself may change when an individual enters or leaves it.[2]

If the democratic process is fairly applied to the group situation, then the summation of a person's contributions to the solution of cognitive problems exceeds the performance he would be able to achieve individually or on his own. He is also important to the group by his uniqueness: No one else can bring the group exactly the same resources or needs. A dynamic group recognizes individual uniqueness.

Each group engaged in democratic cooperative planning is made up of many kinds of individuals. Persons who differ from the majority within a group can and do make contributions to the group. In fact, more learning is often possible in a problem solving situation from *differences* than from similarities. Therefore it is important that each and every member make his maximum contribution to the total group. The individual who helps in planning and setting goals is more likely to see that they are fulfilled. Pierce and Albright recognized this principle:

> The larger the number of people involved in an undertaking the more effective outcomes should be; broad participations can be at the level of policy determination, problem definition, program planning, program execution, and appraisal of results. This means that all affected by decisions should have a voice in making decisions and that leadership should and will shift from member to member in democratic group efforts.[3]

Group processes used in democratic cooperative planning are not to be dismissed as administrative and educational leadership or supervision gimmicks. They are basic tools for democracy, designed for fair participation. These interactions do more than develop good solutions to the problem: They also profoundly affect the individuals in the group. The learning in problem solving evolves from both situations, and it begins with cooperative planning. According to recent research, learners who participate in decision-making are more likely to carry out responsibilities connected with these decisions. They are voluntary rather than passive group members. Other studies indicate that a high degree of interaction to produce group consensus on goals increases the probability of individual participation in the group.

Democratic leadership is uniquely different from authoritarian leadership or the kind of leadership which tries to manipulate people to do what

---

[2] *Ibid.*

[3] Truman M. Pierce and A. D. Albright, *A Profession in Transition* (Southern States Cooperative Program in Educational Administration, 1960), p. 30.

the leader has already decided they are going to do. Authoritarian leadership depends on forcing people to fit into a pattern of conformity constructed from a fixed notion of education. The authoritarian leader frequently issues edicts, mandates, and directives to which individuals—for example, teachers—are expected to conform. He uses authority as a device to ensure that people carry out a kind of "passive followship." Such demands are contrary to democratic leadership—which thrives on activeness of group members rather than passiveness. An authoritarian leader seldom places any faith or trust in the capabilities of other people. Quite to the contrary, he is likely to feel constantly threatened if any individual questions his decisions or procedures. He will resort to coercive force in order to whip people into line. Fortunately for education this kind of leadership is less prevalent today as a pattern of educational leadership. But it is nonetheless still present. Its use of personal attraction, slick rhetorical argument, or influence cannot be overlooked.

Between authoritarian and manipulative leadership there is no real difference in educational outcomes. But the able school person possibly resents the manipulative approach more than the authoritative because, under the latter, an individual has at least a choice between following the edicts or taking the consequences. He knows at the outset under an authoritarian leadership where he stands. But neither authoritarian nor manipulative leadership techniques has a place in implementing a problem solving-team teaching curriculum.

Implementing Problem Solving System-wide

There is no single approach for a school system implementing problem solving-team teaching. However, some school systems move their schools along parallel lines in so far as in-service education is concerned—with leadership competencies being developed at the central office level. Although principals and classroom teachers will become extensively involved in decision-making if a problem solving curriculum is selected, the top administrative and supervisory personnel would still insist that it is the central office's role to make final decisions on whether or not the system is to move in this direction. In any case it is rare when all the schools within a system implement the curriculum reorganization simultaneously since no two schools are at the same point of readiness at any given point in time. Much more realistic is the realization by personnel throughout the system that, while all schools in the system will work toward the achievement of problem solving-team teaching, allowance must be made for variations among these schools. The central office, then, can concentrate on the schools which are ready to begin the implementation process.

No decision to implement an educational innovation on a system-wide basis should be made without deliberate planning. The system's size and the readiness of its teaching personnel are particularly crucial. With planning and direction, the system-wide approach offers certain advantages. By its size and resources, the school system is able to provide a broad base for support. In actual implementation, central office personnel can use the considerable weight of system-wide authority and prestige. The central office can further draw upon personnel who have had varied backgrounds and extensive experiences and who will be leaders in developing resource units, instructional materials, and other means for implementation. The system-wide approach also has the advantage of securing outside consultants when needed.

Implementation of a new curriculum process must be supported with a sound public relations program to explain the program and to encourage public participation. If key members of a community know about the program; they will be more willing to serve as resource persons when asked. The central office is also able to send teachers for observation of schools inside and outside the system which are using a problem solving-team teaching curriculum effectively. And the system is especially able to act as a clearinghouse, publicizing information through bulletins and pamphlets distributed to schools and individual teachers.

But, despite the advantages offered by the central office in a system-wide implementation of problem solving, success in the process rests critically at the individual school level. In the final analysis how effectively each school uses the central office's resources together with those of the community spells the difference between sound or ineffectual implementation.

Another possibility in implementing problem solving system-wide is through the selection of pilot schools. The influence of these pilot schools would then permeate the rest of the system through devices like inter-school visitation, sharing of in-service endeavors, and publication of materials. To prepare the teachers and principals who will need to work closely with the central office, the implementation planning sessions should include workshops for entire faculties or teams from the involved schools. The workshops might be held on college campuses during summer months or in selected schools to which college faculty members would be invited.

When a system plans to initiate problem solving — whether through campus or school workshops—it should choose carefully the personnel who will conduct the workshops. Such persons—hopefully having a rich background of problem solving experiences—can be valuable resource personnel throughout the school year following the workshop sessions. The experiences could well be repeated later for other teams of teachers within the school system. Or the system might arrange with one or more colleges to provide credit for teachers who take the workshop.

Principals are also key persons in the planning phases. It is not enough that principals be committed to the problem solving concept and want to try it; they must be active from the earliest stage so that they can go on to work effectively with their teachers as the curriculum is implemented. The level of operation in any school will rarely rise above the principal's perception of what constitutes good educational practices in various classrooms. In that respect the principal is a *key person* in program inauguration.

Principals, teachers, and central office administrators are important parts of a system. The system which as a general practice encourages experimentation is likely to have personnel committed to some concept similar to problem solving-team teaching. Perhaps many of its principals and teachers have been implementing such programs without being fully aware what they were innovating. It is these educators who can be most instrumental in helping to initiate a problem solving curriculum; they should be included in the first round of trainees.

Implementing on Individual School Basis

Many school systems interested in implementing problem solving-team teaching prefer to try out the curriculum in one or two schools. They might further rule out involvement by all the faculty within a school on the basis that skills and readiness of its members vary. In these situations the central school office must be sympathetic and offer whatever support is needed. When teams of teachers from individual schools do implement a problem solving curriculum, it is crucial that the entire faculty—including the principal—be sympathetic with and observant of the program's potential. From the author's experience in problem solving-team teaching curriculum implementation, this modest approach might well be the most advisable approach. If efforts are successful in a school with one-, two-, or three-team situations and if the rest of the faculty was in on early plans and on-going evaluative sessions, then the innovation could have impact on the total school faculty. Small-team situations demand exceptionally planned training programs. Team members should attend a summer workshop during which they can practice pre-planning. During the workshops they can draw upon background experiences as they work out philosophical, psychological, and sociological bases for problem solving experiences. A key phase of the workshop will be the development of a comprehensive pre-plan for a hypothetical problem solving curriculum.

While the plan may not be used when each workshop participant returns to his classroom, the practice will prove invaluable as teachers and students together go through preliminary steps.

It is particularly desirable for the principal to attend the summer workshops along with the teachers if he wants to be in a position at a later date to involve the rest of his faculty in problem solving endeavors.

An example of a problem solving-team teaching pre-plan drawn up in one summer workshop is offered below. This plan was developed by a team of fourth-grade teachers from Prattville (Ala.) Elementary School. They were part of a 1971 summer workshop at Auburn University which featured teaching teams from six different school systems. The pre-plan example is representative of the work these teams carried back to their school systems. It is interesting to see how these school systems planned to implement problem solving. Several of the systems were planning additional workshop experiences for their entire faculties during the upcoming school year (1971-72) —with a view that by the beginning of the 1972-73 school year all faculty members would be actively involved in problem solving-team teaching. Other school systems would begin the 1971-72 year with some involvement in problem solving and then give selected teams more extensive training during the following summer.

Pre-Plan Example on Communicable Diseases

Subject Overview: Despite a rapidly advancing scientifically-oriented world and despite advances in the control of communicable diseases, such diseases remain a serious threat to human health and welfare. Much is still unknown about control of communicable diseases and what we do know has not been effectively utilized. Control of contagious diseases becomes more and more essential as the world population increases. Every person must become aware of the problem in order that he not harbor or spread deadly and crippling germs.

We now have methods by which communicable diseases can be prevented and controlled—unlike past civilizations in which thousands perished in plagues and epidemics. But is man presently using his knowledge and methods to the fullest extent to insure healthy citizens? Are our young people being made aware of the methods of disease transmission? What can an individual do to help improve personal health and to prevent the spread of disease?

Criteria for Selecting the Problem: Improving community health by developing ways and means of controlling communicable disease will:

1. Promote changes in feelings and attitudes,
2. Offer a positive goal,

83

3. Fulfill a community need,
4. Help individuals cope with problems arising under similiar circumstances,
5. Improve the health of the community,
6. Provide an opportunity for individuals to recognize a degree of success,
7. Cut across subject-matter boundary lines,
8. Enable participants to utilize a wide range of resource materials, and
9. Be of genuine interest to both pupils and teachers.

Objectives: The student who has studied reducing communicable diseases should have greater understanding of:

1. What communicable diseases actually are,
2. How they are spread,
3. The extent of communicable diseases in his community,
4. Whether specific communicable diseases are increasing or decreasing in frequency,
5. What values and techniques can prevent disease, and
6. The economic relationship between the cost of disease prevention and the cost of curing disease.

In investigating the problem, the student should show evidence of changed behavior regarding:

1. Personal cleanliness,
2. Utilization of the public health service,
3. Controlling of insects,
4. Sanitary preparation of food,
5. Pollution of water supply,
6. Home sanitation,
7. Rest-room sanitation,
8. Lunchroom sanitation,
9. Self-confidence,
10. Taking immunizations,
11. Taking eye and ear examinations,
12. Group inter-relationships,
13. Working independently,
14. Self-control or discipline, and
15. Respect and care for books, materials, and equipment.

Research into the problem should increase the student's respect for:

1. Disease control,
2. Workers involved in the health fields,
3. Accomplishments in the past toward disease prevention,
4. Need for research on the subject,
5. Man's dependence on good health,
6. Group work and cooperation, and
7. The ideas of others.

As the student researches and discusses the problem he will be acquiring skills in:

1. Library use,
2. Letter-writing,
3. Report-writing,
4. Gathering and organizing information from many sources,
5. Oral presentation,
6. Development of graphs and posters,
7. Note-taking,
8. Computation,
9. Graph and table interpretation,
10. Handling many types of materials,
11. Spelling new words,
12. Democratic group interaction,
13. Assuming of responsibilities,
14. Input into group discussions,
15. Basic laboratory techniques,
16. Self-evaluation,
17. Working independently, and
18. Setting up and maintaining a room library.

Initiating the Unit: Two or three days before the unit begins, a cough plate and a control plate should be prepared. The teachers might encourage student participation in the preparation. Also decorate bulletin boards with pictures or photographs like a person sneezing, polluted water, flies and mosquitoes, cream pie and potato salad, and a rusty nail. It will fall to the teacher's judgment as to how venereal disease should be portrayed.

Create an interest center with textbooks, pamphlets secured mainly from the county health office, magazine articles, and newspaper clippings. Prepare an exhibit table with materials like a hypodermic needle, syringe, thermometer, stethoscope, vaccine bottle, alcohol sponge, soap, shoes, a glass of water, and cough plates. Use these items to lead the class into a discussion of how each item is related to disease or its prevention.

Ask the group to name diseases and have one of the participants list them on the board. Using the list, divide the students into sub-groups for investigation of which diseases are classified as communicable. A sub-group spokesman is to report the findings back to the group.

Developing the Unit: Present a film or films (for example, from the film catalog of the state department of public health) on better health, germs, catching a cold, or microorganisms). The filmstrip "Communicable Diseases" by McGraw Hill is excellent. The group, in preparation for discussion of the scope and trends of communicable diseases, should divide at this point into sub-groups based on individual interests.

Sub-group 1 — Investigate the effects of some of the great plagues on social and economic communities, particularly cause and extent, cure, mortality rate, superstitions, sociological aspects, protection, and scientific advancements.

Sub-group 2 — Research the spread of communicable diseases carried through air, water, food, insects, and mechanical means. Each sub-group member can investigate diseases within a particular area.

Sub-group 3 — Check out which communicable diseases are most prevalent in present society. An outside resource speaker, perhaps the country health nurse, school nurse, or public health doctor, can provide initial facts and figures. The students can then illustrate how specific diseases are affecting their county—using charts and graphs based on age, prevalence, or location.

Sub-group 4 — Find out which communicable diseases are increasing and decreasing by writing the country health department for comprehensive materials on medical, epidemiological, and control aspects. Use the Communicable Disease Center in Atlanta as a starting point for tracing what effect the Vietnam War has had on the increase of malaria in the U.S. An investigation of the recent upsurge in measles cases in the country can underline the importance of immunizations. Biographies of men like Louis Pasteur, Robert Koch, William Gorgas, and Edward Jenner can demonstrate the progress in controlling communicable diseases.

Sub-group 5 — Discover the controls presently used for preventing disease through quarantine laws and their enforcement, immunization, sanitary conditions, waste disposal, food preparation, protection of the water supply, and personal hygiene.

Sub-group 6 — Investigate the economic relationship between the cost of disease prevention and the cost of curing a disease. To do this, develop the cost of an immunization program for a particular disease. Recent information can be obtained on polio and measles immunizations. The students can arrange a visit to the public health officer and draw up a full list of questions before the interview. In exploring the cost of curing communicable diseases, the students must consider time lost from a job in terms of cost to the employee and cost to the industry. An interview with a local hospital administrator should yield data on hospital costs.

Culminating the Unit: These experiences can draw together the individual and group efforts —

1. Arrange a field trip to the country health department and possibly the state's department.
2. Have each sub-group prepare a notebook of individual research efforts.
3. Prepare posters and leaflets for store window display and home use dealing with communicable diseases and their impact upon the community.
4. Ask each group whether it wants to present individual or group reports to the class and have them proceed with the preparations.
5. Help the student make transparencies and posters which can illustrate the final reports, with emphasis upon selecting main ideas and taking good notes.
6. Work with the students in preparing an interest center in the school lobby.

Correlating Learning from the Disciplines: A unit of this type is designed to develop individual student skills and interests. The problem solving emphasis enables students to use scientific principles and procedures as they become aware of individual responsibility in controlling communicable diseases. The impact of past plagues provides the students with a historical perspective. News media articles accent the contemporary view. Spelling, letter-writing, and composition skills necessary in contacting resource people and in conducting interviews will draw upon language arts. Mathematics is involved in the interpretation of graphs. Computation of averages and percentages used in assessing disease control versus disease cure provide additional practice. Abilities in the arts are applied through posters, bulletin board displays, and illustrations.

Suggested Materials: Books —

1. Atkinson, D. T., *Magic, Myth and Disease.*

2. Dubos, Rene and others, *Health and Disease: Life Science Library*. New York: Time, Inc., 1965.
3. Dubos, Rene, *The Unseen World*. New York: Rockefeller Institute Press, 1962.
4. Eberson, Frederick, *Man Against Microbes*. New York: Ronald Press Co., 1963.
5. Fabricant, Noah, *The Dangerous Cold*. New York: Macmillan Co., 1965.
6. Fiennes, Richard, *Man, Nature and Disease*. New York: Weidenfeld and Nocolson, 1964.
7. Hancock, Lucy, *Community Nurse*. New York: Macroe–Smith Co., 1944.
8. Leaf, Munro, *Health Can Be Fun*. New York: Lippincott, 1943.
9. Shipper, Katherine, *Men, Microscopes and Living Things*. New York: Viking Press, 1955.
10. Wilson, Charles, *Men, Science, and Health*. Indianapolis: Bobbs Merrill Co., 1962.
11. Schwartz, William F., *Teacher's Handbook and Student's Manual on Venereal Disease Education*. Washington, D.C.: American Association for Health, Physical Education, and Recreation, National Education Association, 1965.

Pamphlets — These materials are available from the Alabama Department of Public Health's Division of Health Education and Information: "How to Order and Use Health Education Materials," "Dictionary of State and National Sources," "Diphtheria," "Tuberculosis," "Rabies," "Immunization," "Sanitation," "Hookworm," "Venereal Disease," and "Vital Statistics."

Filmstrips —

1. "Communicable Diseases," Community Health Series, McGraw–Hill Book Co., 330 West 42nd St., New York 10036.
2. "Invasion by Disease," Number 121185, Fighting Disease Series, McGraw–Hill Book Co.
3. "Community Sanitation," Number 400059, Community Health Series, McGraw–Hill Book Co.

Instruction for Preparing Cough Plate — These materials are needed: two commercially prepared trypticase soy agar slants, two sterile petri plates, one test tube holder, boiling water, aluminum foil or newspaper, and scotch tape.

Follow these steps:

1. Slightly loosen the cap on the tubes containing the agar and immerse them in boiling water. Leave the tubes in the water until the agar melts.
2. Using sterile conditions, pour each tube of agar into each sterile petri plate. Replace the top of the plate and slightly rotate to distribute agar evenly.
3. Allow the mixture to harden.
4. Cough or sneeze on one of the plates, then replace lid and secure it with scotch tape.
5. Wrap the plate in aluminum foil or newspaper and place in a warm spot (not over 37°C) out of direct sunlight.
6. Examine after 48 hours (or 24 hours if plate has been placed in an incubator).
7. Use the other prepared sterile plate as a control.
8. After the experiment, the plate may be disposed of by heating a pressure cooker to 15 pounds for 15 minutes. If cooker is not available, ask a local medical technician at a hospital to dispose of the plate for you.

Evaluation — With continuous evaluation, the student is able to pinpoint bite-sized objectives in order to realize a long-term goal. In taking part in this unit, he should realize a better understanding of the effects of communicable diseases. Fairly early in the unit — possibly one week after it has begun — each child may complete the first evaluation or progress report. As the unit progresses, students will be sharing accomplishments and research problems in their particular areas.

The second report can sustain interest, perhaps focusing attention on the student's role in the group endeavors and encouraging him to formulate his future plans.

Near the end of the unit each student could use the third progress report as a self-evaluation. At the same time the team of teachers might record their evaluation of each student. Similarities and discrepancies within the total evaluative process could be discussed with each student.

Each student is responsible for two reports: "How Can I Protect My Family and Myself Against Communicable Diseases?" and "How Has Study of This Unit Affected My Awareness and Understanding of Communicable Diseases?" The unit is completed with discussion of each student's understanding and reactions.

These specific evaluative materials were used in the Prattville pre-plan:

Progress Report 1
1. What is the problem on which your group is working?
2. What reading materials are you using to obtain information?
3. Have you recorded the sources of information for a bibliography?
4. Whom do you plan to interview for data and opinion?
5. How else do you plan to get information?
6. How are you getting along in the group?
7. What plans are you making for illustrative materials?
8. How do you plan to report findings to the class?
9. Do you need help in any way?

Progress Report 2
1. When does your group plan to report to the class?
2. How does it intend to give the report?
3. What have you done to illustrate your findings?
4. Name the books, magazines, pamphlets, and other printed sources you have used for information and tell where you found them.
5. Name any other sources of information you have used such as letters, interviews, phone calls.
6. What next steps do you plan to take in the solution of the problem?
7. Do you need more time on this project? If so, tell how much and why.

Progress Report 3
1. Did I accept responsibility by: (1) getting my work done on time, (2) bringing library books in on time, and (3) keeping research materials up-to-date?
2. Did I practice self-control in committee meetings, class discussions and meetings, the absence of the teacher, and controlling my emotions?
3. Do I have good attitudes toward students, myself, work, materials, and responsibility?
4. Has my oral and written work been correct in spelling, grammar, punctuation, sentence structure, paragraphing, clarity, order, and approach?
5. Have the letters and reports I have written been acceptable in penmanship, form, neatness, and condition?
6. Have I been able during research reading to understand scientific material, graphs and tables, oral presentations, and general instructions?

90

7. How much have I participated in class meetings and discussion, voting, and group activities?
8. How wisely have I utilized free time, committee time, and individual work-time?
9. Have I contributed to the making of posters and lettering projects?
10. Was my art work neat, original, and organized?
11. Have I developed skills in averages, percentages, constructing of graphs, decimals, and large numbers?
12. Have I developed skills in the use of laboratory equipment, in its care, and in applying the scientific approach?
13. Have I gained an understanding of new ideas and opinions, scientific principles, the general subject of communicable diseases, and some ways these diseases can be controlled?

Teachers used these self-evaluative questions:
1. Did I use the problem approach and was the problem itself of value to the students?
2. Did I use experiments to help solve the problem, answer questions, and develop concepts?
3. Were the experiments — when used — performed under controlled conditions so that results would be comparable?
4. Did I rely on the "teach–tell" method or did I help the child discover facts for himself?
5. Once the unit had been initiated, did I then "abdicate" at the right moment so that group leadership and organized action could evolve?
6. Was the learning one step at a time and on the child's level of experience?
7. Did the children have a hand in planning and did their involvement in the earliest phases result in worthwhile group and individual experiences?
8. Were the materials clear and easily obtained and did the students have a hand in making and using them?
9. Was my classroom interesting looking and did it help to generate group enthusiasm?
10. Did the unit learning experiences lead the students to change concepts and values?

This bibliography is suggested for the team of teachers in the unit:
1. Anderson, Gaylord, Margaret G. Arnstein, and Mary R. Lester, *Communicable Disease Control.* New York: MacMillan Co., 1964.
2. Bingham, Alma, *Improving Children's Facility in Problem Solving.* New York: Teachers College, Columbia University, 1963.

3. Coulson, W. R. and C. R. Rogers, *Man and the Science of Man.* Columbus, Ohio: Charles E. Merrill Publishing Co., 1968.
4. Doll, Ronald C. and Robert S. Fleming, *Children Under Pressure.* Columbus, Ohio: Charles E. Merrill Publishing Co., 1966.
5. Hanslovsky, Glenda, Sue Moyer, and Helen Wagner, *Why Team Teaching.* Columbus, Ohio: Charles E. Merrill Publishing Co., 1969.
6. *Improving Educational Assessment and An Inventory of Measure of Affective Behavior.* Washington, D.C.: Association for Supervision and Curriculum Development, 1962.
7. Kelley, Earl C., *In Defense of Youth.* Englewood Cliffs, N.J.: Prentice–Hall, 1962.
8. *Perceiving, Behaving, Becoming.* Washington, D.C.: Association for Supervision and Curriculum Development, 1962.
9. Popper, Samuel H., *The American Middle School.* Waltham, Mass.: Blaisdell Publishing Co., 1967.
10. Renfield, Richard, *If Teachers Were Free.* Washington, D.C.: Acropolis Books, 1969.
11. Schulman, Lee L. and Evan Keislar, eds., *Learning by Discovery.* Chicago, Ill.: Rand McNally and Co., 1966.
12. Taba, Hilda, and Deborah Elkins, *Teaching Strategies for the Culturally Disadvantaged.* Chicago: Rand McNally and Co., 1966.
13. Vars, Gordon F., *Core and Interdisciplinary Team Approaches.* Scranton, Pa.: International Textbook Co., 1969.

Implementing Problem Solving at Team and Group Levels

It is characteristically American to believe in the worth and dignity of the individual and to believe in the inherent right to life, liberty, and the pursuit of happiness. Unfortunately, it is also a harsh fact of life that such democratic beliefs are more easily pronounced than practiced; it is easier to pay lip service.

Perhaps one of the most substantial arguments for a problem solving–team teaching curriculum is that it involves practicing the principles in order to be a sound learning experience for its participants. Within this context, the role of planning is crucial: The planning phases — done *jointly* by teachers and students — establish a blueprint for the anticipated experiences with the tacit understanding that the plan be flexible enough to allow that group and individual interactions become abundant opportunities for learning experiences. Certainly it should not resemble the authoritarian subject-oriented plan which insists that the student fit into standardized procedures. Instead it should chart a direction which teachers and students feel can lead to learning experiences while a solution to the problem is being sought. Such cooperative planning can pave the way for a student to experience the following:

1. Intelligent, direct involvement in situations touching upon the student's own well-being;
2. Acceptance by the student of responsibility for his own actions and for the obligations which the larger group places upon him;
3. Behaving cooperatively in that he assists others and allows them to have their own views;
4. Developing a clear understanding of both his own and others' individual problems with the positive view that these problems can be worked out;
5. Respect for, within the democratic setting, the value of problem solving in recognizing and trying to resolve conflicts by planning a definite course of action leading toward a solution;
6. Familiarity with the tools of problem solving, particularly the gathering and applying of pertinent information toward a solution.

Citizenship, according to George B. D. Huszer in *Practical Applications of Democracy,* cannot be taught.

> It is a skill which must be acquired by constant practice. It is attaining of certain attitudes and habits of actions which make democratic living together possible. . . . How can we expect democratic results from authoritarian process in education? We often try what cannot be done to obtain one kind of results using another kind of means. We need an educational system which is democratic in structure which will build human beings capable of living together rather than dominating each other.[4]

During cooperative teaching team–pupil planning, teachers have the chance to develop a comprehensive understanding of the students. It is an excellent opportunity to establish feelings of belonging and friendliness. The getting-acquainted period is time well spent, and teachers need not feel anxious about any apparent lack of academic achievement during this planning time. At the outset the team of teachers must assume leadership and take an active role in introductions: introducing themselves, having students introduce and interview one another, and involving participants in memory games and other devices. Teachers as the implementers in the early stages of problem solving must search constantly for means of know-

---

[4] George B. D. Huszer, *Practical Applications of Democracy* (New York: Harper and Brothers, 1947) , pp. 52–56.

ing the students better. These means can help: anecdotal records, socio-metric material, the California test of personality, self-made question-naires, interest inventories, open-ended discussion, informal writing, con-tacts with students in their homes, on the playground, and in the class-room, and a careful analysis of school records. A team of teachers at the team–pupil planning stage must begin as soon as possible to encourage leadership abilities and other unique talents of the students.

Team–pupil planning takes place at several levels. There will be some general planning in the form of identifying and selecting problems for development in terms of valid criteria (see Chapter 5 for specific criteria). Other phases of the planning program will take place at the small-group level where various team teachers will work with student sub-groups. At this level it is essential that the situation be informal — preferably with a teacher sitting with the students in a circle or around a quadrangle of tables. Here particularly the teacher's role as facilitator rather than as authoritarian is apparent in a problem solving experience. Teachers are placed as members of the group rather than apart from or above the group. They guide, not control, the group as it thinks together, identifies possible approaches to the problem, and selects instructional materials for the unit.

Both the problem solving planning and learning phases must be im-plemented in such a way that every group member's ideas are recognized and weighed. Much is left to the teacher's skill in group situations. The danger is always present, particularly in the beginning, that the teachers might dominate the situation, reducing the students to passive roles. In truth, teachers need to change their own behavioral patterns before they can try to involve students in genuinely cooperative planning. Too many are bound to the rigid lines of a formal classroom. But it is just as much a danger for the overly anxious teacher or team to turn the responsi-bilities over to their students, relying on them too extensively before the students are ready to assume these responsibilities. Either danger threat-ens the problem solving learning experience. There must be a reasonable balance between teacher and pupil involvement at the outset — with a gradual decrease in teacher involvement and an increase in pupil involve-ment as the project progresses.

The team teacher involved in a problem solving unit must develop deft skills in group work — small- and large-number groups — as well as skills for facilitating individual activities. Knowledge about handling group processes in education have to be acquired. Generally students have not previously taken part in group problem solving or any group effort re-quiring cooperative efforts. Even teachers, by and large, lack experience in

94

group learning situations. Hopefully a team of teachers will begin to recognize and use the skills during summer workshops or by observation of an effective problem solving unit.

How well teachers can guide students through the problem inquiry process is critical. While they must not dominate the group situation, they nonetheless need to point out pitfalls and offer constructive suggestions for improving the group processes if the students are to move ahead. Once the students have begun to grasp the tools of group work, the teaching team members can move around the sub-groups more freely for work with various students. Each teacher can visit from sub-group to sub-group — just listening or injecting a word here and there. This technique can direct the group toward constructive goals without making the teacher a dominant figure. The teaching team can also measure group and individual progress through group reporting and written reports. While verbal reports can provide an on-going picture of subgroup activities, the written reports provide indices to how the members of a given group have organized and presented their thinking in accordance with declared goals. Also the teacher has an opportunity to comment on group strengths and weaknesses and offer constructive changes.

Each teaching team must engage students in continuous evaluation *as a two-way communicative process*. Such cooperative evaluation is, frankly, a slow and cumbersome interactive process which cannot be mastered in a short period of time; but, with mutual patience and perseverance, it is not only possible, *but very important* that teachers and students work together in evaluating what they are doing and determining what the next steps should be. The inexperienced teaching team might best initiate teacher–pupil evaluation sessions at the end of a day, asking questions like "what have we learned today" or "what mathematics experiences have we had." Students might react with the statement that there were no math experiences because no problems in a book had been assigned. But teachers can readily cite some math experiences far more profitable than the traditional textbook assignment. Some students, too, will be sensitive to these less obvious, but valuable math experiences. A teacher can use the same approach in language arts, science, art, music, social studies, and other experiences the students may have had. Otherwise the equating of lesson assignment with learning which is part and parcel of the traditional classroom activities might obscure real experiences. A student may go home and have his parents ask what he did in math or language arts today. If he replies that there was no work in math or language arts that day, then the end result could well be a call to the principal's office to express the parent's concern over what *is* happening in that school.

Just as it is important that students participate in planning problem solving learning experiences, they should be active in all evaluative phases. Evaluation of course begins with planning. In initial planning, the students will set up certain criteria for choosing problems; from the standpoint of evaluation, they will also develop criteria which will help clarify their purposes. In this way the students have an active voice in determining the objectives towards which they will be working. As teachers and pupils become more and more involved in evaluative processes, they will realize a higher degree of competency and a sense of continuing worth. They are not only learning how to evaluate the immediate, but also learning in terms of long-term goals and experiences which they can apply in future situations. Through the involvement and decision-making in planning and evaluative sessions, the students can grow in many ways. They experience self-confidence. They are practicing the important tool of research by reading and extracting pertinent material from printed sources. They are learning how to synthesize their understanding and how to draw basic generalizations and conclusions so that they can cope with the problem at hand.

For students who will become citizens in a country which places a high premium on group and democratic processes, the group experiences of a problem solving curriculum are valuable preparation for life situations.

Involving Parents and Other Laymen

Hopefully a parent would not need to call the principal's office to find out "what is happening in that school." Parents and other lay citizens who represent a cross section of the community's socioeconomic and ethnic structure should be involved from the outset in the implementation of a problem solving–team teaching curriculum. They might constitute an advisory group to the board of education or the school faculty. Initially, parents and the lay public could be oriented to the problem solving concept through a large meeting during which someone with a rich background in problem solving–team teaching experiences can explain the structure and advantages.

It is particularly helpful for the lay public — including parents — to organize a citizens' advisory committee to work during implementation with the involved faculty. Paralleling the lay committee should be a professional advisory committee representing a cross section of all teaching and administrative personnel — those from the central school office, the principal, and classroom teachers — at various operation levels. The two committees could effectively sponsor community surveys to assist with the program implementation; they might further identify problem areas. Joint findings of these committees could be publicized in local and state-wide newspapers.

The committees could survey individuals who attended or graduated from schools in the community and particularly those who went on to higher education institutions and vocational schools to determine what kinds of problems they had encountered while in the school system: adequacy of the school curriculum, counselling situations, degree of personal encouragement for the individual, and extent of any follow-up actions. It is recommended that this be done approximately at the sophomore level after leaving high school.

The lay advisory committee might survey drop-outs to find out why they left school. In particular, these areas might be covered:

1. Adequacy of the school curriculum in terms of relevancy, meaningfulness, purpose, and challenge during the student's time in school;
2. Extent of homework assignments and whether or not the student felt that the homework was reasonable or valid;
3. Kinds of pressures to which students might have felt they were subjected in order to earn high grades or make the honor roll;
4. Analysis of prevailing impersonal relationships for their impact upon the student;
5. Necessary conditions for effective work and study in the home and at school.

Findings of this survey should be given wide publicity throughout the community.

Workshops could be jointly planned by the lay and professional committees — not only for the benefit of the lay public, but also for the teachers' need to have nonprofessional views. In the workshops both groups might discuss just how effective they think the present school program has been in helping the home, church, and other community segments to influence in a positive sense student behavior, values, ideals, appreciation, understanding, and knowledge. They should keep before them the basic question of how a more meaningful program could solve the problems at hand.

The two committees could serve a clearinghouse function between school and community, issuing periodic bulletins about the project and publishing informational articles in the local media.

In involving parents and other members of the community in curriculum reorganization through problem solving, the leaders in planning and implementing need to affirm these principles:

1. The community not only has the right, but *the obligation* to participate in defining the school program in a problem solving situation.
2. Communication channels are *two-way:* The school needs public opinion just as the public must have information about its schools.
3. Informed community citizens are the best defenders of the school against possible ignorance and misunderstanding on the part of regressive forces advocating false economy, special interests, or causes undermining public education. It is easy to promote a cause against something and particularly a concept as new as problem solving–team teaching. Educators should not be expected to stand alone; it is also the community's responsibility to defend the schools from these regressive forces.
4. The community should cooperate constantly with the school system in evaluating innovative programs like problem solving in order to answer the broader need of determining the purposes and experiences of an educational institution.
5. Initiative for school–community cooperation originates within the school system and with professional personnel like the superintendent, principal, curriculum coordinator, and teachers. These people must see that the advisory councils are begun so that the lay public will be in on the new project from the start.
6. Lay persons should not be confined merely to consultative roles with respect to planning and evaluating a problem solving curriculum. They should become involved in hard work to gather concrete evidence of program strengths and weaknesses.
7. Educational personnel committees studying the problem solving project should include lay persons — provided these citizens are willing to engage vigorously in surveying community problems. School–community cooperation provides an excellent means for adult education.
8. Those representing the community in any of the cooperative efforts with the school system should be broadly representative as spokesmen for the community's segments — ethnically, geographically, and socioeconomically.
9. Recommendations made by lay advisory groups should be channeled through either the board of education or the individual school — depending on which is the implementer of the problem solving unit. There should be a clear understanding between school and community people that, while such recommendations will be duly considered, they are not necessarily binding. On the other

hand, the lay advisory groups must be more than figureheads and it is the responsibility of the school board or faculty to see that the lay council has an on-going advisory role.

Whoever is involved in implementing a problem solving curriculum — school administrator, principal, teacher, student, lay person — becomes a *working* member. Also he participates from the earliest possible point. If the planning phases have gone well, then the learning experiences will be full and challenging for the individual student.

BIBLIOGRAPHY

Anderson, Vernon E., *Principles and Procedures of Curriculum Improvement*. New York: Ronald Press Co., 1956.

Dubin, Robert and others, *Leadership and Productivity*. San Francisco: Chandler Publishing Co., 1965.

Franseth, Jane, *Supervision As Leadership*. New York: Row, Peterson and Co., 1961.

Goraan, Thomas, *Group-Centered Leadership*. Boston: Houghton Mifflin Co., 1955.

Harris, Ben M. and Wailand Bessant, *In-Servire Education*. Englewood Cliffs, N.J.: Prentice-Hall, 1969.

Hyman, Ronald T., *Approaches in Curriculum*. Englewood Cliffs, N.J.: Prentice-Hall, 1973.

Jacobson, Paul B. and others, *The Principalship: New Perspectives*. Englewood Cliffs, N.J.: Prentice-Hall, 1973.

Leadership for Improving Instruction: Association for Supervision and Curriculum Development Yearbook. Washington, D.C.: ASCD, 1960.

Leeper, Robert R., ed., *Role of Supervisor and Curriculum Director in a Climate of Change*. Washington, D.C.: Association for Supervision and Curriculum Development, 1965.

Lindsey, Gardner, ed., *Handbook of Social Psychology*. Boston: Addison Wesley Publishing Co., 1954.

Milstin, Mike M. and James A. Balasco, *Educational Administration and The Behavioral Sciences*. Boston: Allyn and Bacon, 1973.

Neagley, Ross L. and N. Dean Evans, *Handbook for Effective Curriculum Development*. Englewood Cliffs, N.J.: Prentice-Hall, 1967.

Petrullo, Luigi and Bernard N. Bass, *Leadership and Interpersonal Behavior*. New York: Holt, Rinehart and Winston, 1961.

Pickarts, Evelyn and Jean Fargo, *Parent Education*. New York: Appleton-Century-Crofts, 1971.

Pierce, Truman M. and A. D. Albright, *A Profession in Transition* (Southern States Cooperative Program in Educational Administration, 1960) .

Richey, Robert W., *Planning for Teachers*. New York: McGraw-Hill Book Co., 1973.

Saunders, Robert L. and others, *A Theory of Educational Leadership*. Columbus, Ohio: Charles E. Merrill Publishing Co., 1966.

Schmuck, Richard A. and Patricia A. Schmuck, *Group Processes in the Classroom*. Dubuque, Iowa: William C. Brown Co., 1971.

Smith, G. Kerry, ed., *In Search of Leaders*. Washington, D.C.: American Association for Higher Education, 1967.

Vars, Gordon F., *Common Learnings: Core and Interdisciplinary Team Approaches*. Scranton, Pa.: International Textbook Co., 1969.

Waskin, Yvonne and Louise Parrish, *Teacher-Pupil Planning*. New York: Pitman, 1967.

Wiles, Kimball, *Supervision for Better Schools*. Englewood Cliffs, N.J.: Prentice-Hall, 1967.

Chapter 5. Emphasis on Teaching and Learning

An environment refers to all the interacting forces having impact upon the learning experiences of children. It takes in the human relationships which exist among members of the teaching team, between teachers and students, among students, and between the school administrators and students. It includes feelings and emotional tensions — for instance, acceptance or rejection of individuals — created in the interacting process. And it recognizes the influences of experiences outside the school, particularly the home and community, which help shape children before they ever step into a classroom as well as when they do.

If the atmosphere of a school is friendly, free from pressure or strain and, yet, at the same time a busy and purposeful place, then a good learning environment probably exists. If children are eager to get to school in the morning and reluctant to leave in the afternoon, the learning environment is most likely a sound one. The best problem solving learning environment stimulates the individual to reach constantly for new horizons, understandings, and experiences.

Human relationships are important in an effective problem solving learning environment. In fact, teaching and learning in problem solving depend in large part on *how teachers and pupils perceive their relationships with each other.*

It is the teacher who must make many crucial decisions during the process of helping a student realize his potentialities. Teachers assume many roles in problem solving-team teaching. They are technicians who arrange materials, plan schedules, and apply group techniques. They are social engineers who join with their teammates in selecting out of the cultural heritage those ideas which are of greatest value in helping the students to solve a problem. And they are artists who are sensitive to human feelings and are able to encourage student creativity.

A team of teachers planning out an effective learning environment must work well beyond the simplistic levels of superficial skills and conventional information; it must seek those levels which enable students to come to grips with the more vital developmental tasks confronting them. Teachers themselves are by no means free of anxieties. They are aware that other school people and many members of the community may wish a safer, more conventional classroom environment. But the teaching team which delves into the deeper concepts and the more meaningful learning relation-

100

ships will in the end be able to work more securely with their students—
and eventually with the parents—because the team members are creating
wholesome changes in their students by guiding and facilitating individual
and group growth.

The teachers on the team must work hard at developing a peer-group
relationship among themselves without the personality problems of individual stars, prima donnas, or hermits. As a team, the members must be
free to communicate with each other in the planning, execution, and
evaluation phases of the learning process. None should experience discrimination or belittlement from fellow team members.

Above all, the teachers are sensitive to the ways in which people learn.
Extensive research has shown that a person does not behave in accordance
with the facts as normally seen by other people, but in terms of *how he
perceives the situation at the moment.* Therefore, what a person does and
what a person learns are products of what is going on in his unique and
perceptual field of awareness. A person behaves, then, in terms of those
personal meanings or perceptions which exist for him at a given moment
of action. This process is vastly different from what has heretofore been
perceived as the way a person learns.

Combs has pointed out that "education has done well in gathering facts
and in making them available to people, but has done much less in helping
people discover the meaning of such facts so that behavior is affected."[1]
Kelley has made a similar observation:

> The learning of facts must now be recognized as only the first and
> the simplest phase of the educational process; bringing the facts into
> the meaning world of the learner is the teaching activity which will
> make a difference in the lives of students. If behavior is a function of
> personal meaning or a function of perception, then perception must
> become the center of the teaching-learning endeavor. Perceptions
> must take their place as a vital part of the curriculum if knowledge
> is to be effective in the lives of students.[2]

In problem solving-team teaching, the teaching team must recognize that
the matter of meaning—the beginning of the learning process—does not
make any impact until it takes place in the child's own personal and
unique perceptual field, resulting in changed behavior for the individual.
Accordingly, the job of education is learning how to help students discover
personal meaning in each learning situation. Learning occurs *only* when

---

[1] Alexander Frazier, ed., *Learning More About Learning* (Washington, D.C.:
Association for Supervision and Curriculum Development, 1959), p. 9.

[2] Tape recorded by the author during an address at the Association for Supervision
and Curriculum Development 1962 annual convention.

something happens inside the learner; this action is mostly controlled by the learner, not the teacher. In order for learning to take place, the classroom must be a place in which exploration and discovery of meaning are the central activities. Then, students will learn how to learn — enabling them to continue learning long after they have left school.

In effective teaching and learning, behavior is looked upon as a direct function of human meaning and perception rather than as forces exerted upon the individual. The teacher must not be dictator, maker of rules, or manipulator. He assists, helps, aids, and facilitates the growing human organism in the process of becoming. The teacher is continually engaged in helping children to explore and discover personal meaning of events in their own lives. He skillfully creates an atmosphere which makes exploration of meaning possible on the one hand and encouragement of active discovery on the other.

Individual perception happens when there is a favorable environment outside of the individual which makes it safe for his feelings and ideas to come forth. No one will let his feelings be known if there is danger that he will be attacked and ridiculed for what he thinks and believes. The classroom atmosphere must be made safe for exploration of meanings if there are to be changes in the behavior of students.

Working from the Perceptual View

In the past psychologists and educators were inclined to look at a person's experiences or life history in determining how he had become the person he was. But the perceptual view of causation of behavior has changed in recent years. The tendency is to look at the results of how an individual behaves right now or in the present situation. This immediate view pertaining to behavior emphasizes how a person sees a situation at a given moment, and what he sees shapes his behavior at that time.

If it can be understood how a person is currently perceiving himself, then it is possible to help him change his behavior — even if it is not known how he came to behave that way. Such an immediate view of behavior differs from past approaches. In using this perspective, teachers, administrators, supervisors, and counsellors need not know a student's past history in depth in order to effect change in his behavior. The emphasis, instead, is upon knowing the individual rather than knowing about him.

Proponents of this perceptual point of view maintain that something can be done in school for every child, even though the school is but one part of his total world. Teachers and other educators using this approach can be rescued from much of the paper shuffling and routine case study neces-

102

sary for gathering data about a student's past history. Instead, they can concentrate on working with a student in a particular situation. Nor need they worry about trying to change the student's home and community environments.

Since learning is the discovery of personal meaning, it is a highly personal process. Its success depends not only on what the teacher does and says, but also upon what the situation offers in the way of unique meaning for the learner himself. Mass techniques of teaching and learning present difficulties because they are not objective ways of dealing with the student.

In a problem solving situation, the learning process becomes a *joint* experience of teacher–pupil planning and actions — affording each class member the opportunity to bring facts and information to bear upon his perceptual world. Facts and information are important raw materials for new and exciting ways to perceive the world. Teachers must search for ways that students can experience self-expression; they must sense when self-restraint is also needed. Under these conditions the individual student will come to see himself as a person who can achieve and learn. He will begin to see that, within the group, he matters.

As the learning experiences take place, both teachers and students should come to understand that people do not change their ways of doing things *until* they see what they perceive as a new and better way of acting. They will begin to grasp why different students behave differently within a classroom. Then they can begin accepting a person within the context of each situation and stop blaming him for behaving in ways which are different from their own perceptions.

If a learning environment permits the exploration of meaning, planning is very important. Decisions can be made cooperatively in team–pupil sessions about time schedules, teacher assignments, class size, tools and equipment, and needed facilities. Classes should be large enough so that students can measure their ideas against those of other students within the broad range of interests, needs, and abilities; they need to be small enough for students to test the ideas in some detail. Diversity is possible through both large-group and sub-group situations. There must also be a continuity in time — particularly for junior and senior high students who heretofore have been segmented into six to eight periods per day. Such division or interruption in a problem solving situation fails to allow ample time for any exploration of meanings and feelings.

But effective planning cannot take place *unless* school personnel are willing to be reoriented in their views or concepts of education. Among other things, such variables as feelings, attitudes, convictions, biases, beliefs, doubts, fears, love, hate, anxieties, and values have to be admitted into the classroom. Traditionally, in terms of the learning process, feelings and other emotions have been banned from the classroom. In past practice generally, the iron will of the teacher was imposed upon his students; learning — for students — was the submission and subordination of their feelings rather than trying to understand these feelings and to use them constructively. Therefore, in a problem solving educational program, teachers, administrators, supervisors, guidance personnel, and others must learn to see themselves as helping or facilitating persons. Like their students, educators will change their behavior only when new ideas about people, learning, and effective ways of working come to have meaning for them. They will change as they see the new ideas fitting into and being consistent with their perceptions of the self and their roles as educators, and they must be convinced that the change in behavior will enhance their own roles.

In-service education can help effect such a change — provided these "student" teachers and administrators have the freedom to explore other ways of viewing education than the traditional perspective. Action research and experimentation can also help. If educators reorient their perceptions, the classroom, too, will change into a laboratory for exploration and discovery.

Caring for Individual Differences

In order to provide situations in which students can achieve self-actualization or become fully functioning, adequate personalities, a broad range of learning experiences are necessary for a reasonable degree of success — challenging, but not unduly threatening. A challenging situation is one where, if an individual applies himself consistently and diligently, he can have the possibility of achieving success. Success is *not* guaranteed; it requires effort on the individual's part. A threat, on the other hand, involves a situation in which the person is bound to fail, no matter how consistently or effectively he may apply himself. Once a person perceives that failure is likely to occur, he begins to behave in a way which ensures that failure will take place. In a challenging situation, the individual is generally able to perceive that success is possible and he will start behaving to assure that he will experience success.

As an individualized educational concept built on the premise of a non-graded learning situation, problem solving learning is particularly designed to enable each participant to function in accordance with his own interests, needs, aptitudes, and abilities; in terms of his prior experiences; and in light of anticipated interests and needs. Individualization is achieved through two major approaches. First, the problem which the group has selected is of such scope and nature that it can be subdivided — with each sub-problem having a large array and variety of activities and learning experiences that must be handled if the general problem is to be solved. Learning experiences will be implemented through large-group, small-group, committee, and individualized activities. Opportunities are provided for frequent sharing of individual and group research, making it possible for each student to have comprehensive insights into ramifications of the problem.

Second, skills, basic concepts, and understandings are developed on an individualized basis in terms of each student's unique background of experiences. Each student is taken at the point where he is allowed to develop as rapidly as he is able. Skills are taught primarily from a diagnostic, remedial, and developmental approach. The teaching team must constantly evaluate student efforts, diagnose individual and group deficiencies, and update materials in order that individuals can move ahead. It is precisely this attention to individual needs which leads to maximum contributions by students to the total team effort.

Teacher-Pupil Planning: Cooperative Process

When the team teachers and students meet to plan out the problem solving unit, they should work cooperatively. The sessions can lay the foundation for cooperation during the regular teaching and learning experiences which will follow. Under supervision of the teaching team, the boys and girls are involved in what they are to study, how it can be pursued, and what criteria will be selected to determine success.

In actual planning sessions, a team of perhaps four or more teachers will work with approximately 120 students. They will examine possible problems, weighing the merits of each one and establishing relative significance. A problem can be selected by several means. It might be chosen because the class had previously worked on a problem together; during this period, they might have become interested in an allied problem which is now proposed. The approach, having a built-in intrinsic motivation, is frequently used when teaching teams and students are experienced in problem solving situations.

A second approach might be called the development of a census of problems. The students identify problems which they consider of real concern and valuable to their own education. They would need to consult parents and other community people for opinions on which problems are most acute. Under this approach, it is likely that many problems will be identified and that some valid criteria is needed for final selection.

As a third possible approach in selecting a problem, the teaching team can observe the students in day-to-day interactions and discussions. After the in-depth observations, the teachers can usually find leads to meaningful problems. Here again valid criteria for selection is necessary.

There is no single list of criteria applicable to all learning situations, but the following guidelines can help teachers and students move toward realistic planning. Basically, the problem selected should:

1. Represent persistent areas of a personal–social nature and be common to children and youth in the culture;
2. Be adaptable to the group's level of maturity;
3. Provide growth experiences in terms of values like tolerance, social sensitivity, cooperativeness, civil responsibility, aesthetic appreciation, self-direction, critical thinking, and democratic living;
4. Be a new problem in the sense that the group has not studied it together — although a problem can be repeated if explored from a different perspective or in greater depth than previously;
5. Help the students to learn how to live more effectively today and in the future;
6. Interest most of the group;
7. Lend itself to the use of problem solving techniques;
8. Provide abundant opportunities for cooperative planning, implementation, and evaluation of outcomes and give attention to the unique needs of each pupil;
9. Give chances for generalization past the point of daily student experiences;
10. Offer meaningful and direct experiences such as action research efforts;
11. Integrate knowledge from the various disciplines for the problem's solution;
12. Create opportunities for student investigation, research, reading, writing, library use, and group work and communication;
13. Be a subject on which sufficient information is available;
14. Offer experiences which will develop continuity in emotional, intellectual, and physical aspects of the learning process;
15. Recognize the control role of guidance in a problem solving process, with the team or classroom teacher as the main guidance resource;

16. Help individuals to expand their special interests in those areas uniquely related to their own maturation;
17. Be effectively implemented so that it can lead to concern for the solving of other problems.

Without some guidelines or general criteria, the team and group may well experience haphazard, ineffectual learning situations. Students might be tempted to select superficial problems of immediate appeal and overlook more meaningful and basic ones. The teacher who resorts to the technique of class vote or majority rule should be warned that such procedures are, at best, risky. No group can decide on which problem to study until it has plunged — not merely dabbled — into its parts: extent, scope, severity, trends, causes, effects, and remedies. Only after the students have made a preliminary investigation of potential problems will they begin to perceive that some problems are more worthwhile for study than others. When the group has explored possible problems in some depth, then a group consensus can usually be reached. If the group favors more than one problem for study, then priorities need to be determined.

Once the problem has been selected, the team–pupil planning sessions can decide how to subdivide it. These subdivisions are common in problem solving:

1. *Extent, magnitude, severity, and trends of the problem* — As a group begins to explore the problem — for example, the effects of vandalism and delinquency upon individuals and the community — it will not only cover the local scene, but also make comparisons with nearby or distant communities. While a problem solving experience often begins at the immediate or local level, it inevitably expands to include the broader perimeters of state, regional, national, and global levels. The student then learns about the interrelatedness of the world.

2. *Causes and contributing conditions which account for the problem* — The students examine the physical, social, economic, and psychological forces which gave rise to the problem; they are able to see how the problem is related to man's total living environment and how it may affect the well-being of people.

3. *Costs and effects of the problem, both on individual lives and on society* — Both obvious and hidden costs are pinpointed. In the vandalism and delinquency problem, for example, the students would view costs in terms of restoration of property, legal ramifications, incarceration of the delinquent, and maintenance of cor-

rective institutions. They might also check into social and psychological effects of vandalism and delinquency upon the family and community.

4. *Prevention of and remedies for the problem*—Using data from the first three subdivisions, the students could research the history of the problem and investigate how other communities either avoided or coped with the problem. In the case of vandalism and delinquency, the students would need to consult records in juvenile courts, detention homes, and newspaper and magazine files. If, for instance, the class found that the lack of recreational facilities contributes significantly to certain kinds of delinquency, it could carefully evaluate existing recreational facilities and planned or projected ones.

As the problem is tackled and group activities begin, team-pupil planning sessions must deal with possible hypotheses, particularly as data is made available through research, on-site visits, and interviews. Information which is not of importance or not relative to the problem will be discarded at this point; that which appears valid and adequate can form a basis for generalizations and conclusions to support hypotheses. Possible solutions can be suggested.

Solutions which are posed can be tested with questions. Does the suggested action satisfactorily reduce or overcome the problem? Does the solution promote changes in feelings and attitudes? Does it appear to be long-lasting? Is it consistent with the group's stated goals? Would it be acceptable to those it affects? Does the solution reflect the capabilities, interests, and resources of the student group itself? Have the limits of the solution been clearly defined so that the group can measure its success with the problem? Will the solution help to prevent subsequent problems?

Throughout these team-pupil planning sessions, the teaching team must be successful in impressing upon the students that both teachers and students are there to work *together;* that they are all members of a group; and that, within the cooperative context, ideas will be evaluated in terms of merit, not on the basis of who projects them. The team must be sensitive to the lengths of the sessions. It is all too easy to conduct them hastily —most likely because many teachers feel they have to get along with the problem's information gathering and solution phases. The notion can prove inhibiting. On the other hand, there is just as much danger in allowing students to get too far into the planning process—to the point that they might lose interest in what they plan to pursue later. It is the team's responsibility to strike a balance between the two extremes.

The Human Part in the Learning Environment

In the opening of this chapter, the point was emphasized that how teachers and students perceive their relationships with each other in large part determines what kind of teaching and learning environment will be established. It is very crucial during planning and all other phases of a problem solving experience that, as teachers and students seek data and put together generalizations and hypotheses, they must also learn to accept one another.

Teachers particularly must constantly search for ways to know the students. They cannot facilitate learning for the students unless they exhibit sensitivity to emotions and feelings: hang-ups, hopes, anxieties. The team must be able to understand the pupils' interests, family involvements, leisure activities, travel experiences, and other pertinent information. Through informal interactions and discussions, casual daily tasks, and visits to the homes, the team can begin to sense the students' needs and interests.

While it falls to the teaching team to take initial leadership in setting the problem solving activities in motion, the students will assume more and more responsibility in a relatively short period of time. One rule is useful: Teachers should never do for the students what the students can do for themselves. As the activities progress, students will begin to sense the relationship between cognitive and effective areas of learning. In problem solving the two concepts are inseparable. Human thinking and feeling processes are very important, and one cannot operate effectively in problem solving learning experiences without the other.

In the past, education has relied too heavily upon the cognitive learnings—and particularly its lower levels. Higher cognitive levels like generalization, synthesis, and evaluation have all but been ignored; even less attention has been given to the affective or feeling elements of learning. But educators are coming to realize that the individual is an integrated personality which is constantly in the process of becoming adequate—not only through the knowledge and insights he is achieving, but also through his feelings, alienations, frustrations, and concerns in relation to personal identity and purpose. These affective elements are as important as the basic facts and concepts he is learning.

Most of our curriculums used in classrooms originated through human experiences in which the knowing and feeling aspects were interrelated in a most realistic and meaningful way; but, in the process of ordering and systematizing information, these interrelationships have been lost. Insights and information have been separated from the feelings and emotions accompanying them because education came to feel that time was too short for each individual to relive these experiences which have the greatest impact upon behavior.

Human dimensions must be reintroduced into the classroom learning situation to enhance the individual's desire for learning. It is only as these emotional dimensions are added that the learner will become personally involved to the important degree that learning will result in changed behavior. Because the integration of affective and cognitive learnings is central to its purpose of preparing the individual for life situations through group inquiry, problem solving learning accommodates the human dimensions.

The teaching team in problem solving respects the need for behavioral objectives in the learning situation, and that the objectives cover the three domains of learning: cognitive, affective, and psychomotor. If the team has worked effectively with the students in the beginning by planning sound behavioral objectives and particularly at the lower cognitive levels, the later task of evaluating these students in terms of changed behavior can prove meaningful. The teachers should keep the behavioral objectives in mind during the entire problem solving process. They need also to recognize the different levels of the learning domains involved in the various learning situations. A brief resume might be helpful at this point. Taxonomies of the three learning domains can be consulted for detailed summaries.

The lowest level of cognitive behavioral objectives — knowledge objectives — refers to a person's ability to recall, though not to his capacity to apply the knowledge to specific situations. A knowledge objective might be the ability to recognize a simple sentence or to define a noun and its role in a sentence. Once the student is able to recall such information, he is usually ready to move to the next higher cognitive level, that of comprehension objectives. At this level, the student is not only able to define an objective, but also to translate it into meaningful terminology and further to infer its possible implications. At this level, for example, the student would have the ability to read and interpret information on the increased cost of living or comprehend the impact of the population explosion on the world food supply.

A third level of behavioralistic objectives in the cognitive domain, that of application, implies an individual's ability both to understand principles and generalizations and to see their relationships to new problems and situations. The ability to apply principles and generalizations to a given problem or situation constitutes one of the more complex and difficult objectives of education, and it is a level frequently overlooked. But this third cognitive level is used regularly in problem solving in order that the students can understand the problem's full implications as well as its

110

impact upon human society. Students working on this level would develop, for example, the ability to apply economic principles of supply and demand to the prediction of beef price trends or develop concepts in order to see how Charles's and Boil's laws have direct impact upon home and school refrigeration systems.

Analysis, the fourth level of cognitive behavioral objectives, operates on the assumption that the individual not only can comprehend a specific body of facts, but also view the facts in terms of function. Analyzing a problem is a complex ability, drawing upon knowledge, comprehension, and application; it even goes beyond these steps. The analysis level can be a preliminary step toward creative synthesis. Once a student develops analytical abilities in a number of fields, he can use them in other problems and efforts. If he is well versed in analysis techniques, he can recognize subtle differences between facts and information. For example, he would be able to recognize which parts of a political statement are factually supported, based upon half-truths, or merely propaganda. He can analyze the effects of social deprivation on people with respect to its impact upon their inability to develop adequate self-concepts and learning experiences.

The process of putting together elements and parts of a situation so that it will form a whole is done at the fifth level of behavioral objectives in the cognitive domain: synthesis. When the parts are combined, a pattern or structure emerges which has not been previously seen. Synthesis —closely related to creative teaching and learning — is a kind of self-expression in which a student is urged and helped to produce something different from what an average individual in an average learning situation would produce. It represents divergent rather than convergent thinking; as such, synthesis is one of the terminal outcomes of learning. Students who master this level will be able to produce ideas, plans, and products which are uniquely theirs: writing a creative poem on a sunset or designing a multipurpose recreational facility to meet a community's specific needs.

The evaluation objectives—the highest level of cognitive learning—incorporate some of the confidences which have been acquired at lower cognitive levels: knowledge, comprehension, application, analysis, and synthesis. It involves the processes of making judgments about values, identifying ideas to apply to the problem's solution, and arriving at the ultimate outcome. In evaluation both standards and criteria are used to appraise the extent to which objectives have been met. It is a process used repeatedly by citizens in a democracy who must regularly evaluate social policies, political decisions, and governmental actions. And it is used by individuals involved in solving problems of pollution, war, peace, and urbanization.

The student who has mastered evaluation objectives, for example, will have the ability to judge the artistic quality of a creative painting through use of recognized criteria or can appraise possible consequences of actions advocated in a given situation.

But learning is more than developing intellectual facility; it is the discovery of personal meaning which results in changed behavior. Hence, the emotions and feelings—attitudes, appreciations, biases, and prejudices—enter the learning situation. The way a person feels about a situation frequently has more impact upon his behavior than what he knows or understands about the situation. Educators, then, *must* begin to give increased emphasis to the affective domain of learning.

The behavioral objectives in the taxonomy of affective domain are arranged along a hierarchial continuum. At the receiving level — the lowest one—an awareness is developed of basic things. For example, the student becomes aware of the differences among various social, economic, and ethnic groups. Next the individual develops a sensitivity to the significance of some of these behavioral differences; he is then at a point where he receives a higher order of feeling which can be characterized as an attempt to control some of his own perceptions and feelings. At this point, with respect to the problem solving activities, he will be able to pass judgment on some of the prevailing conditions of the problem highlighted by research. He will then try to respond to these findings by indicating a willingness to adhere to more humane principles, particularly in patterning his own life. With the response, the student gains increased satisfaction and may find pleasure in trying to seek a remedy to the problem.

At this point, he develops a valuing concept and starts accepting specific values—for example, a desire to improve the lot of underprivileged children. As he responds to these values, he will increasingly try to remove some of the discrimination—an indication of his commitment to the worth and dignity of human beings. As he organizes and conceptionalizes these values, he is beginning to formulate judgments relative to societal responsibility in caring for the human and material needs of underprivileged children. As he organizes his value system, he starts to regulate his own actions according to the value concepts he is making. In characterizing the value concepts, the student begins to develop a long list of behavioral reactions which are consistent with his thinking.

He has now reached the critical point in the learning process: He can change his own behavior in light of valid evidence—not only in the problem solving situation, but in future situations. By this time his commitments are so strong that they, by and large, regulate his personal and civic life, touching upon all of his behavioral relationships with other individuals and with general society.

Once the student realizes that knowledge and feelings have a close relationship and that objectives in one domain have counterparts in the other, he will become sensitive to objectives in both domains. Cognitive levels like, say, analysis are closely associated with valuing; those of synthesis and evaluation are tied closely to the organization and characterization of human emotional behavior.

Pupil Roles in the Learning Process

Laying plans for problem solving ordinarily covers three activity phases: initiatory, developmental, and culminating. Some problem solving units will operate more informally than others. If the problem solving has arisen from a former problem undertaken and completed by the group, it will be hard to separate one phase from another. If a group is using the problem solving approach for the first time, activities are usually more distinctly identified.

Initial activities are deliberately designed to develop a readiness on the part of teachers and students to explore how the problem relates to them and others in the group. Effort at this point will frequently be made to arouse interest in group members; whatever motivation is developed, however, should be intrinsic to the problem rather than superficial. Films, filmstrips, and slides might help to identify opposing viewpoints, leading the students into an analysis of the problem relative to conditions in their own communities. If a bulletin board of news items, pictures, graphs, and maps were developed by the students, they could then pose questions suggested through the materials. Or contrasting views about the problem could be collected from the media. As a fourth introductory activity, the group might discuss a unit on a similar problem. In still another activity, the students could survey opinions and attitudes throughout the local community about the problem. They might then compare the community attitudes with those identified by selected professionals working towards some solution of the problem.

At this point the team and students should be in a position to conduct a more intensive planning session. A technique like listing on the board questions raised by class members can narrow the questions down to those the class feels are most important. It would then be possible to make statements of expected outcomes, areas of student interest, and possible obstacles. The key question of how to explore the problem will probably come up, and the teacher might recommend that the class begin with a few specific large-group activities and then identify useful committee and individual projects. Possible materials should also be suggested, bringing the students into the research stage.

One possible weakness of problem solving-team teaching is that the teachers can prepare their students in a superficial manner. Perhaps the team asks the group to define the arguments for and against the problem without going into the processes by which meaningful education results; tools like study skills, research skills, skills in generalization and conclusion, and skills in critical thinking should be used consciously rather than taken for granted. Time should be taken to understand the steps in a reasoning process rather than blindly accepting the final step of a syllogism.

These steps, while partly initiatory, are important to the developmental phase of a problem solving experience:

1. Form committees for each major sub-problem, having them develop and investigate a bibliography of materials and then consider how the information-gathering could be expedited. The committees can use library sources for organizations and agencies concerned with the problem.

2. Make an inventory of community resources, starting with reference listings in the library and checking with local agencies, keeping in mind that persons must be sought to come into the classrooms for discussions and interviews.

3. Survey how the people in the community have been affected by the problem and how they have confronted it. The teachers and students can make maps or charts to identify areas where the problem is most prevalent. Also, the local problem can be compared with state and national levels.

4. Develop multimedia materials—motion pictures, slides, filmstrips— to illustrate the major parts of the problem and how they can be investigated; present the materials during a roundtable or panel discussion.

5. Follow through on how the local community is working to lessen or eliminate the problem. The major findings of the students about the community's actions can be summarized in a chart; the group can examine the chart and draw conclusions about what the community has been doing. Follow through with other conclusions—at this point still tentative—expressed by class members in a role-playing situation or other dramatic approach. Perhaps the drama would portray the impact the problem is having upon individual and

community well-being. Or the class might put on an assembly program depicting the problem's extent and airing proposals for possible solution.

Many other activities could be suggested for committee and class work, but it should be sufficient at this point to emphasize that whatever is selected should be of such range, scope, and intensity to keep the program alive and induce the students to continue toward the problem's solution. Teachers should particularly remember that activities and learning experiences should parallel student abilities, experiences, and interests. It is all too easy for students to get in over their heads by pursuing activities too far beyond their abilities to comprehend and to implement. Such a pitfall should be avoided.

Near the end of a problem solving experience, the knowledge and insights developed by the class through general discussion and committee or sub-group investigations must be brought together for an overview. These activities are aids in the summarizing process:

1. Arrange a school assembly during which an aspect of the problem is presented, including a film or series of slides prepared by the problem solving participants, dramatic skits, and general group conclusions.
2. Plan a similar presentation for the PTA, service clubs, the League of Women Voters, or the Chamber of Commerce—concluding with an open forum.
3. Plan and write a series of articles for the school newspaper which stress the group's conclusions and recommendations for action.
4. Cooperate with a local group having a study program on the problem or allied ones.
5. Present one of the dramatizations developed during the problem solving activities over the school's public address system, the local radio station, or a television station.
6. Exhibit in the public library various charts, graphs, posters, murals, or cartoons illustrating the problem's possible solution.
7. Select topics for further group analysis and study, using them as possible initiatory activities for a subsequent problem.

If the team of teachers and the students *really* attacked the problem during the planning phase, the culminating activities will reflect the fact and the group's conclusions will be well-rounded.

As the class participates in each learning activity, it should put the specific sources and materials used in that activity on a list. The list will need updating, particularly when other sources or materials have to be substituted for those projected in the planning sessions. The list should cover a wide range: bibliographies and other reference books, texts, general and specialized books, technical and research manuals, pamphlets, fiction books, newspapers and magazines, audiovisual aids, charts, graphs, diagrams, maps and globes, photographs, cartoons, slides and film strips, movies, recordings and transcriptions, radio and television broadcasts, community resource persons, materials from government and private organizations, and on-site or field visits.

Determining Learning Outcomes

It is all too common in an educational effort to work very hard in the actual developmental activities and then fail to measure the outcomes to any useful extent. In problem solving the evaluation of both activities and processes is an integral part of the learning process. The evaluative phase—the broad process by which achievement of expected outcomes is recorded—particularly checks back into the initial objectives set by the group in early planning sessions. The objectives covered the areas of behavior, skills, and attitudes.

By now the group is prepared to discuss its progress openly. It can handle questions like:

1. Has the class continued an interest in the problem past scheduled activities and research projects?
2. Have the individual opinions of the group members been influenced by the project?
3. Has the group helped or cooperated with any community organizations which have been actively working on the problem?

There are other indices for determining learning outcomes. Tests and group discussions can help to establish how well the group members have come to understand facts and concepts. Questions asked, sources used, and statements given in class during the regular activities phase can provide clues to learning. Written reports are evidence of the mastery of subject matter and research procedures. Informal questions by the teachers are another means. Since a problem solving group is generally large, the teaching team often must seek a more detailed understanding of how well students have handled concrete materials, verbal skills, and thinking processes by testing them. But, if the problem solving experience has been soundly planned and carried out *cooperatively* by teachers and students, the most useful analysis of outcomes is found in the students' self-evaluations.

Creating a Learning Environment

From 1935 to 1942 the author was supervising principal of a 12-grade school system in Waterloo, Ala. The school was in a most deplorable condition; the buildings and equipment had been badly neglected and vandalized. All the outside doors of one building had been torn off their hinges and every window in the group of buildings had at least one broken pane and in some cases the entire window was gone. Names and other graffiti were scrawled over most desks, tables, and walls.

Community morale was at a very low ebb. During the 1935-42 period, the Pickwick Dam in the area backed water over all of the fertile soil of the Tennessee Valley farmers, leaving only the upland to farm—a relatively unproductive crop area. People neglected their homes and the community itself was generally in a poor condition. Not a single home in the school area had indoor bath facilities. Few of the homes had been maintained, painted, or landscaped. Litter and debris were scattered throughout the community. Churches were in bad need of repair and upkeep. In brief, the community—torn by physical and economic crises—had given up. The school reflected this despair by its lack of landscaping, upkeep, and repair. Practically all of the school's industrial arts, home economics, and science equipment had been either destroyed or stolen.

The picture was dismal when the faculty of the school met for two weeks to preplan before classes began in fall of 1935. The teachers and administrators analyzed the school and community situation to discover ways to rehabilitate the community and to revitalize its educational program. Collaborating with several leading citizens and a group of the older students, the faculty pinpointed four critical areas:

1. Home, school, and community improvement;
2. A diversified agricultural program to enhance economic incomes;
3. An extensive home, school, and community recreational program;
4. Better diets for both children and adults through sound menu planning and improved growth and preservation of food crops.

The entire school—which included grades one through twelve—became involved in the restoration and reclamation of the school building, equipment, and facilities. Buildings were painted; broken windows and doors were replaced; floors were refinished; and furniture was sanded, sealed, and refinished. Each student bore responsibility for improving specific facilities, including his desk. At the same time the faculty made an intense effort to impress the students with the responsibility of caring for public property by stressing that its destruction was really the destruction of their own personal belongings held in common by the entire community.

117

When two new buildings were constructed for the school grounds, the students helped to design and select equipment and furniture. They also assisted in constructing large tables for recreational and study needs. They mixed stains and indoor paints for the walls.

The twelfth grade concentrated on the problem of improving living through reclamation of home, school, and community environments. At the outset, the class surveyed each home in the school attendance area to find out what kinds of improvement could make the homes more livable. Needed repairs were carefully cataloged: additional electrical wiring, plumbing, landscaping, structural improvements, repainting, interior decoration, and furniture refinishing. Next, the twelfth graders did a very effective job of selling the homeowners on doing much of this work and also offered student supervision and assistance wherever possible. Faculty members served as resource personnel: the supervising principal, social studies teacher, language arts teacher, general science teacher, home economics teacher, agriculture teacher, shop teacher, art teacher, music teacher, physical education teacher, and general math teacher. These persons formed a team and, together with the twelfth graders, took on the job of landscaping, sodding, and leveling the school grounds. The task necessitated studying the growth habits of shrubs and flowers, testing for the right kind of soil, and treating the soil so that the shrubs and flowers would grow.

Much of the school grounds, the teachers and students discovered, was thick with blackberry briars, persimmon bushes, sassafras bushes, and general undergrowth. Once these had been cleared away, work was started on reclaiming this portion of the grounds. The school also purchased seven more acres of adjacent land which was badly eroded and unfit for any productive use. The teachers and students formulated plans to reclaim this land also. The purchase served two purposes: (1) to demonstrate the reclamation possibilities of badly eroded land and (2) to have additional playground space.

The county commissioners were prevailed upon to furnish large earth-moving equipment so that a part of the newly purchased land could be leveled off, sodded, and landscaped. The other part of the purchased land was reclaimed through other means. One part was set in pine seedlings; another was set in kudzu vines with check dams constructed to stop the erosion process; within a few years this entire area could be reclaimed for school use.

The school established a small nursery plot on this same land through the propagation of shrubs that were secured through cuttings or prunings of shrubs used in the landscaping of the school and its grounds. The shrubs would be used later in landscaping homes.

Twelfth graders set these objectives to be achieved within the next few years:

1. Elimination of soil erosion on the school grounds and through much of the community;
2. Rapid curtailment of forest fires which had in the past destroyed much of the scenic countryside;
3. Improvement of community homes through painting, repairing, interior decorating, landscaping, and other efforts;
4. Combating the unsanitary conditions from accumulated debris and litter;
5. Installation of sanitary facilities in the school and in as many of the homes as possible;
6. Rewiring of the school building to eliminate fire hazards and improve electrical supplies in both the school and in private homes;
7. Improvement of the waterfront along Pickwick Lake—at that time backed up and surrounding the school on three sides—so that the lake site would become an adequate recreational and commercial fishing facility.

Several new homes were constructed and landscaped with shrubs, flowers, and lawns. Recreational possibilities of the community were publicized in nearby communities to encourage the building of new homes on the waterfront.

A few homes close to the school were in dire need of improvement, but their owners were unable to finance repairs. These homes were selected as projects in which the students could demonstrate the possibilities for improvement. They were painted inside and out with relatively inexpensive paint made by the students. Much of the furniture in the homes was refinished. Landscaping was done.

It is important that the twelfth-grade students had prepared for their huge project. They developed numerous bulletin boards illustrating well-kept and nicely landscaped homes and schools. They collected plans for community settings. School buses took them to several surrounding areas where the schools were properly maintained and adequately landscaped. From selected resource persons, the students learned what can be done through cooperative efforts.

During the project, the students wrote many letters requesting pamphlets, bulletins, and research monographs for information on projects

119

similar to theirs. State and federal soil conservation agencies, the forest reclamation service, several chambers of commerce, and community improvement organizations sent back information and materials. The students even queried other school systems on whether they had ever attempted similar reclamation projects.

Carefully analyzing all these materials, the twelfth graders were able to make some basic generalizations and conclusions about the problem of reclaiming home, school, and community environments. Articles by twelfth graders appeared in the local, county, and state newspapers to publicize the project. Photographs in these articles were taken by the students themselves. A machine for development of photos was made and used.

In order to plant shrubs, landscape grounds, and refinish furniture, for example, the students had to research which materials and methods were best for a given task. They discovered what raw materials were needed for making paints and varnishes, both for the interior and exterior of homes. They checked out how to select materials for upholstering of furniture; they kept in mind the general color scheme in each case.

One of the responsibilities accepted by the twelfth graders was the restoration of the community cemetery. Situated on a high hill overlooking the lake, the cemetery was in a bad condition—with numerous trees growing out of the graves and an enormous amount of erosion throughout the area. The students carried away all the debris and growth on the grounds, and then sodded it. Next they worked toward establishing a community cemetery association to assume responsibility for the continuous care of the cemetery.

As these many activities were taking place, the twelfth graders devised a good way to maintain an overview of the changes in the community area. They constructed a map of the entire school attendance area. The map covered one side of a school room. It was drawn to scale and had all the roads and streets in the area. Then the students went out and photographed each home and, where possible, had the occupants of the home standing in front of the building. These photos were placed upon the map at their respective places, giving the students an accurate assessment visually of the improved conditions. The map was later used in planning sessions after the students' project by the community, both in assessing improvement and in projecting further needs.

As a culminating experience, the students appeared before various civic and church groups, both in the immediate and surrounding areas, to share their problem solving experiences. By the time the 1941 school year had ended, the graduating class's commencement program contained a contrast in photographs: a panoramic view of the conditions in the community in 1935 and the conditions then prevailing in 1941. The story in the program was told in part through scenic backgrounds painted by the students under the supervision of their teachers. At the commencement itself, the students had authored and staged dramatic skits; the stage scenery was built to reflect the varying conditions in the community at different points in time. They also made their own costumes and put together the music and dances which highlighted the contrast in time.

By the end of the problem solving project, the students had not only done an enormous amount of work underlined by a high motivation, but they had also reoriented their thinking about civic, social, and community affairs in terms of improving living. Both the students and the community benefited immensely.

BIBLIOGRAPHY

Bair, Medill and Richard G. Woodward, *Team Teaching in Action.* Boston: Houghton Mifflin Co., 1964.

Baker, Eva L. and James Popham, *Expanding Dimensions of Instructional Objectives.* Englewood Cliffs, N.J.: Prentice-Hall, 1973.

Baker, Eva L. and James Popham, *Classroom Instructional Tactics.* Englewood Cliffs, N.J.: Prentice-Hall, 1973.

Beggs, David W. and Edward G. Buffie, *Independent Study.* Bloomington, Ind.: Indiana University Press, 1965.

Brown, F. Frank, *The Nongraded High School.* Englewood Cliffs, N.J.: Prentice-Hall, 1963.

Chamberlin, Leslie J., *Team Teaching.* Columbus, Ohio: Charles E. Merrill Publishing Co., 1969.

Doll, Ronald C., ed., *Individualizing Instruction.* Washington, D.C.: Association for Supervision and Curriculum Development, 1964.

Dunfee, Maxine and Helen Sagl, *Social Studies Through Problem Solving.* New York: Holt, Rinehart and Winston, 1966.

Frymier, Jack R., *The Nature of Educational Method.* Columbus, Ohio: Charles E. Merrill Publishing Co., 1965.

Goodlad, John I. and Robert H. Anderson, *The Nongraded Elementary School.* New York: Harcourt, Brace and World, Inc., 1959.

Gorman, Alfred H., *Teachers and Learners: The Interactive Process of Education.* Boston: Allyn and Bacon, 1969.

Hanna, Lavone A. and others, *Unit Teaching in the Elementary School.* New York: Holt, Rinehart and Winston, 1963.

Hanslovsky, Glenda and others, *Why Team Teaching?* Columbus, Ohio: Charles E. Merrill Publishing Co., 1969.

Hill, Wilhelmina, *Unit Planning and Teaching in Elementary Social Studies.* Washington, D.C.: U.S. Government Printing Office, 1963.

Howes, Virgil M., *Individualization of Instruction.* London: Macmillan Co. and Collier-Macmillan Ltd., 1970.

Jackson, Philip W., *Life in Classrooms.* New York: Holt, Rinehart and Winston, 1968.

Johnson, Robert H., Jr. and John J. Hunt, *Rx for Team Teaching.* Minneapolis, Minn.: Burgess Publishing Co., 1968.

121

Lurry, Lucile L. and Elsie J. Alberty, *Developing a High School Core Program*. New York: The Macmillan Co., 1957.

Manlove, Donald C. and David W. Beggs, *Flexible Scheduling*. Bloomington, Ind.: Indiana University Press, 1966.

Morine, Harold and Greta Morine, *Discovery: A Challenge to Teaching*. Englewood Cliffs, N.J.: Prentice-Hall, 1973.

Muessig, Raymond, ed., *Youth Education*. Washington, D.C.: Association for Supervision and Curriculum Development, 1968.

Overly, Norman, ed., *The Unstudied Curriculum: Its Impact on Children*. Washington, D.C.: Association for Supervision and Curriculum Development, Elementary Education Council, 1970.

Parker, Don H., *Schooling for Individual Excellence*. New York: Thomas Nelson and Sons, 1964.

Peterson, Carl H., *Effective Team Teaching: The Easton Area High School Program*. West Nyack, N.Y.: Parker Publishing Co., 1966.

Petrequin, Gaynor, *Individualizing Learning Through Modular-Flexible Programming*. New York: McGraw-Hill Book Co., 1968.

Pritzkau, Philo T., *On Education for the Authentic*. Scranton, Pa.: International Textbook Co., 1970.

Renfield, Richard, *If Teachers Were Free*. Washington, D.C.: Acropolis Books, 1969.

Rubin, Louis J., ed., *Life Skills in School and Society*. Washington, D.C.: Association for Supervision and Curriculum Development, 1969.

Russell, Ivan L., *Motivation*. Dubuque, Iowa: William C. Brown Co., 1971.

Schmuck, Richard A. and Patricia A. Schmuck, *Group Processes in the Classroom*. Dubuque, Iowa: William C. Brown Co., 1971.

Shaplin, Judson T. and Harry F. Olds, eds., *Team Teaching*. New York: Harper and Row, 1964.

Shulman, Lee S. and Evan R. Keislar, eds., *Learning by Discovery*. Chicago: Rand McNally and Co., 1966.

Stoddard, George D., *The Dual Progress Plan*. New York: Harper and Bros., 1961.

Strom, Robert and E. Paul Torrence, *Education for Affective Achievement*. Chicago: Rand McNally and Co., 1973.

Vars, Gordon F., *Common Learnings: Core and Interdisciplinary Team Approaches*. Scranton, Pa.: International Textbook Co., 1969.

Chapter 6. Problem Solving in Action

One way the soundness of an approach or idea can be demonstrated is through examples. It is not enough to state that the problem solving curriculum is a practicable concept which works effectively when soundly planned, implemented, and evaluated by intelligent, trained personnel who believe that the method of inquiry can lead to healthy learning situations for the individual student mainly through large- and small-group activities. Through examples, the concept can be clarified past abstract discussion.

This chapter describes five problem solving situations—one (on environment) compiled from the author's observations of programs in three separate schools and the remaining four summarizing actual problem solving units within specific schools. They offer the reader the opportunity to see how problem solving actually works.

The first five chapters have argued strongly that a problem solving curriculum has definite advantages over the outdated subject centered approach, particularly in the problem process's realistic emphasis—given the unsettling context of a complex society—on preparing a student for life situations. Instead of the essentialism, authoritarianism, and materialism central to the traditional classroom, the problem solving curriculum is more humanized—and consequently more humanizing—by its emphasis on the student and on helping him to learn *how* to learn. Shaped from a philosophical base of pragmatism, humanism, and democracy, the process creates a learning environment in which the student can experience psychological growth and social adequacy. The environment operates largely on principles derived from organismic, perceptual, and field theories of learning originally developed in psychology.

It has further been argued in the earlier chapters that the reorganization of a school curriculum along the lines of problem solving–team teaching involves vast and sweeping changes in attitudes and procedures. Teamwork in planning and process relies heavily on multiple resources outside the classroom to explore the problem. It also requires a major change in the teaching role. Whereas a teacher is generally the main resource in the traditional classroom, he becomes a facilitator or enabler of the learning process by directing and assisting students in their progress. Obviously such a role implies considerable intelligence, perception, skills, patience, and energy. But the ultimate change rests with the student who must reach continuously for new understanding and experiences as he pursues the problem with the group. He is not a passive, but an active or contributing member of the learning team.

In examining five specific problem solving units carried out by seven schools, the reader can see how each group utilized inquiry methods, team teaching techniques, large- and small-group discussions, and field activities in the problem solving process. These schools — located for the most part in the author's home state, Alabama — reflect a high degree of professional enthusiasm and skill. Though most of them have been moving in this direction less than two years and many were in the first year of applying the problem solving process, their applications merit close attention. Some have had impact upon their immediate communities; others have influenced surrounding schools and school districts. In implementing a problem solving–team teaching curriculum, they have in common the quality of practices far superior to those of most elementary, middle, and senior high schools in the nation. Each school selected and subdivided a problem, collected pertinent information, formulated and tested out numerous hypotheses, and drew conclusions. But each also pursued the problem according to the needs and wishes of its student participants. In the first situation presented which deals with environment, for example, students were thoroughly sensitized to the subject before they even held preliminary discussions. On the other hand, students in situation 5 knew relatively little about their subject beyond having read a few leaflets on juvenile shoplifting. They conducted a sort of crash course for the whole group, calling on outside speakers for needed facts and figures, before determining the parts of the problem.

The situations described in this chapter range from one- to two-month units which generally involved three to five hours daily, approximately five days a week. The seven levels from which the models have been drawn correctly reflect the broad potential of a problem solving curriculum: Four are higher elementary grades, three are senior high grades, and one is a middle-school grade. Selected problems bear out the interest with contemporary topics; further, the subjects are ones in which students themselves tended to express interest: environment, drug abuse, economic systems, differing cultures, and juvenile shoplifting. Students played some part in the problem selection and planning phases, although more actively in some units than in others. For example, situation 4 on differing cultures evolved from the students' own needs in understanding cultural backgrounds of the school's heterogeneous population. Such motivation took the students far beyond a series of geography lessons.

Each problem solving unit explored its subject in depth — well past the point of classroom lectures and textbook readings. The environmental unit participants described in situation 1 *saw* vividly how resources have been wasted. They visited polluted streams; they observed excessive car and truck emissions; they discovered numerous instances of soil erosion and depletion; they found samples of mineral, oil, and gas depletion. Students in the drug abuse unit talked with former narcotics addicts, private and government agency representatives, law enforcement officers, business persons.

In resolving the problems, teachers and students crossed subject boundaries freely. Oral and written communications were carried out; special vocabularies had to be mastered; statistics were compiled and interpreted; research was done to obtain background data and discussion material. These materials became tools to pursue the problem. In order for students to carry out their inquiry on environment, for example, they had varied learning experiences in language arts, science, music, art, and career education.

Teachers within the respective teams — as facilitators of the learning experiences — assisted in discussion, raised questions for study, and suggested possible resources. Their most proficient skills were utilized: Some were excellent organizers, others fielded the discussions on major concepts and generalizations, and still others sparked small-group and individual projects or promoted debate.

Although these brief outlines of five problem solving situations cannot specifically record the individual learning experiences, the reader has only to compare these problem solving curriculums with what he knows of traditional classroom "learning" to see that the process is much more than a lecture and a set of reading assignments. For the student, the difference between passively carrying out an assignment in a traditional classroom and actively learning through the problem solving curriculum is crucial.

SITUATION 1: A PROBLEM IN RESOURCES AND ENVIRONMENT

Background of the Unit

This hypothetical problem solving example, based on activities in three separate schools observed by the author in October and November of 1972, is presented here as a single unit to be done by a tenth grade class or approximately 120 students. The three schools observed are located in the Tennessee Valley area of northern Alabama. The unit is intended to cover two months, including five days a week and four hours each day. In draw-

125

ing up this single example from three actual situations, the author has tried to illustrate how a full or comprehensive problem solving curriculum can work.

Teaching roles were assigned according to specific skills. Four teachers made up the team from the areas of social studies, language arts, biology, and career education. Helping them were: one full-time teaching aide, one part-time clerical worker, and four resource teachers in art, music, home economics, and guidance. Of the teaching team itself, the social studies teacher was unusually capable in teacher–pupil planning and in large-group and individualized interactions. The language arts teacher was skillful in expediting work. She excelled in helping the students to plan small-group and individualized projects in which they summarized, generalized, and synthesized learning outcomes through news articles, booklets, letters. In particular she worked with students in the process of writing and acting out the dramatic skit — a culminating experience intended to show how the group had worked towards resolving the problem. The science teacher was strong in documentary research directly related to the problem and its parts. A member of the community for many years, the career education teacher was in close contact with most area government and social agencies. She proved a key resource in lining up outside resource people and arranging for field trips.

Initial Group Activities

The students had already been sensitized to the environmental problems in their community, particularly those detrimental to health, recreation, and general welfare. They had closely checked various newspapers and magazines as well as television programs concerning problems of the Tennessee River: pollution of the river and its animal and plant life and the threat posed by an atomic energy plant. Students and teachers had visited polluted streams; they had observed how much wells and springs were polluted in areas surrounding the city. They had seen air pollution caused by industrial poisonous gases and fumes and they were aware of harmful car and truck emissions. They knew that a large amount of industrial waste was being dumped into streams, making them unfit for recreation. They had visited fields and woodlands to see the problems of reforestation and of soil erosion and depletion which deprive man of nutritional foods. They were further aware that petroleum, natural gas, coal, and minerals had been depleted.

Armed with a sound grasp of the problem, the student began to define it. They developed this description:

126

There are two Americas. There is the America described in the song "O beautiful for spacious skies, for amber waves of grain, for purple mountains majesties, above the fruited plain." We agree that this is the America of which we sing. This is America the beautiful, America the bountiful. This is the America we inherited before we defaced it.

But there is another America whose spacious skies are filled with factory soot, smog, noxious chemicals, and poisonous gases. There is the America whose amber waves of grain have been replaced by clouds of dust and smog. There is the America whose purple mountains majesties stand amid the stumps of cut trees and charred ruins of burnt forests that have been depleted of the mineral contents through mining and oil and gas depletion that is making life less tolerable. There is the America whose fruited plains are now gullied by erosion and washed away into rivers. There is the America whose clogged streams and lakes are polluted with sewage and industrial waste, destroying much of the plant and animal life and making them unsafe for recreational, industrial, and commercial purposes. This is the America we have made through destructive wastes — without regard for the future welfare of the upcoming generations.

We conclude: These are the two Americas. It is late, but we must try to save or restore much of the America we have inherited. We need to save or rebuild the precious six to nine inches of topsoil that lies between us and extinction. We need to save or reclaim much of our forests, clear water, and wildlife. We need to pass on to our youth the rightful heritage of a fertile soil, clean streams, fresh air, and a supply of fuel that will not be readily exhausted. Through such processes the recreation, beauty, peace, and spiritual value of an un-spoiled out-of-doors can be enjoyed by present and future generations.

With this general statement, the students then subdivided the problem into four areas:

Subproblem A "Causes and Effects of Man's Abuse and Misuse of the Natural Environment" included: depletion of the soil, of our forests, and of wildlife; exhaustion of minerals, oil, gas, and underground water supplies; and pollution of streams and lakes and of air.

Subproblem B "Prevention and Remedies to Correct the Misuse of the Natural Environment" covered: reclamation of forest resources; elimination of forest fires and indiscriminate cutting; curbing wildlife depletion or extermination; providing food and shelter for replenishing wildlife; curbing soil erosion and reclaiming the depleted soil; using and conserving water resources wisely; curbing water pollution; curbing mineral, oil, and gas depletion; and curbing air pollution.

Subproblem C "Extent, Scope, and Trends" took in an enormous amount of research, investigation, and energy, including countless experimental first-hand studies performed by students. The subproblem involved:

127

soil erosion, stream pollution, wildlife depletion and destruction, mineral depletion and wastes, petroleum and natural gas abuses, air contamination, and water pollution.

Subproblem D "Costs and Effects of Our Resource and Environmental Destruction and Abuses" involved: cost of commercial fertilizer to replace plant nutrients and minerals lost from soil depletion; cost of reforestation; cost of curbing stream pollution; ill effects of unsafe water for recreational and industrial uses; effects of depletion of recreational facilities in our streams and forests; cost of rebuilding topsoil; effects of malnutrition from soil depletion; asthetic effects of our natural environment's destruction; and dangers to human health stemming from all such depletions.

Next, teachers and students jointly selected specific objectives to pursue.

They set these understanding and information objectives:

1. Determining what natural resources man has inherited and how he has used them;

2. Observing how the food we eat, the clothing we wear, and the shelter we make come directly from plants, animals, and mineral content in the soil;

3. Exploring the destruction and unwise use of our resources and environment which has caused increased handicaps to man's struggle for survival;

4. Tracing the interdependence of all plant and animal life and, in turn, their dependence upon soil, water, and fresh air;

5. Establishing the relationship between the geography of natural resources and the geography of industry and commerce and the locations of large cities and centers of wealth;

6. Studying the effects of soil erosion and of man's influence upon the physical features of the earth;

7. Realizing how soil, water, plant, animal, and mineral resources can be both conserved and used effectively;

8. Discovering how the future prosperity of all individuals, communities, states, and nations depends upon wise use of environment and resources;

9. Considering that ownership of land, water, and mineral resources is really stewardship;

10. Interpreting the role of governmental agencies in conserving various soil and mineral resources and in protecting human life from the hazards of a polluted environment;

They pinpointed these skill objectives:

1. Increasing proficiency in techniques of democratic living — particularly cooperative planning, group processes of problem solving, self and group evaluation, sharing ideas, projects, and materials, and acceptance of the self and of others;
2. Reading, understanding, and interpreting the significance of materials from books, magazines, newspapers, charts, pictures, and audiovisual aids;
3. Examining and interpreting information from government personnel such as forest rangers, state and federal experimental station workers, soil conservation workers, water pollution board members, and air control agency employees;
4. Using oral and written communications well in expressing all findings;
5. Utilizing an expanded vocabulary for the assimilation of information to the various groups through communication channels;
6. Expressing ideas through art, music, rhythms, monologues, languages, pantomimes, graphs, movies, and skits;
7. Thinking critically and analytically in order to summarize findings;
8. Using research techniques to explore original findings and documentary materials;
9. Working harmoniously with others and accepting responsibilities.

They selected these objectives bearing on attitudes:

1. Developing value concepts to govern behavior in terms of relationships with other individuals;
2. Encouraging a sense of responsibility to carry a task to its completion;
3. Developing a willingness to evaluate contributions by others;
4. Fostering an appreciation for the beauty of nature;
5. Developing an appreciation for wildlife and the importance of their native habitats;
6. Cultivating an appreciation and respect for laws governing the protection and improvement of those exhaustible and renewable resources here for man's use, but not abuse;
7. Acquiring a sensitivity about man's dependence upon his natural environment for his own survival;
8. Learning to appreciate and to have pride in the community from the perspectives of past, present, and future;
9. Accepting that other people have rights and responsibilities;

129

10. Learning to withhold judgment and feel comfortable amid differences of opinion and judging opinion on its own merit;
11. Achieving a willingness to help improve the asthetic surroundings of the home, school, and community.

The group set these behavioral objectives:
1. Assuming responsibility for conserving and improving natural resources such as water, soil, forests, wildlife, and air;
2. Using renewable resources more extensively and, at the same time, minimizing the consumption of nonrenewable and exhaustible ones so that many exhaustible resources can be recycled for future use;
3. Promoting positive habits like the prevention of forest fires, elimination of water pollution, conservation of soil and mineral resources, and protection of health;
4. Showing the relationship between resource exploitation and wise resource use in relation to human health, happiness, and well-being;
5. Formulating habits of working with groups such as garden clubs, home demonstration clubs, and civic organizations in promoting cleanup campaigns, eradicating litter, and reclaiming devastated areas.

Ongoing Learning Experiences
Language Arts Activities. Students wrote many creative stories and poems about water and air pollution, strip mining, forestry depletion, wildlife destruction, and soil erosion. They made a list of the vocabulary needed to pursue this unit, learning to spell and use words correctly in oral and written reports. A daily diary recorded the problem solving activities. They wrote letters to Ralph Nader, the U.S. Department of Interior, the water pollution board, Atomic Energy Commission, Tennessee Valley Authority, and other governmental agencies or private sources related to the proper use of natural resources. Countless oral reports were prepared and presented to civic clubs, church groups, the local Chamber of Commerce, and other community-minded groups. Students wrote articles for the daily newspaper. As a culminating experience, the total group wrote, staged, and acted in a dramatic skit which is discussed in more detail as the project finale.

Science Activities. Assisted by the biology teacher, the 120 students made a thorough study of plant and animal life in their community and surrounding rural areas. In conducting documentary research on the balance of nature, the students discovered that it had been upset through various exploitation activities within the community over the past few decades.

130

They investigated ways and means to restore the natural environment to some productive state of equilibrium. They performed extensive soil borings, testing the amount of erosion in various local urban and rural areas. The soil borings in the city determined the amount of topsoil and the kind of subsoil in the students' own yards. Samples of these borings were sent to Auburn University for analysis to determine which plant foods were deficient and how the soil could be treated for more productivity. The borings done in rural areas involved some forest areas, badly eroded hillsides, meadows, and other specific places.

Another project was the building of a balanced aquarium and terrarium. Also the students set up a number of controlled experiments for both plant and animal life to determine the kinds of food and nutrients necessary. Many of these animals and plants were tested after being deprived of some nutrients and food. Experiments were then conducted to try to overcome these deficiencies through proper treatment.

Potplants were placed in the classroom. Many of the students landscaped parts of the schoolgrounds and resodded other parts, using necessary fertilizer and soil treatments to encourage vigorous growth. They propagated a number of shrubs from the cuttings and plan to landscape around their own homes with the shrubs. They found out, in the landscaping projects, that many of the soil areas required treatment for acid or alkali conditions in order to have plants thrive. Peatmoss, leaf mold, fertilizer, and other substances were added to prepare the soil.

The science teacher, the local water pollution board, and a soil-testing laboratory helped students to analyze soil and water samples so that means could be devised to prevent soil destruction and water pollution. Other experiments, done first-hand, helped establish amounts of pollution emitted by various makes of automobiles and studied practices to eliminate industrial pollution of both air and water.

Audiovisual Activities. Films, slides, filmstrips, videotapes, pictures, charts, graphs, and similar media reinforced the learning process. Students heard and saw tape recordings and television and radio programs about the wise use of the environment. They collected articles on problems in nature — for example, those about skeletons of young birds found in nests destroyed by fire, charred stumps of trees, burned bark from various trees, deteriorated insects, and leaf mold. Each student made a scrapbook about his own experiences in the different projects, including photographs he might have taken or collected from articles. A major effort was the preparation of miniature model farms and city homes for display downtown and at the county fair.

Musical Activities. The music teacher worked cooperatively with the team teachers and 120 students in supervising interpretative dances, rhythms, and games, both during the on-going activities and in the culminating activity (a skit). Its role will be discussed later. Numerous assembly programs were performed by unit participants before the entire school. Songs in these programs included: "America the Beautiful," "This Land is Our Land," "The Farmer in the Dell," "The Mulberry Bush," "The Ballad of the Boll Weevil," and "Trees That Grow So High."

Art Activities. In part-time work with the unit, the art teacher assisted the students in interpreting many of the concepts they had observed through art. Some students translated the beauty of the forest, its wildlife and clear streams, through needle tapestry. Others participated in painting scenic pictures and murals for room and hall display in the school building. Many helped to paint backdrops as part of the stage scenery for the final activity. Many worked on puppets as props for the culminating musical project. One group designed numerous posters illustrating good and bad practices with reference to man's use of natural resources.

Social Studies and Career Education Activities. The two team teachers from these disciplines planned field trips to devastated areas, rural as well as urban. Trips were made to a water filtration plant, neighborhood farms and fields, burned-over forests, muddy streams, wildlife reservations, experimental farms, fish hatcheries, tree nurseries, the Tennessee Valley atomic energy plant, and headquarters of the Tennessee Valley Authority. Resource personnel were brought from many agencies. Films, filmstrips, slides, and photographs were studied. Many of the groups' experiences in these two segments led to generalizations and conclusions helpful in producing skits, news articles, and assembly programs.

The social studies teacher particularly helped the subgroups make an intensive survey of the history of natural resource depletion in this country and throughout the world, covering Babylon, North China, The Holy Land as well as the United States in detail. The study led them to conclude that, when natural resources are depleted or badly polluted, man's survival is jeopardized. The students were able to show — aided by a math teacher — graphs depicting the economic relationship between community, state, and national well-being and the use of natural resources.

The career education teacher specifically helped with lighting in the final skit; he also evolved sound effects depicting the drab, depressing environment versus a joyful and healthy scene of nature and made some excellent props.

132

Culminating Activities. These final phases of the unit study covered three activities: making a movie, producing a skit, and evaluating the entire experience. The movie showed how to use and conserve the environment and natural resources. Many persons beyond the students became involved in its making. Parents, board of education members, chamber of commerce representatives, and persons from government agencies helped to develop maps, charts, and time lines designed to trace the learning process. Creative efforts like artwork, poems, songs, and stories went into the movie.

The major experience intended to illustrate the students' activities, findings, and generalizations was a skit written by several of the participants who were gifted in organizing, systematizing, and writing up information. The skit had three scenes. Scene one showed what the white man had found when he first came to this country: abundant forests and wildlife, free-flowing and clear streams, mineral resources, fertile soil, and a rich civilization. There began to evolve a predominantly rural America and the resources were still plentiful. Musical background, lighting effects, scenic costumes, and art displays reinforced the scene.

By the second scene, man's abusive acts had begun to upset the balance of nature. Streams were contaminated with human and industrial wastes, soil was continually depleted, forests were burned and cut down, minerals were exhausted through strip mining, and air and water were beginning to carry the ill effects of industrial deposits and automobile emissions. In telling this part of the story, the students used drab music, dark lighting, and appropriate background scenery.

The third scene — through music, art, and words — depicted the kind of America *which is possible* by eliminating air and water pollution, restoring forests, rebuilding the soil, reclaiming grasslands, and doing away with the smog, soot, and grime of industrial wastes. According to the students' conclusions about the problem, this is the America which is possible if our environment and natural resources were used more wisely.

Everyone's talents and energies were used. Those who were not directly involved in making costumes, preparing light and sound effects, or writing and staging the skit became involved in program committees to advertise and publicize the drama or as stage hands, poster makers, mural painters, writers of invitations to parents and other students, prompters, and takers of tickets. *All* students had a participating role in the production.

In the third culminating phase of evaluation, efforts were just as intense. As the students neared the summarization stage of the unit, the art and home economics teachers worked closely with the group to bring in a number of resource personnel from the Atomic Energy Commission, Tennessee Valley Authority, wildlife reservations, experimental farms, fish hatcheries, nurseries, and extension agencies. The team of teachers guided the students in summarizing and generalizing their conclusions drawn from studies and resources.

Throughout these evaluative experiences, the students constantly asked themselves the following questions:

1. Do the group's culminating activities accurately summarize the knowledge, insights, motivations, concerns, and habits necessary to restore an abundant life?
2. Have such activities helped to evaluate those purposes which were set forth at the project's beginning?
3. Has this particular problem solving experience stimulated democratic living and sharing?
4. Have we drawn upon information sources which would enable the group to confront and cope with the problem more realistically?
5. What new skills have been acquired during the learning experience which members of the group now use in day-to-day life?

In the evaluative phase students and teachers made full use of self appraisal, small- and large-group discussions, teacher and team assistance, and outside aid. Each student was evaluated in terms of individual progress and contributions weighed against his own capabilities — not in terms of any class, school, or national norms. It is interesting that, according to the evaluation, most of the objectives listed earlier in this chapter had been achieved.

Nor did the students' work stop with the assessment. The group further contacted a large number of industries in the state, sharing its research and conclusions and urging the companies to cooperate in eliminating abusive practices. In replies five large and 32 smaller industries pledged to work for an improved environment. The governor, several members of the Alabama legislature, and congressmen from the state were also contacted. Several replied with pledges to assist in solving the problem of man's need to use his environment and natural resources more wisely. These actions illustrate that the impact of the problem solving unit — both on its participants and on those who became involved as resources — extended far beyond the four walls of a classroom.

SITUATION 2: A PROBLEM IN CURBING DRUG ABUSE

Background of the Unit

During the 1972 winter quarter at Auburn University, 15 graduate students — 12 of them teaching supervisors, counsellors, and administrators and 3 full-time students — planned a problem solving curriculum on "Improving Health and Civic Responsibilities Through Curbing Drug Abuse." Participants in the seminar identified these four subproblems:

1. Extent, scope, severity, and trends of drug abuse;
2. Causes and contributing forces;
3. Costs and effects of the problem;
4. Preventive measures and remedies.

Four separate schools were selected to implement a subproblem: Tuskegee Elementary School (sixth grade), Tuskegee, Ala.; Auburn Middle School, Auburn; Phenix City Senior High, Phenix City; and Baker Senior High, Columbus, Ga. The three full-time graduate students went into three of the schools to help with basic research on the drug abuse problem, though not the learning experiences.

The unit in the schools lasted six weeks (not counting preplanning by the graduate seminar), involving three hours a day, five days a week. An average of 80 students in each school worked on the project. Each school had three teachers on its team.

As each school worked on its particular subproblem, its committee shared the findings and developments with the three other committees. Under this structure of communication, each group developed its own objectives more or less independently and set up activities and learning experiences without too much duplication or overlapping among the four schools.

The author has consolidated these efforts into a single unit.

In terms of understanding the problem, these objectives were set:

1. What are the present trends in drug abuse treatment?
2. How severe and widespread is the problem in cities, counties, states, and nations?
3. Which drugs are most abused and most harmful?
4. Where in the United States and other parts of the world are drugs most widely used?
5. Which social, economic, and ethnic groups tend to use drugs the most?
6. Trace the history of drug abuse.
7. What legal penalties exist for drug use?
8. How have other schools and communities combated the abuse?
9. Which drugs have a flashback effect even when no longer used?
10. How does drug abuse break up homes, shatter families, and alienate young people?

11. What personality traits generally figure in the development of a drug abuse?
12. Which types of individuals seem prone to psychic dependence — that is, a desire for the drug which is independent of physical symptoms or needs?
13. Which types of abusers suffer from personality disorders and seek escape from reality through drug use?
14. Learn the nature of environmental factors in drug abuse: poor home conditions, antisocial attitudes, inadequate family relationships, disillusionment with life, inability to achieve worthwhile goals, peer pressures to misuse drugs, indifferent attitudes, and the generation gap.
15. To what extent does a state of affluence allow the time and money for drug abuse?
16. Do setbacks in goals, drives, and motivations contribute to abuse?
17. Does the leisure-time problem contribute to drug abuse?
18. What effects does drug abuse have in terms of individual salary loss, cost of supporting a habit, long-term addiction, health dangers, loss of civil rights, impairment to mental faculties, and possible birth defects for babies of drug abusers?
19. What is its impact on communities in terms of law enforcement, institutional care, crime prevention, property destruction, preventive education, loss of human resources, court costs, and drug abuse in the schools?
20. Why is drug abuse dangerous in a mechanical society like ours in which ownership of guns, fast automobiles, mechanical equipment, and laxness in parental control due to parents working away from the home are emphasized?

These values and attitudes were selected as important in surveying the drug abuse problem:
1. Gaining positive values and attitudes about costs and effects of drugs for the individual and the community;
2. Appreciating drugs for beneficial or licit purposes;
3. Recognizing the connection between drug abuse and criminal activities;
4. Realizing that drug abuse can cause birth defects in an addict's offspring;
5. Viewing drug abuse as a serious health hazard;
6. Seeing its harmful effects in terms of job opportunities, social responsibilities, mental capabilities, and economic proficiencies;

7. Understanding it as a serious social problem to be faced and confronted;
8. Realizing that commonly used drugs in the home can also be dangerous;
9. Appreciating the possibility that marijuana use can lead to hard drugs;
10. Viewing the long-term physical effects of marijuana as generally unknown;
11. Comprehending the full consequences of drug abuse for the individual, the family, and the community.

These objectives for behavioral outcome were set:
1. Avoiding drug abuse in the school,
2. Discouraging others from abusing drugs,
3. Working with social agencies in the community to combat the problem,
4. Avoiding places where drugs are known to be used regularly,
5. Helping those who use drugs to learn what aid is available,
6. Providing better communication and interaction with groups of former habitual drug users,
7. Accepting the fact that medicine cannot be expected to cure all of man's ills,
8. Working to eliminate personality disorders in themselves and in others,
9. Helping people to face reality and problems without the harmful crutch of drugs,
10. Trying to improve those environmental conditions which contribute to drug abuse,
11. Working to change harmful attitudes about drug use,
12. Promoting better interaction between students and adults in the community about drug abuse problems,
13. Developing more self-confidence and an improved self-concept through the activities of this problem solving unit,
14. Fostering better interaction between students and parents,
15. Developing negative attitudes towards the effects of drugs, and
16. Engaging in activities which serve as alternatives to drug abuse.

Initial Group Activities

The 320 students did a number of things to familiarize themselves with the subject of drug abuse. Their first action was to take a pretest about drugs to establish how much information they already had in hand. Under the supervision of teachers, they burned wafers of marijuana in order to know its distinct odor; they studied pictures of the plant. Films they viewed included: "Tomorrow May Be Dying," "Psyche," "Weed," "Acids," and "Up and Downs," followed by discussion and reaction sessions. Following the films "Hooked" and "Losers" the students discussed some of the reasons why the young people in the film became addicted. They also listened to rock records like "Things Get a Little Easier."

Aware that much misinformation existed about the problem they had selected, the students requested materials dealing with both facts and fables on drug abuse from the National Clearinghouse for Drug Abuse Information of the National Institute of Mental Health. Pamphlets were received from the state health department and the Drug Action Committee in Montgomery; special posters were sent by the Scott Paper Company.

After interviews with former drug abusers, the group did some role-playing to reflect the effects which they thought that drugs had had upon these individuals.

Books were key sources. Portions of Malcolm X's autobiography, Jerome Larner's *Addict in the Street,* and Carter Brown's *Blonde on the Rock* and *Hangup Kid* were dramatized. After reading sections of J. Benteen's *Trail Ends in Hell,* the students identified particular facts and ideas within the book which influenced their individual conceptions of drug abuse.

In order to build up reference materials, the group clipped articles from newspapers, magazines, and other print sources, posting them on bulletin boards. They also displayed pamphlets, posters, pictures, fiction and non-fiction books, and other materials.

During a special student assembly, former drug addicts and a state narcotics agent offered insights into the effects of drug abuse. The students also conducted a survey on school and community attitudes toward the drug abuse problem. A question box was put inside the school so that students could submit questions about prescribed drugs which alleviate physical, mental, and social discomforts. Finally, a discussion session dealt with why the drug abuse problem is more dangerous in our mechanical society than it would be in a less complex one.

By the time regular activities began, the students knew their subject.

Ongoing Learning Experiences

The group and parts of the group became involved in a myriad of activities:

1. Using maps drawn by group members and by commercial concerns, the students pinpointed areas of drug abuse in nearby communities, the state, nation, and world.

2. A selected group discussed a chapter from Louise Donaldbee's *London Scene.* The chapter — "Turning on in Stockholm" — covered the great marijuana debate.
3. A clearinghouse was set up to give information to the school and its community.
4. Policemen spoke to the unit participants about how many young adults in the community actually had problems with drugs. Also, representatives from Narcotics Anonymous addressed the students.
5. A histogram was made showing the increase in the use of harmful drugs as well as a map showing where various drugs originate and a chart illustrating which crimes are most associated with drug abuse.
6. Television coverage of the problem was monitored and discussed.
7. Students invited resource speakers from the local mental health center, law enforcement agency, toxicology department, and half-way house to discuss the harmful effects of drugs.
8. Numerous free or inexpensive materials were obtained for use in the clearinghouse.
9. Field trips were taken to mental health centers, correction institutions, and departments of toxicology to assess the impact of drug abuse.
10. Drawing from countless research reports and first-hand observations, the students wrote and presented a public play and pantomime on the problem.
11. Scrapbooks were put together from magazine and newspaper articles, and a dictionary was compiled on special terms in the drug abuse field.
12. A radio and television program was written about the harmful effects of addiction.
13. Posters dramatizing the problem were placed in store windows.
14. Articles were written for both school and community papers.
15. Local drug companies, physicians, and pharmacists donated advertising charts demonstrating the large number of dangerous drugs. Brand names for barbiturates were listed on the charts.

Culminating Activities and Evaluation

Nearing the end of the six-week unit, the group took a post-test to determine how much its participants had changed in attitudes and understandings. Not surprisingly, the students' in-depth study had increased their own awareness of the problem's complexity and of the need to disseminate accurate information. For example, the difficulties a former drug

139

addict has in getting a job was underlined in the group's interviews with businessmen who said that their companies were very reluctant to hire persons with drug abuse records. These interviews were followed by role-playing sessions in which one student posed as an employer and another, a prospective employee having a record of drug use.

In a second role-playing session, students depicted how a drug pusher operates and how two of the people he approaches might react: a weak and willing student who easily yields to persuasion and a stronger-willed one who successfully counters the pusher's arguments. Both the student body and PTA watched the skit.

As part of an effort to make available information and help, the group performed these services in the final phases:

1. Presented a panel discussion on drug abuse trends,
2. Counselled a crisis center on drug abuse problems and reported the findings to the group,
3. Prepared a list of recreational and social opportunities for teen-agers and other youths in order to minimize the boredom which can lead to drugs, and
4. Participated in several group discussions, fielding questions like what changes might be made in present laws or what new laws could help to curb misuse of drugs. During the discussion students assumed the role of the state legislature, formulating bills which they thought would alleviate the drug abuse problem.

Evaluation of Learning Outcome

A number of devices tested out what the unit participants had learned. In an open-ended test, they dealt with questions like why has marijuana use increased in the last 10 years; what is the extent of drug abuse in this community and in other sections of the state; if someone offered *you* a joint, what would you do; and what do you feel a person can do to halt the spread of drug abuse? Each member of the group gave an impromptu oral report on what he had experienced. After evaluating themselves in terms of growth, development, and learning during the project, the students then went into small-group evaluative sessions. Afterwards, teachers and pupils held conferences to discuss what kind of outcomes had been achieved and what might have been done differently. Students were observed by the teachers in various activities to see how much the students continued to participate in community activities related to the drug abuse problem outside of the classroom situation. The net result of these evalua-

140

tive actions demonstrated that the students had become aware of particular situations:

1. Appreciation of the consequences of misusing drugs,
2. Realization that pills and medicine should be taken only under a doctor's supervision,
3. Respect for safety labels and agencies which govern the use of medicine and drugs, and
4. Self-awareness of the harmful effects of drugs on the body and, inevitably, a resistance to individuals who might suggest using drugs.

Possibly the most valuable knowledge gained by the project participants was this self-awareness of drug dangers, supported by intensive investigation of the problems. Reading a newspaper article may or may not convey the impact of the drug problem; interviewing a former narcotic addict, the students found, does convey the impact.

SITUATION 3: A PROBLEM IN HOW ECONOMIC SYSTEMS ARE DEVELOPED

Background of the Unit

Parents, faculty, and students in the Pepperell Elementary School in Opelika, Ala. were in the process of reorganizing the school's curriculum. As an I.G.E. (Individually Guided Education) school, Pepperell was a part of the regional program coordinated by Auburn University's School of Education. The parents, faculty, and students decided to implement a problem solving process for six weeks, three hours a day for five days a week in the sixth grade curriculum. The role of the three team teachers was particularly critical: They shared the decisions for assigning teachers to subject areas, grouping the students, dividing up the space, using available equipment, and coordinating the entire sequence. Helping were two aides, one additional resource teacher (the principal), and five outside resource persons.

The 87 sixth graders worked with the teaching team in selecting a problem from a list of suggested social science goals evolved earlier. As students progressed through the problem of how economic systems are developed and gained an understanding of the parts of the problem, they would be evaluated on the information, skills, and values shaped during the learning experiences.

The teachers worked out a distinct pattern of learning experiences, specific enough to delve into particulars and flexible enough to let the participants pursue their own ideas, concepts, and observations. In a

141

sense these learning experiences replaced the process of subdividing the problem, and Pepperell's approach is outlined here as a contrast to the first two situations on environment and drug abuse. The experiences were designed not to confine the students to those parts of the problems which the team wanted them to examine, but as starting points. Such a dynamic quality, however, which is necessary to the problem solving curriculum is more easily observed than described. The topic itself offers the reader insight into *how* the students and teachers saw the unit. Rather than "studying economics systems," they elected to see how economic systems are developed; the first involves facts and the second, understanding of facts and ideas.

Unit objectives were, in the main, set by the team of teachers. These cognitive objectives were selected:

1. Knowing the interdependent groups of an economic model,
2. Describing relationships of interdependent groups within an economic society,
3. Knowing the differences between a command market, mixed economy, and mature economy,
4. Recognizing the relationship between choices of the American consumer and advertising in the country,
5. Stating definite characteristics of the U.S. economy,
6. Knowing the relationship between government and economy in the U.S., and
7. Recognizing how government planning and economic choices by interdependent groups within a command economy are related.

These value-seeking objectives were set:

1. Given four economic decisions, what would be the consequences of each decision?
2. Given a nation with a newly developing economic system, what interaction takes place within the system and with other nations?
3. Given a set of groups within a society, what would be the relationship between the values of the group making economic decisions and those economic systems in the society?
4. Given the question of who has the right to participate in economic systems in the United States, how might its various members respond?
5. Given four long-range national goals, discuss economic decisions involving these goals in terms of the values of the group.

142

These process objectives were emphasized:

1. Study decision-making in three different economical structures.
2. Discuss and study the bases for five different economic decisions.
3. Compare four economic systems.
4. Predict the consequences of five economic decisions.

Unit Learning Experiences

First Experience:

> Mode — independent
> Materials — paper, pencil, documentary and audiovisual aids
> Personnel — teacher
> Vocabulary and Spelling Skills — unlimited

The students were given this hypothetical situation: If they could have everything they ever wanted, what would they want? After making up lists, they discussed these questions:

1. Did they write down *everything* they would like to have?
2. If not, why were they unable to complete the lists?
3. Did they think they could ever have everything they wanted?
4. Was there perhaps just one or two more items they might wish to add to the lists?

Discussion brought out these points: We can say that our wants and needs are unlimited, *but* — because money and resources are limited — we have to choose what we want and need the most. Examples were given to illustrate this limitation.

Second Experience:

> Mode — group
> Materials — dealing with opportunities, handicaps, and possibilities for services and promotions
> Personnel — teacher and four students
> Vocabulary and Spelling Skills — goods and services words

Students, playing the roles of doctor, patient, store clerk, and customer, acted out two situations: visiting a doctor and buying items at a store. Discussion brought out the difference between services and goods. The doctor provides a *service* and is paid for it; the customer buys *goods* at a store. Then, the students discussed goods they had bought lately and people they knew who, like the doctor, provided services.

143

Third Experience:

> Mode — training, group inquiry
> Materials — varied resource materials
> Personnel — teacher, group leader, and five students
> Vocabulary and Spelling Skills — words about the labor force, capital, material items and their relationships

Within small-discussion groups, the students responded to these questions:

1. Where do goods originate?
2. Who makes them?
3. Who provides services?

Then they merged into a single group and these points are developed: There are two kinds of resources, natural and human. Money is also a resource and it is called capital. In order for goods to be made and services provided, three kinds of resources are needed: land, labor, and capital.

Fourth Experience:

> Mode — personal discovery
> Materials — books, magazines, and other sources
> Personnel — teachers and aides
> Vocabulary and Spelling Skills — any new words encountered in materials

Students and teachers held a "learn-in," sharing the information each had gathered on his own and placing it in perspective in terms of the problem itself.

Fifth Experience:

> Mode — groups
> Materials — store items and references on individual countries
> Personnel — teachers
> Vocabulary and Spelling Skills — new words discovered

In a simulation exercise based on the concept of decision-making, students subdivided into five groups, with each representing a new country. Each group selected four items from the following: five apples, twenty sheets of paper, ten lemons, a pack of cloves, five crates of eggs, one bottle of glue, two coat hangers, one stick of modelling clay, ten pipe cleaners, one pack of crayons, one sheet of toilet tissue, and one roll of paper towels.

Each country proceeded to make a product from the materials. The products were, in turn, shown to the entire group, with these questions raised:

1. Why did different countries have different products?
2. How do the materials used affect the products?
3. Did any of the five groups or countries use the same materials?
4. If so, were the materials used similarly or differently?

Sixth Experience:

> Mode — training
> Materials — items made in previous experience
> Personnel — teacher
> Vocabulary and Spelling Skills — words relating to production and consumption of goods and services

Drawing upon the fifth experience, the students set up a store to sell the products they had made. After goods were sold, discussion brought out these points: The people who made the goods are *producers* and those who bought them are *consumers*; when a group of producers and consumers work together, there is an *economic system.*

Seventh Experience:

> Mode — training, large groups
> Materials — film "Roma and His Elephant" and book on India
> Personnel — team teachers
> Vocabulary and Spelling Skills — many new words

After viewing the film "Roma and His Elephant," students made these points: Most boys in India have had little chance to go to college; instead, they usually help with farming, starting at a very early age; and the family grows most of the things it needs. Also, Roma's sisters must help their mother. Modern conveniences like dishwashers, washing machines, clothes dryers, and vacuum cleaners are absent. India, over the years, has not changed much; its economy is a *traditional* one. After explaining what the word traditional means, the students explained why India has a traditional economy. Group discussion brought out that, until Indians gained independence in 1947, the country had been under British rule. Now independent, the country is trying to work toward a more modern economy — one having industries, factories, and modern equipment like the mature economy of the United States. A mature economy is an industrial one which can make whatever it wants.

Eighth Experience:

> Mode — personal discovery
> Material — mathematics
> Personnel — aide
> Vocabulary and Spelling Skills — terms like a la carte
> and carte blanche

Initially, the students independently answered these questions:

1. What does efficiency mean?
2. Do you receive an allowance?
3. How efficient do you think you are with your money?

Then each selected what they considered the most efficient ways in two situations.

Situation one: You want to buy a pair of skates. The local toy store has them for $10.99. A department store, located five miles away, has skates on sale for $8.95. It costs $1.30 round-trip on the bus to the department store. If you are an efficient spender, where would you buy the skates?

Situation Two: You and your parents are ordering lunch in a restaurant. You have a choice of ordering carte blanche or a la carte. Under the former, you order a complete dinner (two pieces of chicken, a baked potato with sour cream, tossed salad and two rolls) for $1.75. Under the latter, you would pay for each item separately. Two pieces of chicken cost $1.00; the baked potato with sour cream is 52¢; the two rolls are 15¢; and the tossed salad, 25¢. Which way to order is the most efficient?

Ninth Experience:

> Mode — personal discovery, group inquiry
> Materials — speaker and resource materials on India
> Personnel — speaker
> Vocabulary and Spelling Skills — words used by
> speaker and in resource materials

Before hearing a speaker from India talk about "Improving India's Economy and Developing Its Industries," the group did some research into what methods were being used to improve the country's economy, are Indian schools being upgraded, and what help is the country getting from other economies?

Tenth Experience:

> Mode — personal discovery
> Materials — television, math
> Personnel — teachers
> Vocabulary and Spelling Skills — new terms used

146

In small-group discussions, the students considered these questions:

1. How do manufacturers in our country know what products to make?
2. How does the factory owner measure whether or not his product will sell?
3. You are in the business of making and selling records. Record A, a "hard rock" song, had sold 1 million copies. Record B, a slow-moving soul song, sold only 100,000 copies. In the future, what kind of song would you want to produce: hard rock or slow-moving soul?
4. Even though you have made 1 million copies of the soul song, it has not sold. What could you do to persuade people to buy the record?

Eleventh Experience:

Mode — group discussion and research

Materials — filmstrip, documentary materials on Russia's economy

Personnel — team teachers

Vocabulary and Spelling Skills — command economy and other related terms

After viewing the filmstrip "Economy of Russia," the students discuss these questions:

1. In Russia who decides what is to be produced?
2. Who decides which resources will be used?
3. How are prices determined in a command economy?
4. In which type of an economy is the consumer likely to find what he wants? Why?

Twelfth Experience:

Mode — personal discovery, large-group inquiry

Materials — occupational pamphlets

Personnel — teachers, drivers, resource people at farm or flower shop

Vocabulary and Spelling Skills — job and career terminology

Part of the students visited a farm and the others, a flower shop to see the processes and skills used at each place. Afterwards, the group examined its own potential job skills:

1. What kinds of skills do individuals in the group have?
2. Could the student use these skills to help earn a living?

147

3. Who plans to attend college? How does a college degree help in earning a living?
4. If a student goes to college in order to be trained for a job, what skills would he primarily use?

Thirteenth Experience:

> Mode — personal discovery and small-group inquiry
> Materials — products in a local supermarket
> Personnel — teachers and parents
> Vocabulary and Spelling Skills — terms for market products

In order to see the competitiveness of a limited supermarket, the students visited one, checking out prices. The group divided up and applied these guidelines in assessing prices: price per ounce, appearance of package, number of producers competing, differences in ingredients, and what the product promises. The competitiveness was particularly apparent in products like laundry soap and breakfast cereals.

Fourteenth Experience:

> Mode — large- and small-group inquiries
> Materials — paper and pencil to compute prices and quality
> Personnel — teachers
> Vocabulary and Spelling Skills — consumer product terms

Students were asked these questions about the supermarket trip:
1. Which laundry soap would you buy? Why?
2. Would it be better for the consumer if only one laundry soap were on the market?
3. What would you do without money to spend?
4. If you were physically unable to work, how would you get money to buy necessities like food?

The small groups then merged and exchanged their ideas and answers.

Fifteenth Experience:

> Mode — small-group inquiry and research
> Materials — paper, pencil, and pamphlets and monographs on economic problems
> Personnel — teachers
> Vocabulary and Spelling Skills — terms on industrialization, a mature economy, and capital

148

Seeking the relationship between industrialization and the American economic system, the class formed small groups to discuss these questions:

1. What are some of the economic and social problems related to industrialization?
2. Are social problems related to economic ones?
3. Do an individual's economic decisions affect the lives of others?
4. What changes in our economy could be predicted for the future?
5. If he were able, what might the student want to do to change our economic system?

Sixteenth Experience:

> Mode — personal discovery
> Materials — reference book, pamphlets, and encyclopedia
> Personnel — teachers
> Vocabulary and Spelling Skills — terms interaction, collective bargaining, and monopoly and related words

Two research problems were assigned: Check into the Sherman Anti-Trust Act of 1890, the Federal Trade Commission Act, and the Clayton Act of 1914 to find out about laws enacted to control monopolies. Then look into what laws have been passed to ease and clarify the relationship between business and labor like the Wagner and Taft–Hartley Acts. When the research had been done, the students held a role-playing session on a collective bargaining dispute over longer vacations, gun control, pollution control, and higher wages.

Seventeenth Experience:

> Mode — large-group discussion, interview, and discussion
> Materials — books, magazines, newspapers, merchant interviewed by students
> Personnel — teachers, speaker
> Vocabulary and Spelling Skills — boycott, corporation terms

Students were asked to research boycotting so that the term was familiar.

A local merchant visited the group to relate how his business was boycotted. In the discussion which followed the interview, many of the students recalled recent boycotts by various groups in the United States.

Culminating Activities:

> Mode — small-groups and personal discovery
> Materials — items used to set up the store; slides
> and projector
> Personnel — teacher
> Vocabulary and Spelling Skills — review of words

Students set up a school store to sell the products they had made throughout the unit. Products were advertised throughout the school. They then discussed how to invest the modest profit. Finally, they held a slide show of pictures taken during each learning experience. The show proved an effective tool for overall review.

Though self-evaluations, group evaluations, and teacher–pupil sessions were used to assess the six-week unit, perhaps the most obvious measurement of the students' motivations was the fact that a large number continued to work on the unit outside of the regular time-periods: during free school time, after school, and on weekends.

SITUATION 4: A PROBLEM ON DIFFERENT PEOPLE FROM OTHER LANDS

Background of the Unit

Perhaps this unit, implemented during the 1971–72 term at East Elementary School in Cullman, Ala., best represents how a problem solving curriculum can be built around student needs and wishes. Cullman's school population is predominantly white. The town itself was settled in 1873 by Germans. But during the past few years children of other cultural backgrounds had increasingly enrolled. Some were of Mexican descent whose families had come to the town to seek job opportunities; others were of European and Far Eastern backgrounds and whose fathers had married while serving in nearby military stations.

Because children are naturally curious about people who have different national, cultural, and racial backgrounds, they began to make comments about these children. With encouragement from their teachers, the children decided they would like to know more about people of other lands. A problem solving curriculum spanning six weeks, with four hours daily and five days a week, was designed for the fourth graders. The four teachers in that grade became the team with the music teachers, librarian, physical education instructors, school luncheon staff members, and community people as resource persons.

The children decided how the unit was to be organized — arranging for work at large-group, small-group, and individual levels. One country would be studied at a time: Japan, South Africa, Mexico, Germany and Austria, and Brazil. In connection with the segment on Germany, the students presented a one-hour pageant of the German culture during the Cullman 1973 Centennial. As an example of the unit's activities, the study of Japan is presented in this chapter. One of the fourth graders was a Japanese girl whose physical features and mannerisms had fascinated her peer group. Therefore, the fourth graders decided to take their first imaginary trip to Japan.

The group went through all the travel arrangements: selecting the method of transportation, studying the Japanese climate to know what suitable clothes should be packed, and communicating with local public health officials for information about which immunizations were needed. Imaginary forms were filled out for passports and visas. Travel agencies were consulted about ticket rates for air and water transportation, time schedules, points of interest and major tourist attractions, and other information. The children, meanwhile, were researching the country — reading books and articles and viewing filmstrips on Japan's geography and history. The mother of the Japanese girl taught the children some basic Japanese words and demonstrated the artistic lettering which is a part of the country's language.

On a visit to the Huntsville, Ala. air terminal, the group boarded a DC-9 jetliner — with an added touch by the pilot and stewardesses who staged a mock takeoff and landing. They next made an imaginary trip to Japanese gardens and a small fishing village by using various art media to construct these scenes. The gardens took shape on sand tables and chalk murals. A fishing village was formed from cardboard arranged on blocks of styrofoam.

In a theater, aided by the physical education and music teachers, the children learned Japanese folk dances. They wore costumes made by the mothers and which were used also in a later project.

Some of the group prepared menus of typical Japanese foods. Oriental art was explored: Fans and colorful lanterns were constructed for scenery in the culminating activities. On still another tour, the children were able to explore both old and new sections of the country through films and filmstrips. Bringing from their homes many items which had been made in Japan, they became aware of the country's bustling industries.

Before leaving Japan the students enjoyed a dramatic hour of stories re-emphasizing religious practices and other national customs of the people.

Unit Culminating Experiences

As a final activity the children planned an international week. Foods representing the countries visited in the unit were served by the lunchroom staff. Each day the lunchroom was decorated to suggest the country highlighted; children dressed in native costumes were hosts and hostesses. As far as possible native customs were practiced. Chopsticks, for example, proved an interesting experiment.

Posters, bulletin boards, and art displays transformed the atmosphere of the school. The children participating in the unit expressed through several evaluative sessions a better understanding of the backgrounds of students in the multicultural classrooms. The understanding was demonstrated as the year progressed through better peer relations and tolerance of differences.

The wide range and variety of experiences in the problem solving curriculum cut across subject areas. Spelling, writing, and punctuation improved with the numerous reports and letters to travel bureaus and communities resource persons. Practical arithmetic helped to compute travel distances, costs, and time schedules. Much talent and energy went into art and musical activities. Climatic features and weather factors provided a basis for science studies. Planning menus for adequate diets and emphasizing immunization requirements for travel pointed up the importance of health for the traveler.

SITUATION 5: A PROBLEM ON JUVENILE SHOPLIFTING

Background of the Unit

Because of the sharp rise in shoplifting losses to merchants in the Prattville–Montgomery, Ala. area and subsequent rises in prices to cover the losses, the local YMCA Hi-Y Council began an anti-shoplifting program. As part of the program, area merchants sponsored an essay contest, offering $50 for the best entry from intermediate, junior high, and senior high students.

Most of the students in the Prattville Intermediate School were interested in the contest, but knew nothing about the problem of juvenile shoplifting. These sixth and seventh graders also needed to learn the fundamentals of essay writing — a new area of expression for most. A team of four teachers — in multi-media communication skills, language, social science, and mathematics — developed a problem solving–team teacher unit for thorough study of the problem. The 152 students in the ungraded school who participated in the unit were slightly above average in reading and communication skills.

The team teachers held a week of daily 50-minute planning periods to set up the problem. The unit would run for five weeks, involving three hours a day and four days a week. Assisting the team would be an aide, the principal, and an instructional supervisor. Six resource persons from the community were scheduled as speakers. A large room which was easily subdivided was selected as the center for activities by the 152 sixth and seventh graders. The team of teachers gave the social science instructor the key task of introducing the unit.

Initial Group Activities

Although student motivation was tied to the appeal of a community-wide contest combined with the direct appeal of competing for $50 by writing an essay, the social science teacher had to involve the students in a problem about which they knew very little, juvenile shoplifting. She chose to sketch an overview of the problem, carefully supporting generalizations with facts. In essence she said to the students:

> Crime and particularly the crime of shoplifting is on the increase all over the country. According to the F.B.I., shoplifting arrests have increased 221% between 1960 and 1970. While exact national figures are nonexistent, it is thought that juveniles make up more than 50% of the shoplifting offenses. The impact of shoplifting on merchants' profits can be staggering — with estimates of losses to storeowners running up to four billion dollars annually. For example, if a supermarket operates on a 1% profit margin, then it must have $500 in extra sales to make up the loss of a $5 theft.
>
> It has been found that youngsters rarely steal out of economic need. One explanation for this thievery is that many young people have never been taught to think of shoplifting as a crime or of themselves as criminals when they steal from stores. To them it is more like a sport or a game. The problem is as serious in affluent suburbs as it is in low-income areas. Complicating the picture is the youngster who is on hard drugs and must steal to support his habit.
>
> Most retailers now prosecute to the fullest extent of the law. This was not true a few years ago when it was difficult to secure a conviction in many courts.
>
> Social attitudes play their part in a problem like juvenile shoplifting. For example, how a parent feels about dishonesty can be a major factor in a child's decision to shoplift. A child, perhaps, hears his father talking about how he cheated on his income taxes or how he had a traffic ticket fixed. Soon he becomes keenly aware of the discrepancy between what parents say and what they do. Stealing is one possible and even predictable outcome of such awareness.
>
> Shoplifting is not a sport or a game. Not only are its legal punishments severe, but the social consequences can damage a lifetime. A larceny conviction can limit job opportunities, college and military experiences, and other economic and social avenues.

During this first meeting, students read a leaflet "Shoplifting is a Crime!" and then discussed whether the problem was important enough — in the group's opinion — for study. Although most of the students had heard about instances of shoplifting in the community, few knew how major a problem it had actually become. The group voted in this first meeting to explore the problem of juvenile shoplifting and to take an active part in the community essay contest.

A series of speakers were invited to talk to the 152 students in the school auditorium. The first outside speaker — country deputy sheriff — spoke for 30 minutes and then frankly answered questions, providing facts about juvenile shoplifting at the local level. Later speakers like the chief county probation officer and a detective for a large department store in town rounded out the facts-and-figure picture. The students were most interested in:

1. Average age of a shoplifter,
2. Penalties for the crime,
3. Why people shoplift,
4. Consequences of the act,
5. Apprehension,
6. Role of youth-aid divisions in large cities, and
7. Newest forms of tag-switching and stealing.

The speakers handled the subject in a straightforward manner, neither inflating nor depressing the facts. One description visibly impressed the group: conditions in detention homes. A speaker emphasized, in talking about the legal and social consequences of shoplifting, that the student should stay in school. A second stressed the fact that each person is responsible for his own behavior.

Incidentally, each speaker's remarks were mimeographed in outline form so that the group would have full, accurate facts and observations in hand. The materials were put into each student's notebook.

Ongoing Learning Experiences

Language Arts Activities. The students, aware that they knew little at the outset about juvenile shoplifting, had considerable research and inquiry before them. The tools with which to do this assignment were important. For the sixth and seventh graders, much of the terminology connected with the writing of an essay needed clarification. What exactly is an essay? What is meant by an opinion as distinguished from a fact? What is prejudice as related to opinion? In an essay what are "pro" and "con" points? The questions were fielded *as they occurred* so that meaningful distinctions could

154

be established to reinforce the concept of language as a tool in self-expression. Lucile Payne's *The Lively Art of Writing* was a helpful resource.

During the five-week unit, students practiced effective language communication through research reports, summations of speeches, correspondence with resource persons, and continuous oral discussion. Every student was responsible for one specific report which was displayed on bulletin boards and walls. The reports became sources. They were used in relevant discussions. New words which appeared in them — such as larceny, detention, penalty, offense, and felony — went on vocabulary lists kept by the language teacher. Mathematical statistics in them were used by the math teacher in constructing problems the group would be asked to solve.

But more direct practice was done on a sequential basis. Starting with one-sentence opinions, the group then selected facts to support these opinions. Eventually the students dealt with the more complex matter of convincing a reader by believable and logical arguments, illustrations, and examples. Separate sessions dealt with the parts of an essay: introduction, body, and conclusion. Putting the parts together, the students wrote a complete trial essay. The language arts teacher used sample essays throughout the practice sessions to give the young writers the guidance and confidence they needed.

Work was also done on sentence structure and patterns. The Payne book gave illustrations of the two types of sentences: the strung-along sentence which has a basic statement with facts added to it and the periodic sentence which has a basic statement with facts within it.

Items which had generally been considered under the labels of grammar and composition — sentences, words, rhetorical devices — became the tools or means in the juvenile shoplifting unit. As means rather than mere object in themselves, they were important to the individual learner.

Math Activities. Students were encouraged to use and develop problems which gave them experiences in all of the basic mathematical operations as well as in the construction of graphs and charts for projects. Some of the problems developed were:

1. Experts have estimated shoplifting's cost to the consumer as around 15% of all merchandise sold in the U.S. If a man purchased a suit for $155, shoes for $65.95, a hat for $30, and miscellaneous goods for $80.15, how much money did the shoplifting "game" cost the buyer?

2. It has been cited that employees steal about $10 million a day from their employers. How much money is lost during a period of nine months and 15 days?

3. Data was obtained through local sources that Montgomery, Autauga, and Elmore (Ala.) counties have approximately 50,000 boys and girls ranging from 6 to 18 years of age. If — as revealed by one of the speakers — 2% of the boys and girls between these ages are guilty of shoplifting, approximately how many should be arrested each year?

4. The Federal Bureau of Investigation reports that crime increased 11% in 1970 (over the previous year), 12% in 1969, and 17% in 1968. If there were 4,285,000 crimes committed in 1967, what was the number of crimes in the following years: 1968, 1969, and 1970?

5. For practice in mathematical ratio and proportion, the class decided to compare the ratio of crimes committed by males and females. It learned that five females to one male are shoplifters. The students were given various numbers representing males and asked to find the proportionate number of females.

6. The class wanted to make graphs to convey data, using as the unit of measurement a picture graph with symbols. The numbers involved were too large to show all figures; therefore, a single male or female symbol represented the number of 1,000. In some instances fractional parts of the symbols were used.

7. During the 1970–71 school year there were 1,978 boys and girls apprehended for shoplifting. If the records reveal that 64% were boys, how many were girls? Convert the percentage for boys to numbers.

8. Theft and drugs work together. Experts say that 95% of the money used to buy hard drugs was obtained illegally. If it takes $30 a day to support a heroin habit and the fence only gives the thief 10% on stolen merchandise, how much does the addict have to steal each day?

9. A large local department store reported that an average of $150 a day was stolen from the store during the 30 days preceding Christmas. How much money was lost by this store?

Culminating and Evaluative Experiences

The final experience, of course, was the writing of a final essay for the community's contest. About half of the unit participants entered the contest, even though such action was not compulsory. But there were other culminating experiences. In a language session students gave spontaneous shoplifting skits illustrating attitudes and reactions to specific situations. A final essay test measured technical mastery, organizational abilities, and effective expression.

156

In every community where a unit such as this one has been offered or where citizens have been informed of the problem, economic losses and arrests have declined. The Prattville–Montgomery area was no exception. During this unit on juvenile shoplifting it was learned that many students had previously shoplifted without knowing or understanding the consequences of their actions. Largely because of the students' own interest in the problem, valuable information was transmitted into the homes and to many of the students' peer groups. For the first time in many instances, parents, brothers, sisters, friends, and acquaintances also became aware of the seriousness of shoplifting.

The students began the unit with little knowledge about juvenile shoplifting; they completed the sequence with considerable facts and observations, not the least of which were the moral and ethical values they had themselves learned during the five-week inquiry process.

Chapter 7.   Focus on the Learner and His Uniqueness

The free man, according to the American dream, is the ultimate goal for a democratic society; education is a primary tool for realizing this goal. It is important here that "free" does not imply license or self-indulgence; a free man can learn to seek a satisfying life and in such pursuit he shoulders his responsibilities as an individual and as a citizen within the larger social structure. Man, therefore, is free to seek his ordinary interests with the tacit understanding that if he chooses not to seek them ethically, he risks the loss of his freedom.

The school can enable an individual to prepare for a satisfying life, but regrettably freedom within the classroom is all too easily smothered by the materialism and conformity prevalent in a subject centered curriculum. The material or subject matter — not the individual student — becomes the focal point for "learning." If the survival of our nation is to be measured by the health of its democratic institutions, then teachers must analyze the times and help the student to interpret them rather than settle for the safe and rigidly charted course of a curriculum which demands the set answers and comfortable conformity. Students *must* play the hazardous roles of free persons, and it is the teachers who can enable them to do so.

This concept of freedom in the classroom is not the same as that of reformers like Admiral George Rickover and James B. Conant. They would equate freedom with devices and with a return to classical traditions; they would further insist upon emphasizing mathematics and science, toughening coursework, following European selectivity and discipline, and scuttling all program parts not directly related to college preparation. Accordingly, the view that education must prepare an individual for adjustment to life has been — just as problem solving–team teaching will be — a target for critics like Rickover and Conant who refuse to admit the dual function of the school. They rail at education for assuming functions which they claim belong more properly to other institutions like the church and the home . . . and, one might add by implication, those of the workhouse, the pool hall, and the reformatory. Indeed, the sobering statistics on juvenile delinquency, mental illness, family instability, violations of the natural environment, and social irresponsibility point to the schools assuming more and more of a role in the lives of youths.

The dilemma is not totally conscious. Educators would not knowingly destroy the basic American concept of education that every individual should have an opportunity to learn. Certainly much of the curriculums and extra-curricular activities which educators have been forced to adopt by vested interests or the common culture itself have been, in hindsight, ridiculous. Possibly out of ignorance, though, many amateur critics of education have scuttled some of the necessities of a first-rate school, particularly in areas of guidance, problem solving teaching and learning, physical and recreational programming, activities, experiences in the arts and humanities, and student governing. The educator in the future will be forced to evaluate closely the perspectives of special interests — no matter how the henchmen of special interests argue for more mathematicians, more typists who can spell better than the boss, more free enterprise indoctrination, more nonhumanistic directions. The educator's commitment remains the task of producing a thinking, well-informed, confident, and basically democratic American citizen.

If the community wants intellectuality in the schools they may have it, but the choice will have to be a deliberate one. The choice must involve matters like willingly investing in school libraries and laboratories on a scale comparable to that of athletic plants, cutting off the sport of anti-intellectual posters in the common culture, securing the position of scholars and teachers with a decent teaching schedule and a bulwark of true academic intellectual freedom, and supporting the methods of intelligence. Such concerns are by no means a retreat to the conforming illusions of tradition; they entail a dynamic adventure in exploration and experimentation most promisingly through problem solving–team teaching.

The problem solving–team teaching curriculum is solidly rooted in progressive educational experiences, although it avoids the extreme child-centeredness of the latter by emphasizing both the individual and social development of students. Admittedly, progressive education labored in enough confusion to warrant the charge that it lacked an adequate philosophy. The likely assumption is that it neglected to operate consistently on the profound insights which were then available. Because it attempts to humanize, problem solving–team teaching holds some devices in low esteem since they have nothing to do with the substance of education. Devices like instructional television, teaching machines, and program learnings are set up to dehumanize and depersonalize education in our contemporary society. Problem solving does not use gimmicks.

Possibilities of Educational Equality

Perhaps, as John Dewey long ago suggested, what the best and wisest parent wants for his child is what all the community should want for all its children. Any other idea of our school is narrow and destructive to a democracy. Yet, democracy is somewhat in peril today because the community has not wanted for all its children what the best parent wants for his own child. As a result the public schools are failing dismally in what has always been regarded as one of the primary tasks — in Horace Mann's words, "to be the great equalizer of the conditions of men." Such concern could facilitate, among other things, the movement of the poor and disadvantaged into the main stream of American economic and social life. But the schools have been far from equalizing. They have in fact helped to perpetuate the differences in conditions or — at best — they have done little to alleviate the conditions. American schools will have to do an incomparably better job than they have done or are now doing in the educating of youngsters from minority groups and lower-class homes and communities.

The failure is by no means recent; it has been tolerated in this country for centuries. Our public schools have never done much of a job in educating youths from the lower class or from immigrant homes. According to Lawrence A. Crimmin, we have greatly exaggerated the commonness of the common school while in actuality the American school has always been a middle-class institution — primarily controlled and operated for the benefit of the great middle-class artisans, storekeepers, and large-scale farmers. Where homogeneity prevailed — say, in the region beyond the Appalachian — due to little social, religious, ethnical, or racial discrimination, the school was allotted as a common school. But where heterogeneity prevailed — especially in the South and in large cities throughout the country — the schools were not very common and, consequently, they served the lower classes badly, if at all. The schools have tended to romanticize their role in stimulating social and economic mobility for immigrant and native lower-class peoples. They have had some success in achieving mobility for the Japanese–American, the Greek, and the Eastern European Jew. But others like the Irish, Italians, Poles, Slavs, Mexican–Americans, American Indians, and Negroes have experienced failure in achieving mobility.

More accurately, by their reflection of a middle-class life style, our schools have been largely unavailable to the peasant culture. Nor was education that important to the new immigrant. For example, the predominantly peasant groups which left Southeastern Europe during the late 19th and early 20th centuries did not tend to view education as important either in itself or as a means for mobility in the new culture *until* the groups began to be absorbed into the American middle class. As a matter of fact, members of these groups began to realize that coveted middle-class status was normally achieved not through education, but through politics or business or even crime — the latter being closely related to the first two sectors.

Ironically but not surprisingly, American schools borrowed heavily from European curriculums and methods. European schools, it must be remembered, traditionally instructed their upper classes. Under this influence, American schools did not attempt to understand the special needs of their new students; rather, the students were expected to do the adjusting. Compounding the problem was a feeling which many Americans brought into the classroom — that of being ashamed of their parents and of a heritage. Also, children and parents from the working class were made to feel that they were low and unintelligent; naturally, teachers — themselves from the middle class — sought to correct these "deficiencies." The tragic end result was the estrangement of the school from the life of the working-class community since the middle 1800's. For a democratic society, the estrangement has been costly.

Horace Mann, while secretary of the Massachusetts State Board of Education, went to Europe in the spring of 1842 and was very impressed with the harmony and affection which then existed between teachers and pupils in Prussian schools which were using the methods of an educational reformer, Pestalozzi. During his six weeks in these schools, Mann did not see a child in tears nor did he hear of a pupil being barred because of misconduct. In fact, he noted, the teachers' manners were even more tender and vigilant than those of parents because the teachers did not have the foolish dotings or indulgences to which parents are prone. Upon returning to the United States, Mann urged adoption of these methods observed in the Prussian schools in order to make learning pleasurable — an approach, incidentally, which would have destroyed the prevailing schooling habits of discipline and obedience so ingrained in American education.

Undeniably, nothing is likely to yield more mischief or be more subversive to happiness than mistaking a child's present attitude for that which secures his lasting satisfaction. But the school people in America took an even more extreme attitude: That placing a child's needs and interests first could only threaten the welfare of both individual and society by sending forth the sickly and thereby encouraging idleness and pleasure. Such was the prevailing feeling among educators in the early part of this century when the progressive educational movement advanced by Mann and others was beginning to take root in some American schools.

Our public schools are possibly the best schools in the world — with maybe the exception of the English Open School. Yet they are saddled with a set of rigid rules and traditions which tend to block out the very children that schools in a democracy were established to educate. The schools continue to sort out some students and certify others for mobility — a process dooming many youths to remain at the lower-class citizenship level. Under the system, a student might be labeled early as a "nonreader" and repeat grades until he settles down to a stay of eight to ten years, after which he is released through a chute to the outside world to perform lowly tasks.

Hollingshead continually argued that the whole lower-class family life and culture did not prepare adolescents to adjust to school. Nor did the school, for the most part, adjust itself to the needs of lower-class students. Administrators and teachers, enforcing their own middle-class values, have put down lower-class students. No matter how much the schools have tried in the post-war period to educate minority group and lower-class citizens, they have made little progress. Success in educating the remainder of the population has not been realized, either: Urban and rural slum schools which have been detected as failures, merely reflect in large part, the failure of American schools as a whole. Essentially, the schools are not educating all men to full humanity.

It is known that lower-class youngsters start with severe educational deficiencies, and the school cannot be blamed for all of them. The school is but one of a number of institutions which affect the youngsters' academic achievements. But a democratic society should expect its schools to be a significant influence in opening opportunities to its young people — regardless of social origin. It must become possible for students from every social, ethnic, and racial group to secure basic skills and confidences necessary to live as effective problem solvers in a democratic society.

Problem solving–team teaching does not accept as adequate the facile doctrine that education is preparation for life; it insists that education must become a part of the everyday life process. It is quite common for many people to link natural selection with experientialism, the educational theory of John Dewey. It is proposed here, however, that despite a rather wide acceptance by the experientialists, natural selection is regarded as too limited or narrowly conceived. Experientialists in the past have argued that education does not teach students to adjust to life or to fit life situations; but rather enhances the quality of human life by promoting selective experiences. Intelligence is involved, to be sure: An experientialist using problem solving–team teaching wants man's intelligence developed as fully as possible. But mental development is only one step towards building a system of values for social living.

Knowledge alone is not adequate; it must be reflected in day-to-day living experiences. Therefore, education begins with helping individuals to do the things successfully which the experiential world demands of them. The true center for the school should be social reconstruction: planning, preparing for, and shaping a new society. This concept of education makes it possible, given present technological know-how, for men across the globe to acquire the goods necessary for human life. But that power needs to be harnessed for the best interest of the human race rather than for a privileged few. Students must learn to project goals for the whole of mankind; such action calls for a reconstructed culture or world-wide order based on the central belief that general knowledge of value is presently available to all men through scientific verification. Education that is properly reconstructed will help students to learn how to exercise the proper use of power for achieving the highest cultural achievement of democracy. If education is to achieve its maximum goal under the problem solving concept, then the student must surely come to know himself. The challenge to this kind of education attempts to guarantee an atmosphere of freedom in which students are encouraged to seek and find human value as the basis for making decisions.

Many critics of education argue that minority group students are unable to move up the socioeconomic ladder — not because of lack of academic abilities — but due to the failure to acquire values and habits such as punctuality and reliability. Employers explaining why they do not hire dropouts or why certain people are hired and not others seldom complain that dropouts cannot read. Instead, they complain that dropouts do not get to work on time, cannot be counted on to do a careful job, do not get along with others in the plant or office, or cannot be trusted to keep their hands out of the cashbox. Failure of the school, according to such argument, is not attributed to the socioeconomic status into which an individual is born, but to the individual's inability to develop self discipline, self respect, or a sense of responsibility.

But, then, can school really mean a difference to the minority student? It must be confessed that evidence runs the other way. The Coleman report seemed to refute the idea that our schools can do the job, arguing that the wide range of differences and the quality of education for minority group students cannot be attributed primarily to variations in educational facilities, teachers, or social materials which are made available. Coleman originally had a feeling that adequately staffed schools and well developed plants with sufficient instructional materials, texts, libraries, and other aids along with average-sized classes and well trained teachers would be appropriate to the point of eliminating inadequate academic achievements among the minority group students. But he was surprised to find that this was not the case. The Coleman survey, limited as it was, found that black schools do not spend significantly less money per pupil than do white schools. Nor do they have substantially larger classes, operate in older, more crowded buildings, and have fewer adequate textbooks. Therefore, Coleman's original suspicion of gross differences between the resources put into predominantly black and white schools has not been substantiated. Coleman and his colleagues found instead that differences in school qualities were not very closely related to differences in student achievement. Quite to the contrary, neither black nor white nor Mexican–American, Puerto Rican, and Asian did significantly better in schools with high per-pupil expenditures, larger libraries, and up-to-date curriculums than those students from schools with low expenditures, limited libraries, and out-dated curriculums.

These findings are not to be misinterpreted as meaning that the schools have no effect on student learning. It means nothing of the sort. The Coleman report suggests only that schools are remarkably uniform in their effects on student learning. Differences in student achievement from school to school seem to be due more to differences in the students themselves than to differences in the quality of schools.

Taking all of these results, the Coleman report concluded that the school brings little influence to bear on the child's achievement that is independent of his background and social context. Further, this very lack of independent effort means that any quality imposed on children by the home, neighborhood, and day care environments is carried along to become the means with which they confront adult life at the end of school.

Yet, problem solving-team teaching proponents would insist that this is not necessarily the case. A school which makes the effort to work closely with the community, they would argue, can help raise the socioeconomic standard of living and help solve the problems of everyday existence. A good problem solving-team teaching curriculum strongly implemented by a school *can* make a difference and particularly in terms of student learning. In problem solving students will not be committed to a life of failure or a low level of social status and job tasks.

Which Fails: Students or Schools?

Writers and researchers have contributed a great deal to understanding why disadvantaged children fail. But very little has been offered on why schools fail disadvantaged students. It is a normal assumption that, if children fail to learn, the fault is theirs rather than the schools'. Whereas schools are perfectly willing to place blame for student failure on poor home environment and lack of personal motivation, they are not at all reluctant to take full credit for its disadvantaged students who succeed.

Most teachers know that lower-class children enter school lacking many of the attitudes and cognitive and affective skills which are critical to success in school. These same teachers have noticed that middle-class children have acquired and are acquiring these same proficiencies from their environment — more or less by osmosis. Some of these teachers might insist that genetic factors may be the primary reason for individual variations in I.Q. Teachers and educators, however, should face up to the reality that they must work with the student's environment as a primary source; knowledge of heredity can do no more than warn them that an individual does have some limitations which can present problems during the learning process.

Schools fail not because of intentional maliciousness on the part of teachers, but because teachers are unable to comprehend the full significance of the uniqueness of each pupil. Educators are still trying to adjust the child to the school program which has been predetermined and standardized to middle-class levels; they make no effort to adjust the school to any unique needs of individual pupils. The literature abounds with research studies showing that it is theoretically possible to boost I.Q. and achievement scores of students who have been subjected to social deprivation. It can be done through head start programs, nursery schools, and kindergartens.

We also have research to demonstrate that these gains are primarily temporary — unless the student's experiences are continued or unless a school is specifically committed to caring for his needs, abilities, and aptitudes. As a result of these findings that preschool experiences must be continued, some noted educators have advocated that we may as well forget such early programs and concentrate on improving current educational programs. But rather than discount preschool and its value, educators should change the entire school spectrum, particularly its middle-class orientation.

Much of the recent research on why students fail in school emphasizes the self-concepts of both teacher and pupil as major determinants in the kinds of learning experiences students will have in school. The teacher's self-concept must be so clearly engrained that it can be communicated to the students; the students, in turn, will gain feelings of adequacy, worth and dignity, and success because, in the teacher's view, they are expected to succeed. Students have a very strong tendency to live up to the expectations that adults place upon them with respect to academic performance

165

and human interactions. The teacher who enters the classroom with the expectation that a large percentage of his students will fail because of deprivation is bound to have made a self-fulfilling prophecy to the degree that his students in many instances will fail. The teacher who expects students to misbehave and be demons also will not be disappointed in his expectations.

The same is true for success as for failure. The teacher who goes into a situation expecting the students to succeed with a reasonable degree of consistency is likely to find that the majority of students will have a high degree of proficiency in succeeding. And the teacher who expects students to be generally well behaved under most circumstances will usually discover that they try to live up to such expectations. Robert K. Merton has stated the situation as a self-fulfilling prophecy — the idea that in most instances people tend to do what is expected of them. Any careful observer visiting middle-class and lower-class schools can perceive readily that teachers vary in what they expect of students. It is most commonly expected in the lower-class school that the children will not learn, and they in turn do not learn. On the other hand in the middle-class school where the teachers have the expectation that the students will learn, most of the students do learn.

Visits to underprivileged schools — predominantly black, white, Puerto Rican, Mexican–American, Indian–American, or any — reinforce the sad awareness that teachers frequently treat students as though they were animals and, further, that teaching is viewed as a training process similar to the training of an animal. Failure for students in these schools is seldom their fault. Their teachers neither understand what failure means to such individuals nor do they seek ways and means to prevent failure. Teachers frequently miss the point that the schools can do only what the ambitions of families being served dictate. Only when the expectations of families as well as those of students have been raised can the concept of self-fulfilling prophecy be realized. Writers have been emphasizing the importance of teachers learning to understand the underprivileged so that their needs, interests, and aspirations can be served more effectively. In practice, teachers are frequently insensitive to these intangibles.

Herbert Kohl, a sensitive writer who has recorded his observations of ghetto schools, insists that children are most often compared to animals. He has described the self-fulfilling prophecy of such individuals:

> After a while the word "animal" came to epitomize for me most teachers' ambiguous relations to ghetto children — the scorn and the fear, the condescension yet the acknowledgment of some imagined

power and unpredictability. I recognized some of that in myself, but never reached the sad point of denying my fear and uncertainty by projecting fearsome and unpredictable characteristics on the children and using them in class as some last primitive weapon. It was pitiful yet disgusting, all the talk of "them," "these children," "animals." I remember a teacher from another school I taught in, a white Southerner with good intentions and subtle and unacknowledged prejudices. He fought for the good part of a semester to gain the children's attention and affection. He wanted the children to listen to him, to respond to him, to learn from him; yet never thought to listen, respond, or learn from the children, who remained unresponsive, even sullen. They refused to learn, laughed at his professed good intentions, and tested him beyond his endurance. One day in rage and vexation it all came out.

"Animals, that's what you are, animals, wild animals, that's all you are or can be."

His pupils were relieved to hear it at last, their suspicions confirmed. They rose in calm unison and slowly circled the raging trapped teacher, chanting, "We are animals, we are animals, we are animals . . ." until the bell rang and mercifully broke the spell. The children ran off, leaving the broken, confused man wondering what he'd done, convinced that he had always been of goodwill but that "they" just couldn't be reached.[1]

Anthropologist Eleanor Burke Leacock has written with exquisite detail how expectations of student academic achievement and behavior differ among teachers in the middle- and lower-class schools and how teachers' expectations in the latter indirectly teach lower-class children not to learn.

> Even with the best will in the world and the application of considerable skill in their teaching, teachers unwillingly self perpetuate a system of inequalities by transmitting to children in myriad ways the message: "This is your station in society. Act, perform, talk, learn according to it and no more."[2]

Dr. Leacock had various individuals interview teachers, asking what is the most important thing to be achieved. In the lower-class schools, the most emphasized concept was discipline. Such teachers insisted on strict conformity, never talking when others are speaking and listening attentively — regardless of whether students were interested. The teachers assumed that there was little time for fun and play; time was spent working toward goals set by the teacher, in terms of both values and content.

On the other side of the coin, middle-class schools answered the question by saying that the most important thing was to be able to get along

---

[1] Herbert Kohl, *36 Children*. New York: New American Library, 1967, pp. 187-8.

[2] Eleanor Kurke Leacock, *Teaching and Learning in City Schools*. New York: Basic Books, 1969.

with one another and to have acceptable standards of human behavior. These teachers emphasized intellectual, social, ethical, and moral development, but their first concern was helping the student to be a human being.

Observation of schools in low-income areas points up the lack of interchange and interaction among students and between teachers and students. Teachers in these schools discuss the nature of the curriculum and the needs of pupils more frequently than do teachers in middle-class communities. Almost without exception, evaluative sessions by the staff in lower-class schools are more negative than in middle-class ones.

Robert K. Merton has written: "It is the successful experiment which is decisive and not the 1001 failures which precede it. More is learned from a single success than from the multiple failures. A single success proves that it can be done. Thereafter, it is necessary only to learn what made it work."[3]

This is an educational fact of life that every teacher should learn. A teacher must be sensitive to the fact that a less mature and less experienced child must have more frequent success and cannot have failure disproportionate to his successes. If he does, he becomes discouraged. Only when an individual matures, becomes more stable, and is accustomed to success can he adjust to more frequent failure. In problem solving–team teaching this fact of life is kept in mind.

Individualizing Instruction

For many decades American educational programs focused directly upon the more typical or average student in a given classroom, disregarding the exceptional students at each end of the continuum. Then, for a brief period of time, educators concentrated on developing programs for the intellectually gifted child. Most recently attention has been given to the handicapped — those with speech and hearing problems, special learning disabilities, low intelligence, mental retardation, and visual problems. While both efforts for non-average students are noteworthy, the more basic issue of educating *all* children for a successful life remains to be confronted. It is not enough to care for any particular segment of the population since this nation is committed to the responsibility for educating and developing each person according to his full potentialities and capabilities.

Educators have always given lip service to the concept of caring for individual differences of students and to the importance of developing each student in accordance with his unique potentialities. But concern has

---

[3] Robert K. Merton, "The Self-Fulfilling Prophecy," *Antioch Review* (Summer, 1948).

usually stopped at the rhetorical level. Many classrooms attempting or appearing to care for individual differences in actual practice demand uniform learning of all students in accordance with preconceived standards that teachers, administrators, curriculum advisors, state departments of education, and agency personnel have formulated. Students, by and large, are still expected to travel at a uniform rate, cover the same materials, and achieve a set amount of proficiency in each and every area they cover. In such situations teachers are still calling for the "correct" answers and insisting on the accumulation of "knowledge," rarely resorting to divergent thinking or problem solving concepts. This is a far cry from caring for individual differences.

The individualization of instruction must incorporate critical thinking and go far beyond the mere transmission of the culture. Citizens must be able to think for themselves and willing to question and dissent. Different viewpoints are necessary to a nation like ours because the diversity provides a climate in which a democracy can survive.

The schools must permit students to make choices and to take the responsibility for these choices. Children and youths must be allowed the experience of making wrong decisions on occasion and then learning to live with the consequences. If everything is decided for them by teachers and parents, students will not be able to bring themselves to make responsible decisions as adults. People need the opportunity to experiment while they are young.

With individualized instruction students can learn self-direction — an absolute imperative if the schools are to turn out citizens capable of independent action and self-motivation. There is disturbing evidence that our nation is drifting toward impersonality in almost every phase of its culture; schooling is not exempt from this trend. Individualization attempted through gigantic organization, assembly line production procedures, standardized demands, computerized personal programs, and mass propaganda for conformity cannot — by any measurement — be self-directing and self-initiating for the students. The schools must help students cultivate themselves and they must further guard against fears of being different which can easily lead to conformity.

The schools have a most profound responsibility to develop an autonomous man who is conscious of himself and directed by his own motivation. Friedman pointed out in *The School and the Defects of the Child* that democratic society calls for inventiveness and creativity while commercial society call for punctuality and uniformity. He feels that our nation is fast becoming a vast industrial, commercial machine for which demand runs

169

counter to its original democratic ideas and dominates its citizens' lives.[4] We cannot stop the machine because we have become entranced by man's age-old dreams of material comfort and security which, mainly through modern technology, now seem within our grasp. But the schools should pay homage to ideas like freedom, individuality, and variety which develop our human resources.

Tyler and Bronell have written that durability and temperament have long been recognized by our society and that — while individual differences are desirable in our culture — widely divergent skills and competencies are essential elements in a society as complex as ours. In fact, nurturing individuality, diversity, and creativity may well be the key to maintaining a nation founded on democratic values.[5]

Most of the participants in an interdisciplinary symposium on creativity held in 1969 at Michigan State University — among them, Erich Fromm, Carl Rogers, Rollo May, and Abraham Maslow — stressed both social and individual needs for creativity in this country. They insisted that the needs created a desperate situation affecting industry, the military, and — most of all — humanitarian living and bordered on a national crisis. Seemingly, American schools need to promote ingenuity, initiative, and creativity if the nation is to maintain both high living and economic standards and develop individual potentialities. Rogers has continuously pointed out the extreme importance of nurturing individuality and creativity. He has insisted that our culture is doomed unless individuals and groups alike discover imaginative ways for adjusting to complex change and to the increased expansion of knowledge, discovery, and invention. Man must adapt to his environment as rapidly as science is able to change it.

Individualization of instruction develops a student's self-concept, making it possible for him to develop into a fully functioning, adequate personality who has a feeling of can-ness, worth, and dignity. This development is essential to the individual's well-being. It is known through psychological studies that learning is an individual and a personal process, and learning can be most efficiently and effectively accomplished if an individual's own unique and cognitive style is recognized and accommodated. Students differ in how they learn, how much, and how they adapt the learning to their own endeavors. The fact of different learning styles, rates, and interests cannot be ignored.

Nurturing individuality is not only essential to the development of a

---

[4] Material has been taken from a prepublication flyer by the publisher Crowell-Collier.

[5] Ralph W. Tyler and Bronell, *Perspectives of Curriculum Evaluation.* New York: Rand McNally, 1967.

student's self-concept; it is also the avenue through which the ego is strengthened by self-discovery, self-understanding, self-determination, and self-fulfillment. As students grow older year by year, they should be assuming a greater role and responsibility in planning, implementing, and evaluating their own learning outcomes. Friedenberg has condemned our schools severely for what he considers the cause of many adolescent problems: "If one is to become self-directed and self-actualizing a person, capable of functioning more efficiently in a democratic society practicing and directing his own activities is absolutely essential because people do not learn to assume responsibility through any other approach."[6] Too frequently, students' assignments are just handed to them; young people do not have the valuable opportunity to practice setting goals or learning to accept mistakes. Students are forced into a pattern of depending upon others to make decisions for them. The situation brings on irreparable damage to individual self-concept and it further makes the person easy prey for those who would like to manipulate him. In this culture it is possible for a pupil to never gain a chance to discover what he can do for himself. Followers — not self-directed individuals — result from the dictatorial, autocratic leadership situation. Plato once defined a slave as a person who executes the wishes of another.

The extent and quality of *individualization* which takes place in a classroom is largely determined by how a teacher defines the term and what role he selects for himself. Today, teachers are setting the goals, planning the activities, and determining alternatives. They are doing the evaluating; they are dominating the scene. Meanwhile, most schools are doing very little except talk about individualization of instruction. Too many teachers are following the concept of St. Paul when he insisted that human nature was mean and that individuals were evil in the flesh. The concept is unsound and must be reversed. Human beings are not innately evil; they learn to be through association and experience, but they are not born this way. So-called aggressive behavior in youths and children is often love frustrated. If love is withheld from a person he may indulge in violent behavior. Unfortunately, it is not the most lovable child who is most in need of love, but the one who is more unloved and disrespected or less likely to receive love and respect.

Developing Self-Directed Citizens

The schools in the past failed students, the education profession, and the society because they have not produced self-directed citizens. Problem

---

[6] Edgar Friedenberg, *Dignity of Youth and Other Atavisms.* Boston: Beacon Printers, 1965, p. 1.

171

solving–team teaching offers a unique possibility to meet the objective. The goals of modern education cannot be achieved without the objective of self-direction. We have created a world in which there is no longer a common body of information which everyone must have. The information explosion has blasted for all times the notion that every student can be fed the same diet. Instead, we have to develop and use a cafeteria principle which will help each student to select, under guidance, what he needs to fulfill his potentialities and capabilities. This entails an unusual amount of student cooperation and acceptance of the major responsibility for his own learning. Earl Kelley has suggested that the goals of education in the modern world must be the production of increased uniqueness.[7] These goals can never be reached in an atmosphere in which all decisions are made by teachers and administrators while students are reduced to passively following predetermined patterns. In such an atmosphere schools cannot possibly achieve the unique purposes set forth for them in a democratic society.

In the past, school curriculums were constructed from the assumption that learning is giving back the right answers; indeed, many present-day practices remain faithful to this basis. Too few curriculums are formed from the assumption of learning. All kinds of gimmicks and attitudes assure a "safe" curriculum, among them, cookbook approaches to learning, hyper-allegiance to rules and regulations, and slavish devotion to materials instead of people.

If learning is the personal and unique matter that psychologists insist, then it cannot be controlled by the teacher; in fact, it can take place only with the cooperation and involvement of the student. Feeding information to the student is not enough: Learning depends upon the learner's capacity for self-direction. Teachers and principals have yet to appreciate the centrality of self-direction in the learning process. Self-direction's qualities of initiative, resourcefulness, ingenuity, and creativity deserve priority over the present obsession with subject matter per se.

A. S. Neill's recent bestseller *Summerhill*[8] has fascinated thousands of educators, perhaps because of his description of the absolute trust he placed in the children under his care. Many teachers and administrators were shocked by his unorthodox procedures and the extreme behavior of some of the children. But perhaps the most impressive point is that Neill was a man who dared to trust children far beyond what most teachers or

---

[7] See particularly *In Defense of Youth* (Englewood Cliffs, N.J.: Prentice-Hall, 1962) and *Education for What is Real* (New York: Harper & Bros., 1947) .

[8] New York: Hart Publishing Co., 1960.

administrators would be willing to risk. Nor was his trust unrewarded. For more than 40 years the school he administered has continued to turn out happy, effective citizens.

Neill's experiences offer a hard lesson, but educators would do well to give up their fears of the human organism and learn instead to trust and use its built-in drives toward fulfillment and self-realization. Responsibility and self-direction are learned, not inherited. Young people must exercise self-direction, initiative, resourcefulness, ingenuity, and creativity throughout their school lives. Ironically, children in kindergarten are allowed more freedom of choice and self-direction than those in high school.

Problem solving–team teaching can increase rather than decrease a student's opportunities for self-direction by developing a favorable learning climate within the school and community which encourages student self-development. Fortunately, in the smaller society of the school professional staff members can in some measure plan the child's environment to his advantage — giving technical expression to insights gained by experience and research — not only in education, but in psychology and related disciplines. While educators are still learning about the optimal growth potential of human beings, they nonetheless acknowledge several basic conditions essential to growth and which — when combined — assure a high-power development.

One of these conditions is stimulation. Increased evidence points to intelligence itself being, to a considerable degree, an environmental artifact. Instead of speaking of an individual's intelligence, educators would do well to think of his *developed* intelligence. There are yet some undefined ceilings to which each child can develop his intellectual powers and very few persons ever reach this ceiling. Far too many live out their lives far below it. Those who rise nearest to it are persons who have had opportunities and encouragement to respond to healthy stimuli within a sound environment. Evidence points to the particular value of early stimulation in a child's life — a time when he is developing most rapidly. Because it is extremely difficult in later years to repair damage which occurred in an individual's early years, the family must bear a heavy responsibility in this area; but the schools must learn to help the family assume such responsibility.

Schools have not traditionally assumed a role of stimulation. Their physical appearance is on the institutional and dismal side: Buildings, halls, and rooms do not invite exploration. In classrooms books are frequently placed out of sight and reach, hardly an invitation to worlds of thought and gratification. A few ingenious teachers actually exist who give their children opportunities to fool around in unconscious creativity connected with arts, crafts, and tools. They also open up the community to the students by encouraging and arranging the use of museums, art galleries, and cultural resources. And they draw resourcefully upon everyday business and living. These teachers have the temperament and technical know-how to encourage children to respond vividly, take risks, toy with ideas, and open themselves up to new stimuli. A few programs have even achieved striking results by opening up the range and quality of stimulation. In such circumstances, children and youths learn to take deep and increasing joy in the very process of learning.

A second major condition essential to human growth is responsible freedom. Few schools have provided the kind of freedom necessary for full development of human productivity — whether productivity is measured in terms of ideas and arts or of economic goods and services. Freedom is a tremendous stimulant to young people; responsibility is a means of touching off the inner fibers of a person, enabling him to rise to full status when the demands upon him challenge him to rise. Without freedom growth cannot begin, and without responsibility growth can never be complete. Of course, responsibility can be harsh and frightening if it threatens a person beyond his capability to cope with a situation — leading to frustration, defeat, and withdrawal. It is a role of the school as well as the home to create conditions for full strength without impossible pressures.

A third important condition which leads to the development of the individual's self-direction is support. No individual can effectively engage in freedom that exercises responsibility and introduces risks with the chance of failure *unless* he has support from those around him. The individual must also experience some success while assuming responsibilities and ventures; without an adequate balance of successes, he develops a defeatist attitude of inadequacy which causes him to withdraw, quit, or give up in despair.

These three conditions—stimulation, responsible freedom, and support— contribute toward a sound learning environment in which the student can grow. All three are present in a problem solving-team teaching situation.

Working through Groups

The uniqueness of each and every individual is particularly cared for through large- and small-group processes. It is as a respected member of the group that an individual has the opportunity to contribute his uniqueness. In problem solving-team teaching, group situations evolve from subgroups and committees which the students form to study the parts of the problem they have selected. Group processes, by their very reliance upon democratic methods in problem solving, offer a superior learning tool to what might be accomplished by a person working alone.

When students and teachers come together to engage cooperatively in activities and to work toward a common goal, they are part of a group. While a group is a plurality of individuals, what it does is performed singly in the sense that, after activities and discussion, some consensus is reached. The group, as a product of participating individuals, is considerably more than the sum of its constituency. It exists in terms of needs, purposes, and goals which have been identified by its members. Members of a group experience a sense of belonging, identifying closely with other members. If the learning environment is positive and challenging, the group members will come to respect rather than suspect the intentions of other individuals within his group.

The leader's role is democratic: Neither above nor apart from the group, he is actively involved in the give-and-take process. He is aware that every member of a democratic group must have a direct voice in group goals, ideas, plans, discussions, decisions, and evaluations. How effective a leader he really proves to be must be judged on the basis of his skill in releasing the potential abilities and contributions of each member. The group leader in this kind of a learning environment should never assume that— because of his status or position—he has superior intelligence or a monopoly on the right answers. Nor should he assert power over others on the assumption that his word should carry more weight in a group discussion because of his leader status.

Such manipulating and raw use of power, designed primarily to urge group members to give unquestioning support to the leader's policies and wishes, is alien to the democratic processes of problem solving. Essentially, the manipulating leader controls through fear. He may rationalize that discipline can be maintained only keeping tight control. In such situations, a leader will have difficulty in securing new ideas from group members because few will dare to challenge the leader's blueprint. A group with this kind of leader is beset by intensive competition, lack of acceptance of all members, buck-passing, avoidance of responsibility, unwillingness to cooperate, aggression among its members and towards persons outside of the group, general irritability, and decrease in work when the group leader is absent.

The situation is no better when a group is saddled with the benevolent, autocratic leader. Then the group loses initiative, regresses to excessive dependence, becomes increasingly submissive, exhibits a lack of individual development, and avoids any added responsibilities. Nor is the situation better under the weak laissez-faire leader under whose direction the group becomes disinterested and indifferent, lacks purpose or direction, obtains no sense of achievement, and fails to produce worthwhile results. In actuality, the laissez-faire leader does not exert leadership, but tends to drift with the tide and lets the currents of events take care of themselves. He is likely to change his position and direction as often as the climate seems to indicate that he is no longer in favor with the group or the hierarchy above him. Whatever the case, he does not have the interests of the group or its individual members in mind.

None of these types of leaders-manipulative, autocratic, or laissez-faire—belongs in a problem solving-team teaching setting.

The democratic leader in a group situation will concentrate his efforts and energies on helping the members operate as a group. He will encourage the qualities of cooperation, enthusiasm, acceptance of increased responsibility, a sense of importance for the work to be done, and recognition of individual worth within the group setting. A leader is expected to participate in discussions, exercise his full intelligence, and give the group the benefit of his best thinking, but his thinking is tested just as carefully as that of other group members. He should not expect his ideas to be accepted as official ruling. Basically, in a group process of learning, the executive or status leader has responsibility for taking the final statement formulated by the group and overseeing its recommendations if specific actions were recommended. Under such procedure an official leader does not lose power; rather, his power is channeled into new areas. He wisely realizes that he is performing his function best when he calls to the fore the appropriate authority in a given situation. Authority is used here in the sense of training and information. Under these circumstances ideas can be advanced without fear of embarrassment. In the group process the official leader—frequently the teacher, but possibly a student who has been delegated leadership responsibility—should place emphasis upon *what* is right rather than *who* is right. In order that group thinking work in problem solving-team teaching, the status leader must eliminate the veto. If a group diligently pursues a problem and develops a solution only to have the responses vetoed, then the group process has been a tool for manipulation.

The effective leader in a democratic group situation organizes experiences of the group; makes the experiences of each group member available to all; encourages group progress through meaningful interactions and valid compliments; coordinates the group's diverse ideas; and assists members in shouldering increased responsibilities. The question of delegating authority is a minor one under the group approach because a total program becomes the responsibility of the total group—with the leader as coordinator. Group processes particularly develop loyalties and individual responsibility for accomplishing group goals. The processes, however, exert certain controls over individual group members. For example, if a given group member decides to operate on his own, it is necessary that group opinion bring him back to the group's goals.

Continuous effort and experimentation by teachers is required to make the group processes work. The more immature the group, of course, the more it needs leadership direction. A good leader can sense when a group is maturing by observing how it is developing internal motivation and a clear idea of direction, how it manifests the ability to improve upon its own procedures, and how its members reflect satisfaction from the total group effort. But, if they are to learn to work together and produce results, the group members need to know the boundaries within which they can work. They must also have the option to change procedure and direction when necessary. Hopefully, if the teachers are relatively inexperienced in problem solving inquiry and the group is working together for the first time, the problem which they pursue should not be too complicated or involved.

In summary, democratic group processes used in problem solving-team teaching draw upon these qualities:

1. An atmosphere which is voluntary, cooperative, and interactive among group members;
2. A willingness to formulate goals, work for achievements, and evaluate results;
3. Recognition that every member is an agent for change as well as subject to change;
4. Acceptance that the group is "we-centered" and that leadership is a group function;
5. Concern with non-administrative tasks such as policy making, goals and objectives, program development, problem analysis, innovation, planning, and evaluation;
6. Jurisdiction by the group over its own matters, particularly in decision-making;
7. Use of group consensus over majority vote, the latter tending to divide rather than unify the group;
8. Application of the group process with the view of training and educating students as well as solving problems.

Small Group and Individualized Activities Provide
Opportunities for Creative Learning

The author has cited on several prior occasions that problem solving–team teaching lends itself effectively to caring for individual differences. The various problems are divided into sub-problems and each sub-problem is further divided into varied activities and learning experiences of a wide range and varying difficulty. For example, let's take the problem "Improving Citizenship Through Curbing Juvenile Delinquency and/or Vandalism." The sub-divisions of the problem might be somewhat as follows: (1) extent, scope, severity, trends and types of delinquency and/or vandalism; (2) the contributing factors or causes that give rise to the existence of delinquency and/or vandalism in the immediate community as well as in the broader social setting; (3) the effects and costs of delinquency and vandalism to the community and society in general; and (4) the prevention and remedies of delinquency and vandalism. After dividing the students into four large sub-committees to make an attack upon each of the respective sub-problems, these will be further divided into smaller groups and eventually into independent research and investigation activities.

Searching

One area of responsibility, with which the various sub-groups would be confronted, would be the searching out of various information, clarifying the ideas and expanding the understandings, as well as opening up new vistas that may have impact upon each of the four sub-problems. These activities can lead children and youth to extend their interests, and use more and more mature skills in their searching, such as reading, art, music and writing. Every youth or child in each of the sub-groups will be searching and confronted with situations which he does not understand, not because there are no answers, but because he has not found an answer for himself. Such questions as "why", "what", "how", and "when" do not stop when the youngster is in the classroom. In fact the well balanced problem-solving-team-teaching situation should provide stimulation each day to encourage children to inquire more and more. Insofar as searching is concerned, as the various groups work on the sub-problems, they will soon learn that problems are not solved once and for all but that one problem leads to another larger one, and that problem solving is one of the great adventures of the full and satisfying life. It is frequently referred to as the scientific approach or the method of reflective thinking. The searching or research done in such endeavors does not necessarily require discovery of the answer, but instead, the group will be seeking possible answers and

178

possible solutions. It is through the development of an attitude of independence, individual seeking that children and youths can gain power in using the scientific method of thinking now in the problem solving type of endeavor. It is only as individuals gain power and self confidence in the searching for answers that such individuals will launch out into the unknown into creative thinking and with confidence and assurance. All kinds of skills are practiced when the various individuals are searching for the varied answers in each of the sub-problems identified heretofore.

Reading becomes one of the many important activities in which students will engage in securing the necessary data and information that is absolutely essential in order to cope with the problem at hand. The students will also do such things as searching for pictures which tell the story or help tell the story. They will seek out and interview experts who can give them added insights into how to more effectively deal with the problem. Students will be constantly testing all alternative possibilities and observing what happens as they test these possibilities. It is absolutely essential that a wide range and variety of resource materials be used in helping students do the independent activities which develop the various searching abilities. It is never enough to give an individual pupil only one source of an answer because, to do so, will limit his development as a potential creative thinker.

There is no challenge for the student who is able to know with certainty where and when to find all information that may be appropriate and how to use it. One of the important challenges in these kinds of learning endeavors is to stimulate children and youth to define new problems which are important for the searcher and researcher to answer. This is a process of continuous learning as the individuals think out problems which are important to the various individuals.

As heretofore cited, the searching activities, and the skills accompanying them, provide an unlimited number of opportunities for independent activities and learned experiences that will enable these students to acquire a relatively high degree of success and develop a feeling of can-ness and adequacy that will help them cope with more difficut problems in the future.

The teachers will be constantly watching for original thinking as well as original ways of expressing thoughts that students may use as they search for the various answers. The teachers will be constantly aiding the students to interview and survey various situations that will give them further insight into the implications of the problem. Moreover, the students will be constantly practicing various skills acqiured from various subject matter and different fields. In addition to reading, writing, spelling and arithmetic, they will be doing original research and investigation in fields of science, economic, sociology and various other areas. The research endeavors could well lead to the establishment of well illustrated bulletin boards showing the various impacts that the learning situation is having upon the boys and girls and society in general.

The students in the various sub-problems responsible for the searching phase of the endeavor will find many opportunities to build rich vocabularies that they can make use of as they explore the various research endeavors. The students will be able to experiment with many new concepts that will arise and will be responsible for success or failure in the final outcome, even though teachers may aid and assist the students in gathering resources and getting the project underway.

Organizing

The students in each of the larger groups responsible for one of the major sub-problems will be further sub-divided again into activities and learning experiences related to the organizing the information secured through the investigation, research and experimentation. Each group will need to organize materials in accordance with some sequential classification or systematized pattern of logging the information for future use. They will be responsible for the creating of stories that will be read by others and for recording the events and achievements into useful form for future use. This also appeals to and provides a wonderful opportunity for independent activities and learned experiences of a rather wide range and of varying difficulties. It enables the individuals to rearrange ideas, to synthesize information from a variety of sources and to practice consistency in the presentation of ideas to the various larger groups. Each and every individual must pause at various intervals in order to organize his facts and his learnings to see clearly and precisely what he has gained and where he is headed. This provided an opportunity for the creative pupil to pull together his knowledge, understandings and ideas into tangible form. The organization of ideas also provides wonderful opportunities for students to do self-testing. It will enable the individual to decide when he has done adequate creative thinking and at what point the original ideas which he has developed are ready for production and for sharing with the rest of the groups. Such ideas may be duplicated into worksheets and workbooks which can develop creative thinking even though such endeavors frequently fail to develop as much creative thinking as we would like. The students will be responsible for keeping records, for planning, preparing, developing and organizing collections extending their common experiences that will enable the total group to see where they have been and where they are going.

The keeping of records requires a host of skills that are needed by all individual pupils later in life. It enables an individual pupil to evaluate his progress and condense his information to a managable form in order to make further plans for studying and action. As individuals present ideas in an organized manner, they will be using skills that can be improved and developed through creative independent activity. They will learn to use simple time sequence outlines by listing ideas in sequential order, by listing materials and books under a given topic, or selecting pertinent ideas from wide reading. This will enable students to recognize the part that records play in social and scientific achievements. They learn to appreciate the works of historians, scientists and teachers. As students participate in making evaluation reports, the teacher can help by emphasizing the importance of self-evaluation. Stressing the importance of continuous progress and evaluation as feedback and guide, teachers can also do periodic evaluations and, by returning them to the students, should encourage them to do more original and more creative work the next time.

The organizational phase of each sub-problem can provide many opportunities for students to engage in a wide array and variety of activities. Such situations can provide opportunities for students to write down their discoveries and sign their name for future reference so that other students may examine them from time to time. The students doing the organizational phases will make varied classifications of the information and will depict these on varied materials that are available for making the information more meaningful and might lead to brain storming at some future time. The various individual pupils working on this phase of each sub-problem may do an extensive job of collecting various things individually and then later contrasting and comparing their collections with the collections of other students. The students responsible for this phase of the learning process in each of the sub-problems will be involved in making various field trips to not only areas of the immediate community to discover delinquency and vandalism firsthand, but to other communities where they may get an insight into what is happening in the other areas of the country. These field trips have to be summarized and evaluated. They necessitate careful investigation and research to see if the ideas that they have observed are in keeping with ideas that are recorded in literature, and then do some organization to determine how they can use the information gained most effectively for the entire class.

The discovery phase of the problem will provide many opportunities for experimentation and investigation carrying the students into new endeavors far beyond what textbook teaching normally incorporates. It necessitates very extensive and comprehensive reading and investigation and effective communication, so that all the ideas and insights gained can be shared with the total class, with the community, and other interested individuals in various and sundry ways. Many newspaper articles and leaflets could be prepared to summarize the findings of the groups and individuals. Certain dramatization skits could be prepared and shared with the total community as well as with other sections of the school. Students gifted in arts and music could translate many of the findings in all of these areas into meaningful communicative skills that might have more impact upon the way people think and behave than the verbalized stories that may be developed by students having different capabilities and interests.

Originality

The third area in which to subdivide the four sub-problems originally stated at the outset of this discussion can be designated as originality.

As children and youths become sensitized to the multitudes of forces in their environment which affect their thinking they can originate new ways of looking at vandalism and delinquency in the problem solving-team teaching situation. They will explore new means to express their ideas and new materials to satisfy their curiosity. As children and youth look at the real things around them they let their imaginations take them into flights of fantasy. As they understand more and more about themselves as individuals with unique potentialities, and as they react to the creative products of others, they will originate ingenious ways of self-expression which they have never used before. They will endeavor to do the things in the environmental problem that would further understanding an application that will affect the rights and well-being of children and youth as well as the well-being of the society.

Regardless of the purposes children and youth have in every problem solving–team teaching classroom, they deserve to have numerous opportunities to work with ideas which are original and unique. They need experiences in finding themselves as growing personalities with distinct, unique roles to play in their own world as well as in the solution of the problem at hand. These are having highly individual, independent and creative experiences that are difficult to provide in today's world of finished products and urbanized way of living. However, when properly implemented in problem solving-team teaching, they can be effectively realized. Children and youth in the past have had few experiences in making their own inventions and creations in the various classrooms and some specific time and attention should be provided for this important part of growing up.

The problem solving-team teaching endeavor will provide a place set aside for independent activities requiring original thinking in the real experiences of the learner. This area usually should be somewhere away from one's home base—the desk for example. The place does not necessarily need to be too large, but it should provide a place where children or youth can serve themselves with the materials needed, and be assured of privacy while working. When classrooms provide areas designated for individual exploration and discovery this encourages children to take responsibility for choosing an activity significant to them as their experiences are directed toward the solution of the problem. Not every kind of self-service center can be available at any one time but over the years the teachers can plan a balance of choices. Among the choices and activities engaged in by the children are those in which they can experiment with materials and explored in order to satisfy curiosity. In the process of originating in these areas children and youths will undoubtedly discover many kinds of insights new to them and new to the class. Original thinking and experimentation with all kinds of materials has been one of man's major preoccupations throughout the ages and one that has helped develop civilization. This creativity out of raw material has a useful purpose as well as aesthetic values. As the children and youths experiment with materials they will need to use skills in art, in woodworking techniques, in body control and locomotion, in music, in safety. The skills should accompany the discovery and invention, not preceed them, if children and youths are allowed their rights to explore for themselves in the world of nature.

Teachers in a team situation can help provide space for construction activities other than those which are classed in small group projects. These can be provided inside or outside the classroom. The teachers should be able to secure from local building and industrial firms all kinds of scrap materials to be used in the center for construction activities. These materials, accompanied by some simple tools, can provide incentives for children and youths to build constructive models that will help portray the story that they are endeavoring to unfold in their effort to solve the problem of vandalism and delinquency. Children and youths working on this phase of the problem should be permitted the opportunity of constructing background scenery and props to be used in dramatizing some of the major insights, understandings and conclusions reached by the full class near the end of the endeavor, which can be a most effective culminating experience and can be shared, not only by the class and the total school, but with the community as well.

In the problem solving-team teaching situation children and youths who are inventive and original in thinking need to be engaged in work with linquistic symbols, letters and numbers to let them try new combinations using symbols and fresh approaches to the matter of recording. The teacher's attitude and interests are key factors in promoting original thinking in new and better ways of doing things, and are valued and recognized. Children and youths will devote time and effort to creative production. Team teachers can make certain that the classrooms environment is rich with curiosity arousing materials and situations, and that the pupils have a place in the room and a time and a schedule to explore on their own, as well as materials to help answer the individual questions pertaining to the problem. The children and youth may be permitted to work on open-ended questions and experiments which will provide new knowledge and new insights for the various individuals. This is the kind of experience that grows out of seeking attitudes, leading to efficient learning and continued motivation to seek further for truth. The teacher should gather resources which can be used in various projects.

Communication

Communicating is the fourth approach that can be used in further dividing the sub-problems that were identified as being pertinent to vandalism and delinquency. Very few important activities can be developed without communicating something of what has been done, of the use that may be made of the products of the activity, of the basic ideas back of the work and the central product derived from it. Whether communication is oral, written or visual the process requires continuous development toward more refined and more effective skills. What happens to communication skills in the creative expressions of ideas is a real task since skills have been developed which can be expected to remain with the learner for further use. It is through the process of observing performance and actual communication that the team teachers can get some clue to further discussion and further activity in which the class may need to engage. Each of the four types of independent activities that have been identified as sub-divisions of the sub-problems have characteristics of the other three. Activities, for example, which have their emphasis in searching may also have value in developing power in the other types. As teachers play to maintain a balance they can be very careful to select activities that will assure children an opportunity to work on their own as well as in small groups, because chil-

184

dren and youths have developed creative power as they search, organize, originate and communicate.

Problem solving-team teaching offers a wide array of opportunities to use original ideas that are characteristic of creative thinkers. This factor in creativity has to be served by some means of communication if the ideas are to be of any value to other members of the class. The team teachers must provide constant opportunities that will enable the students to share their creative thinking in the classroom. As various members of the team work with children and youths, they can designate areas such as the bulletin board and table space for the children and youths to know that they will find materials that will enable them to communicate with other individuals. The individuals working on these small committees should also have a chance and opportunity to invite children from other groups to work with them on projects where there is a common interest. Carefully displayed bulletin board space can be allocated to individuals or small groups so that they will have an opportunity to work out ideas which will result in practicing many communicating skills with those in the area of linguistics and art in particular. The teacher should help the students to select a central theme to be used in expressing their ideas on a bulletin board or table display, so that organization and conciseness will be exemplified at all times. Many books, research monograms, pamphlets, newspaper articles, and magazine clippings can be used to help children share their thinking. As the group or individuals record the information, impressions and ideas they have discovered, they become sensitive to the importance of expressing themselves, so that others will clearly understand what they are writing and organizing. The preparation of both oral and written summaries of the findings of a given group lends dignity to the art of communication and in time results in linguistic arts that are functional, meaningful, purposeful and relevant endeavors having real significance to the boys and girls.

The teacher should constantly encourage all the students to do creative writing, painting, modeling and designing in the classroom which will help them express the wide range of ideas pertinent to the solution of the problem. These diverse activities provide a rich learning situation for increased interest and skill in effective communication. Poetry writing, news writing, publishing magazine articles, making illustrative stories and preparing bulletins and other written activities, can be carried on by individuals and small groups, enabling the students to communicate their ideas effectively to the total class. The students in this group should be prepared to produce an original movie, a play or dramatized skit, which will not only afford occasions for communicating ideas, but will at the same time provide opportunity to share some of the original thinking and creative abilities of the students with the total class, school, and community. Further writing and production of such shows or dramatic skits enable children and youths to value visual and verb art forms as precise expression of man's experiences and man's endeavor to cope with life situations. This group should be charged with the responsibility of developing a well displayed bulletin board that includes some major interest items which have been reported in the news media and reported through television and radio production. Individuals can paint, draw, illustrate and write original stories depicting the kind of learning outcomes that they have acquired through mass media other than the printed media. Self-confidence and communicating ideas through problem solving-team teaching can result in such activities as the making of a book that gives a very careful survey of the major concepts and ideas that have been discovered and used in the solution of the problem of vandalism and delinquency. This book should be well illustrated with pictures, graphs, charts and drawings that the students learn to do through creative endeavors. The book should be neatly written and legible, including original ideas in some sequential pattern using correct meaning and new words acquired through the study, and using clear sentence structure and correct grammar. These books could be widely distributed, not only to other classes in the school, but to the community and even to other schools, to show the kind of learning experiences the boys and girls are grappling with in this very important endeavor.

The type of group participation identified in the foregoing paragraphs indicates a minimum of sixteen separate committees would be necessary to carry on a thorough investigation and exploration of and solution for the problem of juvenile delinquency and/or vandalism. There is a possibility of still further subdividing into even smaller groups. For example, taking subproblem 1: the extent, scope, severity and the trends of delinquency in the local community and in a larger society could easily be subdivided into a minimum of four subcommittees, with each subcommittee further divided to participate in searching, organizing, originating and communicating the pertinent findings. This, in turn, could be divided even further by having certain committees exploring the various facets of this problem at the local level, and other committees exploring the problem at the regional, state and national level, or even at the world-wide level. Each of the other subproblems could also be easily divided into from two to three subcommittees, with each subcommittee further divided into committees responsible for searching, organizing, originating and communicating the findings and proposals pertinent to the solution of the problem.

It is evident from the above that there is almost no limit to the number of subcommittees that could effectively function in a problem solving–team teaching situation committed to the idea of improving citizenship through curbing juvenile delinquency or vandalism. This is equally true of any other realistic problem that confronts the needs of boys and girls, that has its impact upon the society in which they live and affects their well-being. As heretofore said, each of the subcommittees will be further subdivided into individual activities enabling various individuals to engage in exploration and research pertinent to ther particular interests, needs and abilities. These individuals will be allocated responsibilities by the subcommittee with the team of teachers working concurrently with the subcommittees in allocating responsibilities. These allocations will be made in terms of the individual's prior experiences, with the idea that every individual should be working toward a well-rounded program that will result in the full realization and self-actualization of the individual. The assignments are also made in terms of the availability of resource materials to which the individuals have access in the exploration and the development of their particular problems. Through such endeavors the concept of individualizing instruction can be realized to the degree that it has never been realized before.

Individualization of Instruction: A Dream Yet to be Realized

In our country the individuality to which we have aspired for many decades has become inundated by the triumphs of technology and production. Numbers are replacing peoples' names by geographic areas until the individual is usually identified by some digit in a series of numbers. Increasingly, we find ourselves frustrated and dehumanized and even arguing with the machines which mix up the number and notify us incorrectly of the overdrawn accounts. The world is changing its characteristics at a dizzying speed. Technology and scientific achievement, whether they be in space or elsewhere, are helping us to embark on one of the greatest, if not the greatest age of exploration and discovery mankind has ever known. It is generally recognized by leading authorities that we are presently living in an era that can be reckoned as a second grade divide in human history, which is somewhat comparable to the break in historical continuity from barbarism to civilization. More and more schools are confronted with this frustrating situation that has become a creeping glacier, at once closer and more distant from those it was designed to serve. The students are rebelling because they are in search of a way to reduce their indecisions about their own lives. It is no wonder that they resent the irrelevant curriculum and the horror for things that will never be.

Educators throughout the land realize that schools must become the launching pad for tomorrow. But this education cannot be just focused on tomorrow. It must of necessity take care of today and be good while it is going on. *Learning how to learn* must overshadow the learning methods, skills, and knowledge. New problems are constantly confronting us that are very relevant and must be answered. It is true that we must draw upon the past, but we must also focus upon the present and the future. School must increasingly become a place where one goes to have experiences and where there are opportunities for young to find their way. Schools have a function and teachers have a task to provide meaningful opportunities for active student participation in the spectrum of learning decisions, in the nurturing of an environment designed to foster adequate personal development of each individual. We have too long lived under the false assumption and barricade of fear that children are somehow beasts who need to be controlled and tamed. On the other hand, each individual is striving as a human being toward health, both physical and mental, to warrant the self-realization of a full and adequate personality. We are realizing more and more that the student is not our enemy and that the individual needs achievement of adequacy. In order to achieve this, we must develop a flexible and adaptable creative individual who can meet the continuous challenge of change.

The schools must produce a psychological climate, which Rogers describes so adequately when he states that the climate must be such that it will initiate a process of learning to be free. We as individuals, teachers and school administrators are becoming increasingly committed to the concept of individualization of instruction. A great deal has been written in recent years and much lip service has been given to the concept of individualization of instruction, but as is too frequently the case, people only pay lip service to this concept. If one goes into the classrooms or the schools, we find that each individual is continuously confronted with routine endeavors that are uniformly the same for all students, coming predominantly from a uniform textbook, guide, syllabus or course of study demanding mental achievement of all individuals and, consequently, the concept of individualization of instruction has rarely gone beyond the talking and writing stage. It is high time that the schools of America learn how to individualize instruction in the most meaningful and realistic way.

188

The schools must create a climate conducive to the individualization of instruction. A publication of the joint project on the individual and the school made the flat statement: "The foundation of our nation is a supreme commitment to the individual human being." The Rockefeller Panel Report entitled, "Pursuit of Excellence," takes a similar stand when they say, "The greatness of a nation may be manifested in many ways, in its purposes, in its courage, in its moral responsibilities, its culture, and scientific imminence, the tenor of its daily life. But the ultimate source of its greatness is in the individual who constitutes the living substance of the nation."

The true greatness of America does not lie in its military might, its industrial productivity, or the advances in space, no matter how spectacular they may be. The ideal which has made American civilization the envy of the world is the ideal which proclaims the dignity and worth of the individual. Therefore, it is high time that we begin in earnest conviction to realize the potential of each individual and demonstrate that the schools can loosen the creative powers of each individual. Only when such endeavors are realized will we achieve the platform that Jefferson, Wilson and Kennedy visualized for American youth.

BIBLIOGRAPHY

Brennecke, John H. and Robert Amick, *The Struggle for Significance.* Beverly Hills, Calif.: Glencoe Press, 1971.

Cook, Ruth C. and Ronald C. Doll, *The Elementary School Curriculum.* Boston: Allyn and Bacon, 1973.

Doll, Ronald C., ed., *Individualizing Instruction.* Washington, D.C.: Association for Supervision and Curriculum Development, 1964.

Frazier, Alexander, *Open Schools for Children.* Washington, D.C.: Association for Supervision and Curriculum Development, 1972.

Frazier, Alexander, ed., *Freeing Capacity to Learn.* Washington, D.C.: Association for Supervision and Curriculum Development, 1960.

Gillham, Helen L., *Helping Children Accept Themselves and Others.* New York: Teachers College, Columbia University, 1959.

Hamacheck, Don E., *Encounter with the Self.* New York: Holt, Rinehart and Winston, 1971.

Henry, John and Charles Harrison, *Free to Learn.* Englewood Cliffs, N.J.: Prentice-Hall, 1972.

Hyman, Ronald T., *Approaches in Curriculum.* Englewood Cliffs, N.J.: Prentice-Hall, 1973.

Howes, Virgil M., *Individualization of Instruction.* London: The Macmillan Co. and Collier-Macmillan Ltd., 1970.

Jones, Richard M., *Fantasy and Feeling in Education.* New York: New York University Press, 1968.

Miel, Alice, ed., *Creativity in Teaching.* Belmont, Calif.: Wadsworth Publishing Co., 1961.

———, *Independent Activities for Creative Learning.* New York: Teachers College, Columbia University, 1961.

Parker, Don H., *Schooling for Individual Excellence*. New York: Thomas Nelson and Sons, 1964.

Russell, Ivan L., *Motivation*. Dubuque, Iowa: William C. Brown Co., 1971.

Saylor, J. Galen and G. Kerry Smith, *Removing Barriers to Humaneness*. Washington, D.C.: Association for Supervision and Curriculum Development, 1972.

Schmuck, Richard A. and Patricia A. Schmuck, *Group Processes in the Classroom*. Dubuque, Iowa: William C. Brown Co., 1971.

Silberman, Charles E., *Crisis in the Classroom*. New York: Random House, 1970.

Squire, James R., *A New Look at Progressive Education*. Washington, D.C.: Association for Supervision and Curriculum Development, 1972.

Stoddard, George D., *The Dual Progress Plan*. New York: Harper and Brothers, 1961.

Torrance, E. Paul, *Guiding Creative Talent*. Englewood Cliffs, N.J.: Prentice-Hall, 1962.

Van Till, William, *Curriculum: Quest for Relevance*. Boston: Houghton Mifflin Co., 1971.

Vars, Gordon F., *Common Learnings: Core and Interdisciplinary Team Approaches*. Scranton, Pa.: International Textbook Co., 1969.

Waetjen, Walter B., *Human Variability and Learning*. Washington, D.C.: Association for Supervision and Curriculum Development, 1961.

————, ed., *Learning and Mental Health in the School*. Washington, D.C.: Association for Supervision and Curriculum Development, 1966.

Chapter 8.   Need for Specially Trained Personnel

Dr. Morrel J. Clute, *guest writer**

If the teaching role in problem solving–team teaching varies from the traditional lecture-and-assignment approach, then its teacher needs distinctly different preparation during both preservice and in-service periods. Others who will administer and assist in the problem solving learning situation also require special preparation. In particular, preservice training should offer future teachers, administrators, counselors, supervisors, and curriculum workers a different philosophical, sociological, and psychological orientation from what has been given in the past. A curriculum which has been reorganized for problem solving–team teaching is built upon a philosophy of pragmatism, humanism, and democracy. It is grounded in the psychological concepts of the field, gestalt, organismic, and perceptual theories of learning which emphasize individual worth and dignity far beyond past practices. It is further a sociological concept revolving around reconstruction of the society in the school — with the school working cooperatively with other social agencies in bringing about learning experiences by solving social, civic, and economic problems.

Accordingly, educational personnel who will deal with a problem solving curriculum need to be prepared by teacher educators who themselves have had some firsthand experience in problem solving and core curriculums. Their academic program should provide frequent contacts with problem solving–team teaching schools so that education students can find firsthand insights and experiences prior to graduation. These field experiences can happen at several points. First, freshmen or sophomores can begin as teachers' aides in problem solving–team teaching schools — getting a feel of how the inquiry concept works within the field and observing how a school in all its interrelated parts applies it. Second, laboratory experiences should be provided when students are taking the special methods courses in problem solving–team teaching. As the students' understanding of the concept deepens, their laboratory experiences should be extended. Third, in preservice training, the student will work for one full quarter or more in a problem solving–team teaching school as a staff member — hopefully drawing part-time pay from the local school.

*Dr Clute, professor of secondary education in the Department of Educational Administration at Wayne State University, Detroit, Mich., taught for 23 years in the public schools before joining Wayne State in 1954.

But it is not enough to give education undergraduates a series of planned field experiences while in college. It is equally important that the experiences and growth be continuing. Educational institutions preparing problem solving–team teaching personnel must be held accountable for follow-up experiences spanning at least one or two years after graduation — mainly through short workshops and conferences. Those who plan to fill administrative positions in a problem solving–team teaching setting — principals, superintendents, assistant superintendents in charge of instruction, supervisors, curriculum coordinators, and guidance counselors — should have opportunities similar to the teachers and should be able during these internships to work closely with people already acting in these roles. With these administrative experiences and one or two years of teaching in problem solving learning environments, these administrators will probably be ready to move into full-time roles. This internship should be in addition to the one mentioned earlier for teachers while college undergraduates, and it could be conceivably done also at the preservice level. By all means, it should happen early if possible; if not possible, the internship should come at the in-service phase. Both possibilities will be discussed later.

Above all, if the public schools engaged in problem solving–team teaching and the schools or departments of education in colleges or universities which are preparing educational personnel were to form a partnership and to assume joint responsibility for those who will staff schools, the problem solving inquiry concept would have the specially trained personnel it requires.

For example, the administrative role in problem solving schools needs a caliber of leadership far beyond that asked by the traditional school, both at elementary and secondary levels. Administrators should come to the problem solving learning situation armed with first-hand experiences. Then they need to have a *full* participating role in helping boys and girls wrestle with issues and problems. It is only when administrators have had teaching experiences of a successful nature that they can be fully sympathetic as leaders in implementing a more dynamic program for their teachers in the school they are helping to administer.

The principal is the most basic and essential person in a school to understand the total network of problems which involve teachers, lay persons, and fellow administrators at local and state levels. No school operation will ever go far beyond what the principal perceives as being good practice in education. While this observation is basically true in all curriculum endeavors, it is particularly critical in problem solving–team teaching. Only when the chief school administrator is in complete sympathy with a program — viewing it perceptively and ably — can he be in an effective position to assist his teachers in trying out educational innovations with the assurance that teachers will be protected from undue criticism of colleagues, parents, or members of the community. After all, no teacher is willing to venture into innovative experiences when he must struggle to reach solutions of problems unless he is assured it is acceptable to make mistakes.

The school system's superintendent is another important educator in an innovative setting such as problem solving. He too is responsible for creating a climate of experimentation and research in his schools so that teachers and students can seek learning situations. The superintendent, as an educational administrator working with the board of education, provides the resources, personnel, assistance, and in-service education which will develop a faculty for problem solving–team teaching situations. He is in turn aided by the assistant superintendent, supervisors, guidance coordinators, and curriculum directors in helping teachers to increase their abilities to cope with life situations and to solve on-going problems. Their students — within such a learning environment — are learning how to learn, and their skills will hold them in good stead long after they have left the classroom.

The teachers and the principal form a team with the superintendent, the assistant superintendent in charge of instruction, the supervisor, the curriculum coordinator, and the guidance director to solve mutual problems cooperatively. They are using the same problem solving inquiry and group processes that the students utilize; therefore, each is part of a team to make the concept work.

Fallacy of the Teaching Concept

Historically in institutionalized education, there has been widespread acceptance of the erroneous belief that one person teaches another—that is, a teacher transfers his knowing or his wisdom to his students. In actuality, no one person really teaches another; an individual teaches himself. Either he decides to give himself to learning or he withholds himself from it, but the fact remains that every learner is in complete control of his own learning.

Most educators have always known that they do not teach in the literal sense, but they still behave in classrooms as if knowledge were transferable. Not only do teachers demonstrate their acceptance of this fallacy by "telling" students *what they should know*, but school architects as well support the fallacy. Almost every classroom is designed so that there is always a front of the room. In such a design the implication is that information flows from the fount of knowledge in the front of the room to the back of the room. Further evidence of discouragement is found in the arrangement of desks or chairs in straight lines — each facing the fount of knowledge — as if this transfer travels only in straight lines within a one-way communication system.

Belief in the fallacy of teaching concept has made it difficult for teachers to help students teach themselves or to facilitate student learning. Consequences which severely inhibit or damage an individual's interest in learning can result when the fallacy is practiced. Some of the consequences have far more potential damage to a student's enthusiasm for learning than others. Four of the more dangerous stemming from the fallacy that one person teaches another are:

1. That a teacher becomes acknowledged as the sole bearer of knowledge;
2. That, despite that acknowledgement, ironically within local and state educational hierarchies teachers in fact cannot decide basic learning needs of their students or select main resources for study;
3. That learning becomes neatly departmentalized into separate subjects;
4. That belief in a single right answer is encouraged.

The fourth consequence — the belief in a single right answer — is perhaps the most damaging.

The first consequence of the teaching fallacy — the characterization of a teacher as the only one in a classroom who knows anything worth knowing — forces the teacher into an impossible role of having to decide *what* is to be taught and excludes the learner from having any part in deciding what is relevant to him. Decisions about what materials will be used, for example, come down to what the teacher himself knows; under such conditions, learning in any given classroom is necessarily limited to what one person — the teacher — knows. The situation can and does create a very sterile learning environment. The unique perceptions, experiences, and needs of students get lost in the daily shuffle if the teacher believes that he must be responsible for spoonfeeding his own knowledge into the "knowledgeless" minds of students.

The second consequence is the fact that over the years the teacher himself — the individual closest to the learning needs — has been eliminated from making the basic decisions about what is to be taught. School system administrators make that decision — more frequently these days at the

194

state than local level — by the selection of a basic text or texts which then become the determinates of the content of courses. Worse yet, these textbooks in separate subject fields tend to isolate the learner even further from his immediate learning needs by the need for standardization. Children in Alabama or Michigan find themselves using textbooks written by people far away — people who have never been in either state and know nothing about the unique experiences and needs of local settings. Textbooks, for the most part, deal with what has been, and cannot deal with the here and now.

The third consequence of the teaching fallacy is the tendency to separate one subject discipline from all others. Learning in one field is isolated and assumed complete within itself. It implies that the magic of education lies within the subject and that mastery of the content of each subject field somehow provides an integrated whole. A natural result of the practice has been an increased emphasis on improving the quality of the *input* rather than the *outcome*. National curriculum reform has resulted in an increased number of concepts which have been sequentially ordered for learning in each of the subject fields so far studied. Commercial educational packaging companies have worked hard in finding new ways to package the materials. Much has been done — especially with the advent of technology and hardware — to improve both the quality, attractiveness, and usefulness of the material, but efforts have not satisfied the valid complaints and demands of today's students for greater relevancy, involvement, and humaneness in their education.

Although there are probably many other consequences of the belief that one person teaches another, the fourth one discussed here — that content to be taught or transferred demands single right responses to questions asked by the teacher — is the most damaging to the young learner. He who fails regularly to bounce the single right answer back to the authoritarian figure at the front of the room is headed down the road to failure. He becomes labelled, characterized, and disenchanted. If his responses never seem to be the ones the teacher wants, he soon believes less and less in his own worth and more and more that "school is not for him."

Studies by Morris of the University of Michigan found that third graders in schools which use comparative marking and grading practices will tell you that kids getting A's and B's are worth more than those getting D's and E's. It is also now believed possible to identify potential school dropouts by the third grade. Probably no single teacher practice destroys student interest in learning more than the continued use of the single right questions, thus undermining individual feelings of worth and ultimately resulting in hostile student rejection of *all* organized education.[1] In spite of the apparent damage which can come from this weak teaching strategy, the single right answer method still dominates classroom practice throughout the schools of the nation.[2]

In the area of general education — as distinguished from vocational education where a student has made a choice and a commitment to learn those things necessary to the performance of that job — no teacher should ever ask questions to which he knows the answer. Otherwise the teacher will be working against the nurture and maintenance of curiosity and interest in learning, encouragement of creativity and the creative response, student growth in terms of feelings of worth, and development of respect for the rights and opinions of others. No child can learn to respect the ideas of others until he has experienced respect for his own.

When a teacher asks a child questions like:

1. What *do you think* causes this to happen?
2. What *do you believe* explains this?
3. What *do you feel* is a reason for this happening?
4. What meaning does this have *for you?*

he is searching for answers he does not yet know. In asking open questions, a teacher must then accept students' responses as honest indications of what they think or believe. In a classroom environment in which all students are safe in expressing what they really think, there need be no fear on the teacher's part that students might come up with wrong answers because the normal variations in student responses will enable each student to modify his reaction without being told that the answer is wrong.

Teacher as Learning Facilitator

By supporting a static curriculum and believing that a student is taught, educators deny the opportunity for an individual to feel that he has any control over his destiny. The Coleman report found that, of all the variables measured in its survey, the attitudes of students, their interest in school, their self-concepts, and their sense of environmental control showed the strongest relationship to achievement. A pupil-attitude factor — which appears to have a stronger relationship to achievement than do all the other school factors — is the extent to which an individual feels that he

---

[1] For further exploration of the impact of this kind of learning failure, see William Glasser's *Schools Without Failure;* John Holt's *How Children Fail;* and Carl Rogers' *Freedom to Learn.*

[2] John Goodlad and Frances Klein, *Behind the Classroom Door* (Worthington, Ohio: Charles A. Jones Publishing Co., 1970) .

has some control over his own destiny. Schools should cease being authoritarian institutions and educators should stop being determiners of student learning. Instead, both the institution and its professionals must begin at the level where the student is ready to begin: with his own interests and problems as he sees them.

Within this kind of learning environment, the teacher needs to become a facilitator of learning, an inviter into new experiences, and an arranger of circumstances for observation and study so that students are able to find meaning in what they do. Research which is considerable in the area of perception provides basic data regarding this aspect of student learning. Ames's research, for example, found that a student's past experiences form the bases for making meanings out of his perceptions.[3] This dynamic concept of human uniqueness which says that every person living today is different in some way and to some degree from all others is central to a problem solving situation.

Certainly it is human uniqueness which has made human society possible. Not only has this quality made cooperation acceptable among men, it has also made it necessary. Consider the array of human talents, interests, abilities, and capacities which are needed in any society. Why, then, has the school valued uniqueness so little? Traditionally only academic talents have been valued in our schools; the myriad of other human talents — among them, recognition of individual uniqueness — has largely been ignored in a learning situation. Is it not a teacher's role to facilitate growth and development of all talents among his students rather than focus narrowly upon one or two? If the findings from Ames's work are placed on a continuum, the result indicates that people are different and therefore experience differs; consequently, because meaning comes from past experience, meaning will be different for each person. Therefore, the unique responses of each individual require recognition and the practice of saying there is only one right answer is incorrect.

Another contemporary characteristic complicating the teaching fallacy is the knowledge explosion. It has been estimated that the amount of new information being constantly generated is equal to adding 20,000 volumes to the Library of Congress each week. There have also been many estimates — particularly in the technological fields — which indicate that half of all that is known about technical fields today will be obsolete within 10 years. Or to put it another way: Ninety percent of all scientists who have ever lived are alive today.

---

[3] See Earl C. Kelley's *Education for What Is Real.*

With information needs changing rapidly, what should be the focus in education? It would seem that problem solving or skills to apply selected information to contemporary issues — to analyze, generalize, and conclude — would be perhaps the most important of tools to serve a citizen in this country.

Learning Needs

If curriculum is to reflect what students consider meaningful issues, teachers will need to develop competent skills in teacher–pupil planning. To consult his students is perhaps the most important expression of a teacher's respect for them with respect to helping youths to believe in the worth of their own curiosity and ideas. Developing skills in problem solving becomes even more complex when it involves group processes in which several people or more are cooperatively trying to solve problems. Schools have traditionally spent a disproportionately large amount of time in helping students learn how to be competitive rather than be cooperative. This emphasis on competition would seem to ignore the reality that most major decisions which affect Americans are made by groups such as congresses, legislatures, councils, boards, committees. Problem solving inquiry is based upon cooperative group learning.

Open discussion which is directed toward decision-making, policy formation, or action is vital to a democratic way of life. Research indicates that group solution of problems tends to be superior to individual efforts. Further, group activity maximizes the amount of available information needed to solve a problem, introduces more hypotheses for a solution, and permits a greater exercise of the critical function.[4] Problem solving is an effective learning approach for other reasons. Basically, human beings need each other, and an individual's learning of human values cannot take place in isolation from other human beings. In solving problems students work and learn together:

1. Respect for the human personality,
2. Faith in human intelligence to solve problems, and
3. Belief in the ultimate soundness of solutions.

As a method problem solving is founded on many assumptions about people, the nature of learning, and leadership:

1. *Every participant is both a resource person and a learner.* No two people are exactly alike. The differing ethnic, racial, religious, and socioeconomic backgrounds give each individual a unique view, making him a potential resource for others in the group. An effective group situation encourages each person's unique contribution.

---

4 See "What Research Says About Teaching and Learning," *Phi Delta Kappan,* vol. XXXIX (March 1968), pp. 242-304.

2. *Crucial learning is related to an individual's current concerns which he has shared in identifying.* Among social scientists there exists a widespread recognition of the value of member participation in decision-making if groups are to arrive at decisions and if they are to carry out their decisions.[5] This concept implies that purposes are as unique as people and that freedom must exist for individuals to decide the direction of their own learning modified, naturally, by societal needs.

3. *Democratic leadership puts human values first.* In the problem solving classroom, teachers must be cognizant of the foregoing values. The classroom should provide a climate in which:
   1. Students can assume maximum responsibility for their own learning:
   2. Students can identify their current concerns in an area and join with others in study of a common problem;
   3. Students will be able to communicate freely during which they are encouraged and challenged to express views, relate experiences, and present ideas and resources.[6]

The Problem Solving Process[7]

A problem solving study group is most effective when it uses an orderly thought process. For example:

1. *Discovering a Problem:* A selection is made from classroom discussions and consensus. *If* the teaching team has allowed for sound teacher–pupil planning sessions, then the group will be ready for interaction.

2. *Defining the Problem:* When groups within the larger group have been formed, the first step is to find out what the selected problem means to each group member. Possible boundaries of the problem can be roughly sketched by asking these questions:
   a. What do the group members want to know about the topic?
   b. Is this problem actually a combination of several?
   c. If so, on which one should the group begin?
   d. Is the problem within the group's capacity and knowledge?
   e. What can be realistically achieved within the time allotted?
   f. In what ways could the problem be approached?
   g. What results or outcomes might be anticipated?

---

[5] Thomas Gordon, *Group-Centered Leadership* (Boston: Houghton-Mifflin Co., 1955), p. 63.

[6] For a more detailed description of workshop principles and procedures, consult Earl C. Kelley's *The Workshop Way of Learning.*

[7] Citizenship Education Study, *Problem Solving* (Detroit: Wayne State University Press, 1957).

3. *Working Out the Problem:* The group members will assume assignments and projects as they:
   a. Recall information already known by the group.
   b. Determine the need for more information.
   c. Locate sources of information.
   d. Analyze and interpret findings.
4. *Drawing Conclusions:* Taking data from the smaller groups or committees, the total group will:
   a. State possible conclusions.
   b. Determine the most reasonable and logical conclusions.
   c. Reach those conclusions judged valid by the group.
5. *Presenting Conclusions or Plan of Action:* In its final action, the group tries to put its conclusions into some sort of action and it evaluates the learning experiences.

Human Resources

At a recent Michigan student rights conference sponsored by the Association for Supervision and Curriculum Development's Commission on Humanism, students made an appeal for schools to deal with relevant issues in their curriculums. They asked that courses should bear on present-day issues like sex, racism, drugs, the draft, American imperialism, school affairs, community problems, environmental protection, black power, white power, the new left, communism, and the Vietnam War. In a newsletter several years ago, this need for problem solving was expressed:

> School must be a place to prepare young people to take their place in society—not a place where we isolate them from the main currents of our life. Education should become man-centered, idea-centered, experience-centered, problem-oriented, community-centered, and interdisciplinary—this in contrast to the frequent educational experience with its information-gathering, fact-centered, course-centered, subject-centered, grade-setting, and bell-interrupted activity.[8]

In studying a problem it is difficult to know where one subject leaves off and another begins. In a problem solving learning environment the ability to draw upon *any* subject field which contributes to understanding a problem under actual study makes the team and group approaches especially viable. It takes many kinds of human resources to succeed in the inquiry concept: those from the traditional subject fields and those from a learning resource center. Just as there is need for group techniques in problem solving, individualized and programmed instruction are also utilized.

---

[8] Clyde Campbell, *The Community School: Mott Foundation Newsletter*, IX, 8 (November 1970).

Many special skills are needed in the problem solving classroom: planners, discussion leaders, production helpers, record keepers, listeners. Seldom do all these skills reside in one person. The team and differentiated staffing concept allows for persons with varied competences and backgrounds to facilitate student learning.

Staffing Priorities

An old axiom cautions that teachers teach as they were taught. Indeed, the problem solving-team teaching concept has yet to be widely used in elementary or secondary schools or in higher education. It has been said earlier that teachers need special training before they become facilitators in a problem solving setting. Even with this special help, teachers still face classroom problems. One of the more puzzling problems in the teaching arena is the relationship between academic achievement and educational effort. No matter how much on-going experimentation educators conduct, classroom achievement figures continue to be distributed along a normal bell-shaped curve. Research has so far yielded no single teaching method better than the rest. As far back as the *Eight Year Study,* no significant differences in achievement were found between graduates of the study's experimental schools and those of its control schools. Though great differences were found in other areas, the study nonetheless found that, in terms of achievement, experimental students did as well as, but not significantly better than the control students. The teaching method by itself seems not to make the difference in academic achievement.

Similarly the U.S. Office of Education has had to report disappointing results in compensatory education projects — particularly in its evaluation of performance contracting during which no significant differences were discovered in achievement gains between those in the program and those not in it. All of this may suggest that any focus on achievement is the wrong focus. Differences exist in student achievement levels both within and among systems; where differences do occur, teaching methods may explain them. But evidence would seem to say that good results are not due so much to a teacher's methods as to *the teacher himself.*

The Florida Studies in Helping Professions have contributed needed information about the characteristics of teachers whom students view as good teachers as compared with those of teachers who are seen as poor helpers.[9] Study findings clearly indicate that neither the teacher's method nor his knowledge determines whether or not he is a good helper. In general, the differences between good and poor teachers stemmed from

---

9 Arthur W. Combs, ed., *Florida Studies in Helping Professions* (Gainsville: University of Florida Press, 1966) .

how the individual teachers uses *himself* as an instrument to help others learn. Simply stated, *every teacher in problem solving must find and use the facilitating methods of teaching which are most appropriate to his own uniqueness.*

In the four helping professions studied, the same differences were found in at least five areas. But differences in all four were discovered in the frames of reference, attitudes about people, attitudes about the self, the nature of purposes, and the ways in which people related to others involved in the problem. Good teachers generally were sensitive and empathetic to the learners, and they saw students as able and, therefore, responsible. They were also able to convey a positive sense of confidence in themselves which made it relatively easy to give to others. They were furthermore more likely to help involved students with sincerity.

Student achievement would appear to depend more upon how the student feels about a given situation — that is, his involvement and his belief that he has some control over his actions — than it does on the teaching method. There seems also to be a direct relationship between a teacher's expectation or perception of a student and the student's behavior in either a positive or a negative way. Rosenthal and Jacobson found that "when teachers believed that certain students were destined to make great educational growth, those students did indeed turn out to be the ones who made the most growth."[10]

In order to help students learn and achieve, teachers should have some means of determining whether or not they are doing so; the use of a standardized achievement test will not satisfy this need because the testing device does not recognize the unique experiences and backgrounds of students. The only way a child in a classroom can make meaning out of his perceptions is through his own past experience. No basic text or standardized test can serve large groups of students fairly.

There are many ways a teacher can get feedback on his performance. Students are the most useful source because they know best what helps them and what does not. A teacher might arrange daily or weekly feedback sessions with his students. Video- and audiotapes also let the teacher review his classes and work on improvement. He could also have his verbal behavior coded by an observer using the techniques developed by Ned Flanders in "Interaction Analysis." Raths, Harmin, and Simon have provided still another strategy in *Values in Teaching*. The authors' classroom techniques for value identification and clarification do not place students

---

[10] Robert Rosenthal and Lenore F. Jacobson, "Teacher Expectations for the Disadvantaged," *Scientific American*, CCXVIII, 4 (April 1968) .

in the crippling position of having to respond with single right answers. William Glasser in *Schools Without Failure* developed a "rational therapy" strategy which treats students with respect and dignity and which avoids failure situations.

These strategies all indicate an undeniable need for every school to have an in-service program so that each teacher can find and develop those understandings, behaviors, and approaches most appropriate to him. In-service is the only place where former teachers go about "becoming good teachers." It cannot be done prior to the experience of working with students. Administrators, too, need such assistance if they are expected to be part of a problem solving curriculum and to administer to its needs.

In-Service as a Key Teacher Resource

There are at present more than a million teachers in American elementary and secondary classrooms who are not adequately prepared to become effective problem solving–team teachers. Few have had exposure to the concept in action. There are also thousands and thousands of school administrators who have no perception of how to translate the concept into practice. Unfortunately, too many of these persons will never re-enter colleges and universities to acquire proficiency in problem solving. Many of them, teachers for 20 or more years, are busy looking forward to retirement day. Under the circumstances, the in-service route seems the most promising for most teachers in American schools.

An in-service program to retrain teachers in problem solving skills and methods can take several approaches. There can be short conferences and workshops held within the school system and which draw upon higher education persons. At best, the meetings could span an entire summer to give teachers opportunities to become reoriented along the lines of a new concept. Perhaps the schools could work toward securing a foundation grant for re-educating their teachers. But just offering a single working conference or seminar as *the* in-service retraining is definitely not adequate; for most individuals, follow-up sessions are mandatory. For example, workshops within school systems can be supplemented by additional ones held on college campuses. In this second setting, teams of teachers can learn about the problem solving concept with the understanding that teacher education professors will work with their schools *throughout the school year* — particularly in implementing preplans and course outlines developed at the on-campus workshops.

Prior to any large-scale workshops held by school system or college, it is advisable to bring together the educational administrators from the schools to help them establish both a commitment and an understanding of the problem solving concept before any plans for implementation are discussed and drawn. It is sadly true that many administrators — just as teachers — are not really committed to an inquiry approach in education. Such a hope for commitment would be unrealistic — at least in the foreseeable future. But, on the other hand, it is possible to have a rather large network of school systems working in this direction with the idea that their influence will permeate outward into other school systems, setting an example to follow.

It falls to the colleges and universities to work cooperatively in identifying within school systems innovative and confident teachers and administrators. Once some have been identified, it is then time to start arranging workshops.

Staff Relationships

Finding the teaching and administrative staff for a problem solving curriculum and having them work out leadership roles are key problems. There is a rather wide and varied amount of opinion as to whether or not differentiated staffing, according to hierarchial status positions, is desirable over staffing in terms of each individual assuming leadership when needed and followership on still other occasions. Each structure has advantages. It is true, in either case, that someone must assume major responsibility for getting a group organized, oriented, and started toward problem solving. Thus, many administrators prefer to designate one teacher on the team as the lead or major teacher who assumes key leadership roles. The underlying psychology, perhaps, is that what is everyone's business is no one's business, and things will not be done unless someone is held directly accountable for implementation procedures.

While this may be especially helpful at the start, there are also distinct advantages in peer-relationship staffing in problem solving–team teaching. When people work within a peer-relationship basis, it means that leadership evolves or emerges at various times and will fall back into a followship role for that same person on other occasions. No person is equally capable in all types of leadership situations. The peer relationship in staffing, allowing for unevenness, has the strength of improving human relationships: Each participant feels that he is a person of worth and that he is in a position to make contributions to the team. This does not assume that all the team members are equally proficient in all areas. But it does assume that when an individual possesses unusual capabilities and leadership which enable him to emerge as a leader during a given moment, then the process somehow enhances his own feeling of worth. Inevitably, the same process enhances the relationships he has with others on the teaching team.

204

Another advantage of peer relationship staffing is that it creates a professional and cooperative environment in which the entire group is continuously taking responsibility for the total problem solving project in that each member at some time is holding the others accountable for their share of the responsibilities. Of course, some individuals will make greater contributions to the total effort than others, but this fact does not mean that those making the lesser or less frequent contributions should be looked upon as inferior teachers.

This type of staffing also helps each teacher in realizing that he has a followship as well as a leadership role.

In light of the above factors, the writer is strongly committed to the concept of peer relationships in team teaching — with the understanding that someone will always be needed to get the group started. Once it has begun, though, this same individual may move back into a followship role, and the specially trained team will be challenged to apply the ideas and skills hopefully acquired through preservice and in-service training.

BIBLIOGRAPHY

Baker, Eva L. and James Popham, *Expanding Dimensions of Instructional Objectives.* Englewood Cliffs, N.J.: Prentice-Hall, 1973.

Campbell, Clyde, *The Community School: Mott Foundation Newsletter* IX, 3 (November 1970).

Citizenship Education Study, *Problem Solving.* Detroit: Wayne State University Press, 1957.

Combs, Arthur W., ed., *Florida Studies in Helping Professions.* Gainsville: University of Florida Press, 1966.

Glasser, William, *Schools Without Failure.* New York: Harper and Row, 1969.

Good, Carter V., *The Dictionary of Education.* New York: McGraw-Hill Book Co., 1973.

Goodlad, John and Frances Klein, *Behind the Classroom Door.* Worthington, Ohio: Charles A. Jones Publishing Co., 1970.

Gordon, Thomas, *Group-Centered Leadership.* Boston: Houghton Mifflin Co., 1955.

Harris, Ben, *In-Service Education.* Englewood Cliffs, N.J.: Prentice-Hall, 1969.

Holt, John, *How Children Fail.* New York: Dell Publishing Co., 1964.

Jacobson, Paul B. and others, *The Principalship: New Perspectives.* Englewood Cliffs, N.J.: Prentice-Hall, 1973.

Kelley, Earl C., *Education for What Is Real.* New York: Harper and Bros., 1957.

————, *In Defense of Youth.* Englewood Cliffs, N.J.: Prentice-Hall, 1965.

————, *The Workshop Way of Learning.* New York: Harper and Bros., 1951.

Richey, Robert W., *Planning for Teachers.* New York: McGraw-Hill Book Co., 1973.

Rogers, Carl, *Freedom to Learn.* Columbus, Ohio: Charles E. Merrill Publishing Co., 1969.

Rosenthal, Robert and Lenore F. Jacobson, "Teacher Expectations for the Disadvantaged," *Scientific American* CCXVIII, 4 (April 1968).

Waetjen, Walter B., ed. *Human Variability and Learning.* Washington, D.C.: Association for Supervision and Curriculum Development, 1961.

"What Research Says About Teaching and Learning," *Phi Delta Kappan* XXXIX (March 1968).

Chapter 9. Complementary Facilities

DR. WAYNE JENNINGS, *guest writer**

How effective instructional practices can be depends primarily upon the talents and experiences of the instructor. Of secondary importance is the equipment at the instructor's disposal and the facilities in which he must render his services. But, facilities — though secondary — can either complement or complicate educational processes.

Traditionally school buildings have been constructed with separate and isolated classrooms resembling little individual "stockades of learning" characterized by dictated, compulsory learning practices. In their earliest setting in our country, these rooms were barricaded little "birch-rod centers" which bore little, if any, relationship to one another and in which mutual recognition among teachers of each other's talents and contributions to the whole child and mutual agreement on the major goals of the school. Instead, there seemed to have been one objective: Stuff the students with facts and knowledge based on the myth of 100 percent retention and effective learning transfer and application.

It is just as true that some of these isolated classrooms were blessed with master teachers of superb talents. Despite adverse facilities, these educators — only a small number — somehow conceived and initiated programs which generated excitement and which culminated in the positive learning outcomes advocated in this text through implementation of a problem solving curriculum. They and their students planned and investigated pertinent subjects of mutual interest and of social importance, conducted research for information with which to evaluate the important questions, and deliberated *together* in devising solutions. Such activities were carried out in isolation because these few teachers could hardly penetrate the fortress-like classrooms of their colleagues without causing major disruptions. Another teacher's talents or materials were virtually inaccessible, and one's own concentrated facilities tended to discourage any sort of small-group activity in or out of the classroom.

It is impossible to provide outstanding instructional programs under an inadequate roof of discreetly partitioned rooms. Indeed, with appropriate

---

*Dr. Jennings, director of the St. Paul, Minn. Open School, is a past president of the National Association for Core Curriculum, and a former core teacher and curriculum consultant for the St. Paul public schools. Dr. Jennings was assisted in writing this chapter by Earl Daniels and Nancy Pirsig.

equipment and facilities, educational programs can improve immensely in effectiveness. Competent teachers can instruct more effectively, too, in well-ventilated, acoustically controlled, and well-lighted learning laboratories than in the confines of dimly lit, clamor-ridden, and isolated cells.

The problems experienced in a school building with built-in adverse conditions handicap the learning procedures and outcomes. A few of the worst conditions are readily identifiable to most teachers who have functioned under such physical diversity: distracting and distressing effects of too much noise, interference and "static" from small student groups competing with each other for audibility within a limited area, and absence of acoustical measures which would help to insulate sounds. Other distressing elements are the inaccessibility to resource materials or, still worse, the lack of them; the long process of acquiring learning materials; maintenance of the room's physical equipment; and repair of audiovisual and other accessory learning equipment through antiquated school requisition systems. Unknown to the public, many teachers use personal funds and their own resourceful talents to repair the many breakdowns continually harassing their patience and morale. Everything from a faulty pencil sharpener, a torn blackout shade, a broken sash cord on a window, a steadily blinking fluorescent light fixture, and dozens of other distracting elements conspire to reduce instructional effectiveness. These and many other factors can increase tension, catapult frustration, disrupt teacher–student rapport, and create an on-going source of discontent.

Many schools today are being planned as architecturally open schools. In such schools students are able to move freely, seeking and acquiring resource materials. Teachers in these schools are able to group and regroup their students to facilitate various learning purposes and to promote an environment of mobility, interaction, and alertness. Such seating and room-size flexibility features are compatible and complement whatever instructional reasons or objectives which already exist. There is a campus-like atmosphere in an open school which gives students a sense of freedom to self-direct their courses of action.

Of course, architecturally open schools in themselves are no guarantee of modern instruction, and there are many cases of treadmill types of subject centered curriculums in the physical open-school setting which still rely on the teacher stuffing information into students' receiving apparatus.

Planning a New Facility

All too often schools are located where land is available. It would be far more advantageous to locate schools accessible or adjacent to activities in the community — or at least near major transportation arteries.

207

Schools of tomorrow will be full-fledged community centers for lifelong learning with day–night, year-round activities for all ages. The days of the 3 p.m. lock-up are numbered, and educators are beginning to realize this. Public facilities are a major investment for communities; as such, they *must* yield major benefits. Thus schools can no longer be stuck in remote neighborhoods with locations dictated solely by the walking range of its children. The location of shopping centers and other institutions and agencies are usually planned carefully in terms of accessibility and placement within areas of intense activity.

It is pedagogically sound that students use the resources and learning experiences tailor-made and provided for by the community. In common-sense terms, it breaks down to learning how to live and adjust through observation and active participation in a "life-learning" laboratory. What is needed today is a physiological relationship with the life-giving pursuits and activities of a community rather than the obscure and tired imagery produced by lectures, filmstrips, verbal theorizing, and stilted discussions culminating in a "postponed visit" to the community after a student has graduated. It is reckless educational procedure, indeed, to turn the kids loose suddenly — without prior experience or exposure in the community. What meager preparation was offered in school for living in the community is soon dismissed from student minds because it was taught theory-wise and was without follow-up use of the community's business operations, public libraries, employment agencies, public health centers, recreational centers, citizen and civic service centers, courts, police departments, theaters, cultural centers, museums, and the remainder of an inexhaustible list of opportunities. "Use" as intended in this discussion does not mean simple, routine field trips; it covers investigations, reports, interviews, evaluations, and classroom presentations of problem solving experiences and it includes the techniques students use in their confrontations with the public in the work-a-day world and in their leisure pursuits.

It is like standing in the rain: A student cannot help but become wetted by community activities and he cannot avoid stimulation from the appetite for life and for the prospects of becoming an accepted member of the adult world. After such an intimate learning experience, the student begins to think about himself: He begins to experience moments of solitude, meditation, and ever deepening concern regarding the future. He is thinking and, in his way, learning how to study and solve some of his own problems.

It is essential to accept the critical nature of locating a school site where it will be most appropriate and accessible to both the school's and the community's mutual benefit. Schools can be located in business or downtown areas. They can be on major bus or other transportation routes, near shopping centers or freeway exits; they can utilize air rights by using the space over freeways or the joint occupancy of space over schools; property is precious. Schools can be near the areas of community activities for other reasons. One stop can provide both consumer shopping and involvement in the educational, recreational, cultural, and civic centers.

Interior Design

Emphasis should be placed on designing and creating a built-in and stimulating learning atmosphere with physical interiors and features compatible with the learning concepts generated and inherent in curriculum reorganization through problem solving.

An interdisciplinary study of problems does not necessarily imply that there would be no separation of subject areas within a school. It is not old-fashioned to locate materials and resources so that they are convenient and organized for students and teachers. Schools will probably continue to have the usual departments for a long time—though the names are changing (for example: the humanities course is sometimes renamed "communications"). But there will be more teamwork and working relationships among the subject areas. Though still physically separated, subject areas will be related—even unified—in problem solving situations. For example, if a class is working on American Indian life, a group may construct wooden looms in the shop while artistic needs are answered by the art department. Thus, the project would be interrelated between two subject areas.

In some schools learning will actually be integrated. For example, in a bread-baking unit, students would learn cooking, math in measuring the ingredients, science in terms of why the dough rises or fails to rise, discipline in following directions, verbal skills in decision-making, and self-confidence through their perceptions.

To an increasing degree, especially as independently planned study periods are determined by students, various subject areas will require additional space for student use individually. But the situation must function smoothly so as not to interfere and disrupt a class which might be in the midst of a crucial discussion when individual students come to work on a particular project. Privacy areas for instruction or meetings must be provided, or at least facilities should be flexible to the extent of being closed off without shutting out other students who need access to the resource center or open lab. Glass can separate and yet provide visual supervision.

209

Materials for instruction are already monumental in quantity and they continue to multiply. Thus, storage and display space must be provided. There are increasing instances of schools in which their students exceed in knowledge and experience the resources which they have available. The kaleidoscopic interests of today's students are further evidence of the need to find space within a school for housing the incredible range of needed resources and materials.

School areas must serve many purposes. The day when a student's industrial arts participation was limited to boys at both junior and senior high schools is over. Industrial arts should be offered to students at all grade levels and of both sexes and on a vastly expanded front: construction of equipment and formulation of project ideas to enhance the school; student peer teaching through the coordinating of their combined interests and abilities; instruction of younger students by older ones to give leadership opportunities for the extensive energy levels of teen-agers and to have models for the younger children to emulate; students assisting in school maintenance functions, thereby reducing willful acts of theft and vandalism. Industrial arts should also promote and provide student layouts, designs, and printing of school yearbooks; it should handle photography, drama announcements, tickets, bulletins, and other functions in the past delegated to professional services. Using professional services is not only extravagant for the school budget; it also robs students of tailor-made learning projects.

The industrial arts facilities, therefore, can be quite extensive, and the design of its area should receive careful planning. Some might require separation due to high levels of noise, smoke inhalation factors, and offensive fumes and odors. Most likely adequate soundproofing and ventilating systems could greatly alleviate the architectural expense of separating these areas while at the same time maintaining an integrated, industrialized, and modern factory-type facility with its interrelated departments. Alcoves within a larger area can integrate various industrialized functions and operations.

From the industrial arts example, some picture of a far more extensively arranged school complex should be emerging to supplement the qualitatively different kinds of learning experiences possible with a problem solving curriculum. Learning is by experience or by doing real jobs. Learning in shop is more than operating a machine. It involves planning, thinking, decision-making, and selection of materials; it is workmanship and pride; and it is also some math, English, technology, career education, science, and reading.

The school, it should be emphasized, is *not* in the business of producing sanding blocks, breadboards, and dustpans. Today's industrial arts project requires many machines and processes ranging from simple to complex. Students are beginning to be taught new operative skills ranging from mechanical, hydraulic, electronic, modern printing processes to chemical and plastic injection molding apparatus and the latest in photographic equipment.

Teachers may still isolate a particular skill or teach how a certain type of material is best handled, but such things will no longer be performed in large classes with every student duplicating the same assignment at the same time. Such assignments, though essential, can be put onto filmstrips or taught by advanced students or teachers' aides at a particular time *when the need arises*. Thus, the entire industrial arts program is being reshaped to allow students to work at their own natural momentum.

The whole approach adds dimensions to a student's thinking about generalized abilities and his own sense of "can-ness" and it helps produce people who can see what is actually involved in running and maintaining a technological society.

The home economics department would operate much like industrial arts—that is, for boys as well as for girls and with no age levels excluded. The department can play a role similar to industrial arts in servicing the school. It might explore some interesting features which would be natural and spontaneous learning lab experiences. Perhaps its students could explore the purchasing of materials and eventually design and sew choir robes for the school group. They might cooperate with the music and commercial art departments in designing the robes.

The cooking part of home economics might work on seasonal or ethnic luncheon treats and other specialties and also assist the school kitchen personnel in the daily preparation of school lunches. It is much dependent on the architect's and the builder's integrity and talents in physically fashioning a home economics lab conducive to these needs and plans.

There is an overwhelmingly natural learning process involved in the integration of subject matter areas for the solution of problems. The integration encourages a team promoting and advertising their events and activities throughout the school year. The art department could handle seasonal decorations throughout the building. English, social studies, art, typing, and graphic arts areas could provide talents in journalism, advertising, and publishing to launch a school newspaper. Its circulation and subscription processes could be handled by the English, social studies, math, and business departments.

The math department could provide statistical data wherever needed and assist in the inventory of the school's physical assets; the science department might furnish and maintain plant life and flower arrangements throughout the building.

This is but a limited list of suggested responsibilities enabling departments to contribute to the life, functions, and events during the school year. It is obvious that the typical skimpily furnished and meagerly equipped school subdivided into tiny rooms—each shut away from the other's resources of skills and talents and focused on packing in facts by the spoonful—will never do.

James Coleman wrote in the February 1972 issue of *Psychology Today* that our society today is information rich and responsibility poor for youths. In former times it was information poor and responsibility poor, and schools understandably concentrated on information and knowledge in their earlier days. But it is now outdated. Youths need responsibility, tasks, functions; school facilities must complement these needs.

In a problem solving educational program nothing should be overlooked which could supply students with learning experiences, and good facilities play an enabling role. Audiovisual equipment must be accessible for easy student use. Electrical outlets need to be placed at frequent intervals; in "wall-less" buildings, floor receptacles or drops from the ceiling are necessary. In addition, there must be raceways or ducts for future wiring to accommodate new electrical devices: computer terminals, responders, a profusion of teaching machines, dial access retrieval systems, wireless instruction, self-tutorial booths, and who knows what else.

Learning materials like books, magazines, films, and multimedia tools must be vastly expanded and updated in tomorrow's schools. Present materials in school libraries and resource centers are often meager or simply obsolete. If students wanted to investigate pollution, for example, it is likely that the school library would have a scarcity of materials on the subject. If the students consulted *Reader's Guide to Periodic Literature,* they would probably have to go to the public library to find the magazine articles listed. Furthermore, pollution is an enormous and involved subject area which divides into categories like noise, air, water, and litter. It is entirely likely that school materials would be totally inadequate.

If one goes beyond conventional sources like books, magazines, pamphlets, films, and recordings, he would make the sad discovery that few schools are really equipped to provide modern avenues to learning. To overcome the situation, school facilities must be prepared to greatly expand the amounts of space, shelving, and facilities for study. A subject such as pollution illustrates the kinds of materials which must be available in schools or, at the least, assessible. Television networks have produced over 50 programs on the subject of pollution. These programs should be available within school buildings.

Storage and display space represent major challenges until microfilm technology is more widespread. There exists a great need for storage creativity, a direct and meaningful challenge to architects who plan school interior design and furnishings. Shelving and cupboard doors, for example, should be versatile not only to house materials, but also to provide other uses as well. Cupboard doors might be made out of bulletin board material. Shelves particularly should be adjustable.

Carpeting and other acoustical features are essential for modern educational buildings. Not only are they cheaper in the long-run, but they also provide a more favorable learning environment. Tomorrow's schools and some already in existence have students moving about and meeting in large and small groups. To avoid strategic places from becoming intolerable noise traps, acoustical treatment is necessary.

Air conditioning should be strongly considered from the standpoint of outside noise and air pollution and from the likely prospect that schools will be on a 12-month basis eventually. Where air conditioning cannot be installed, provision should be made for its later installation.

Many schools have failed to provide adequate provision for darkening so that audiovisual devices are practical. The new arclamp projectors and special devices are not yet in common use, nor are they sufficiently developed to reduce the need for careful planning of light control, both artificial and natural. It is extremely frustrating to view a motion picture or opaque projections on a washed-out screen because the room cannot be sufficiently darkened. Almost as bad are total darkout rooms in which the contrast of a brilliantly lighted screen is harsh to the eyes and distracting. Light control is frequently found to be inadequate in schools, and educators continue to fail to perceive its influence upon instructional effectiveness and flexibility.

Physical blueprints designed specifically for problem solving-team teaching facilities will require careful planning and innovative ideas with respect to sizes, shapes, capacities, and arrangements of classrooms, alcoves, hallways, stairways, multimedia and multipurpose rooms, drama areas, large auditorium and gymnasium space, and other needs. Students will be constantly working in various sizes of groups. At times, students will leave the large groups and work as individuals, requiring a private area or "turf" wherein they can lay out materials and return from time to time for more work.

However, private study areas cannot be wasted or abused by vacancies

213

caused by student absenteeism, infrequent working habits, or total abandonment of projects. Private "turf" areas should be constructed so that they are versatile and adjustable enough to accommodate several students at one time who may be working cooperatively on a given project. In such areas, it should be possible to move walls without summoning a carpenter or the custodian. Furniture too must be portable and innovative in construction so it can be shifted freely as the area changes from individual study to a small-group session, for example. The emphasis is on multi-use interiors and furnishings to conserve space and maintain an integrated facility. Schools are looking for ingenious innovations and, perhaps, even revolutionary creations. For example, folding walls may be useful, but there will be new ideas in wall portability that will surpass them.

Careful selection of audiovisual equipment is important. All too often money is spent on equipment of poor quality and features. For example, using a small, home-type slide projector in a large group setting of 200 to 300 students is tantamount to using a flashlight to highlight an Olympic event. The small slide projector belongs in the small classroom. In the case of large-group viewing, the arclamp slide projector *with an appropriate lens* is essential.

Few rooms in today's schools are designed for multimedia viewing which involves two, three, or even four projectors. Such rooms simply do not have sufficient projecting space and the postage-stamp screens are another headache. Large pull-down screens and the more modern concave stretch nylon types are better. Large, uncluttered walls are excellent for projecting. Electrical pointers can spot-light a feature on the screen with an arrow. Responder systems built into desks enable students to comment or ask questions. A first-rate quality sound system is essential. Many schools today are burdened with public address systems which are inferior to a cheerleader's megaphone. Inadequate communications systems harass rather than communicate with an audience; somewhere the message is lost in the noise. It remains amazing, for example, that $300,000 can be spent to build an auditorium and only $500 allocated for sound projection—thus nullifying the entire purpose.

Typical furniture for problem solving situations would be large countertops or tables. Needed are large desk-type adjustable sloping tops and tables with built-in leaves and pull-out writing boards, one at each side, on which to place supplementary materials. In subject centered schools, small desks were adequate since they carried a few books and supplies. Students in problem solving activities will be laying out many materials,

214

constructing charts and diagrams, making posters, or reorganizing piles of research data or materials.

There must be tailor-made provision for facilities in problem solving projects which are designed to stimulate student use—day and night. The facilities must be carefully designed and laid out to enable a student to be absent all day long on field projects, out of town on further research, or involved in a "drop everything" project. These situations are comparable to those in the daily living of the working adult. Such students must be allowed entrance into the school in the evenings to continue work on their undisturbed projects. Some students may be at work during mornings of the school year and only be able to work in the school building in the afternoon and evening hours. Thus, school materials must be accessible.

Such an area is more of a home base for the student working on problem solving activities—far different from the private "turf" area mentioned earlier which served both individual and group needs. The more permanent home base area would need ample size in case a group teams up on a specific problem or project. Adequate cupboards and cabinets must be provided for storage of resource materials, tools, craft items, and student materials. Some security provisions and locker facilities should also be included.

When students team up on a project, it is helpful to provide a small committee room for their use. Perhaps an intercom arrangement would be necessary for teacher-student communication and monitoring devices (glass wall, for example) for teacher supervision if the area is to be enclosed to avert distractions.

Generous bulletin board space and display cases should be placed throughout the entire building, displaying various student research and achievements from all areas and departments.

The *openness* of the school building should be as stimulating and as appealing as today's shopping center complexes. These huge buildings feature a centralized courtyard punctuated by decorative flower and plant arrangements, spectacular fountains, and aquariums. Open space provides students with more interaction and freedom to move about instead of confinement to classroom cells. The courtyard or commons interior should be centralized, providing students with some panoramic view of the school's varied activities and resources to stimulate curiosity and active participation. This is an ideal natural force at work in helping guide the students by encouraging self-direction. Walking around in such openness, students encounter activities and discover friends or acquaintances. Such a central, open commons can house the cafeteria and refresh-

215

ment stands. In the area would be lounging furniture and tables. Many students who simply cannot work in the quiet, formal atmosphere of a conventional library would use a "Times Square" kind of library.

Teachers' lounges and work areas can be strategically located in the immediate resource and materials area for easy accessibility by both teacher and student. It might include also some space provision for private teacher facilities for research, study, and student counseling. There would probably be a need for faculty, student council, and advisory council conference space.

Space for community people within the school conclave might require an area since it may be in constant use by PTA, teachers' aides, volunteers, social agency and human relations people, and other community persons. If the school is a true community school, then policies of cooperation must be resolved so that community members can use various school facilities.

The school's auditorium, theater, and small drama facilities should carry a heavy yearly schedule of events—used by professionals, parents and community members, and students and teachers for dramas, concerts, musicals, choral offerings, talent shows, school plays, movies, special events, gymnastic exhibitions, guest speakers, and general public meetings.

Renovating Facilities

Older facilities may not be as efficient and as effective as properly designed new buildings, but many of the physical, resource, and innovative features described earlier can be duplicated.

If the facility location is not accessible to community resources, it is wise to purchase a bus or several mini-buses—making them readily available on the school premises so that learning is not limited and confined to the boundaries of a conventional classroom.

A cosmetic rehabilitation of an old school or a commercial building will not do—it takes more than paint. Walls must be punched out, more space provided to open up the space and mobility. In many places walls can be removed without having the roof collapse. In others, columns can be left or installed. High ceilings can be lowered, making space for piping and electrical wiring. Electrical outlets and lighting fixtures may have to be changed or added; rooms might need rearranging; stairways and hallways would need modification; windows and doors would need changing; and other interior changes have to be made to complement a problem solving-team teaching learning environment. In sound, older buildings it may be necessary to gut the building, leaving only the exterior walls and supporting columns. School and commercial buildings have been made functional and attractive by reducing the building to its shell and totally restructuring the interior.

School programs which are cramped for space may be forced to explore the purchase of an adjacent house and use it as a school annex or to rent a commercial space in the immediate area. It may be possible to make arrangements with the public library or some other community agency which does not have heavy use during school hours.

If the budget permits, older structures can be developed along the lines suggested earlier in the chapter. However, tight budgeting will force priority decisions.

One of the most unusual illustrations of a limited budget and tight time-table was that of preparing the St. Paul (Minn.) Open School for occupancy in *13 days* and with a budget of $25,000. The school is an example of the curriculum and methods advocated in this book; it exists as a research, demonstration unit of the St. Paul public school system and it serves 500 kindergarten to twelfth-grade students. The building—a 45-year old factory—was acquired just two weeks before school was to open.

The initial step was to seek out volunteers sufficiently dedicated to work without pay. Such a labor force was not difficult to mobilize, with some 200 students and parents anxious and eager to make such a school a reality. What is more, they enjoyed working together in such an adventur- ous enterprise. There was a spirit of enthusiasm and pride not found in many companies and firms with salaried employees. The reason for such a phenomenal response was simply the feeling of working for themselves— that is, their own enterprise. Despite the dependence on volunteer help, it was still necessary to hire a person of competent managerial qualities. Such a person was found among the volunteers. The project was further aided by some token work from the central school system's labor force of plumbers, electricians, carpenters, and other tradesmen.

The building project was a natural and tremendous learning experience for the students as well as their parents, and the learning outcomes cannot be overemphasized. The hired man who superintended the entire operation worked closely with the school principal and other lead persons. There was, in fact, a lead person for every floor level and every department: electrical, plumbing, carpentry, painting, and general miscellaneous work. The man who superintended the whole renovation operation—competent and knowledgeable in architectural and constructional operations—was recep- tive to ideas and suggestions of others and he managed to utilize all the volunteer talents. He possessed leadership qualities that managed volun- teer help by instilling a sense of inspiration, enthusiasm, and cooperation among the volunteers.

Students and parents as the volunteer labor force in renovating an old building found a landslide of tailor-made learning experiences, rich with profusion and challenge. With the strike of the first hammer blow, the school's unique learning curriculum began—even though not one classroom was ready. What a golden educational opportunity also for the faculty and administrative staff, not to mention the tremendous budget savings in man-hours of work.

The St. Paul Open School renovation project was an achievement shared by students, parents, teachers, school tradesmen, and even innocent bystanders who got pressed into service. It was a first-hand learning experience of enormous educational significance and fulfillment; it was implemented in natural environmental surroundings and performed in an atmosphere of harmonious participation by a large group differing widely in socioeconomic, ethnic, and racial backgrounds. Despite the project's enormity, the job of renovating the building was finished in 13 days at a cost considerably below a comparable job by professional building and remodeling contractors.

But then, the original idea behind the St. Paul Open School was sound. It was conceived and initiated by a group of St. Paul parents who were seeking alternatives in education to reach the young people; many parents recognized frankly that some of the children were turned off by the regular public school system. They sought out educators who were knowledgeable in the philosophy and concepts of open-school learning approaches and techniques.

In accord with the original idea for alternatives in education, the school curriculum and open-school atmosphere continues to be run by a compatible staff oriented towards the needs of young people. Students enroll in the Open School voluntarily. They have actually booed when holidays have closed the school and they have cheered when they find out it is going to be open. The students and their parents share, accept, and belong to the Open School because it was devised, designed, and operated to fit their peculiar needs and convictions. The parents—and also their children—were disenchanted with the public school curriculums and with the learning and disciplinary procedures. They enrolled in the Open School, filling its 500-student capacity and leaving a waiting list of more than 700 more.

Students in the St. Paul Open School were either chased from or dropped out of the more rigid, traditional public schools. Since the time these youngsters enrolled voluntarily in the alternative Open School, they have been attending daily with a tenacity heretofore not characteristic of their original behavior in the public schools. The change in student behavior can be considered a restoration of learning desire and directly attributable to a major change in educational organization and philosophy.

For 50 years at least educators have neglected the principal educational commitment of this nation: That all American children are to be educated in accordance with each individual's unique potentialities, interests, and needs. This is not a vague curbside commitment to be shrugged off for another 50 years. The commitment includes all children of low socioeconomic status and of all ethnic and racial cultures. But somehow a preposterous and unpardonable enigma in our nation's educational goals and pursuits has resisted the broad commitment; the lower socioeconomic, ethnic, and racial cultures were not provided the same educational opportunities as was the Caucasian race. This educational injustice has had a negative influence on American minority cultures—most obviously in political, social, economic, esthetic, and cultural disadvantages and inequalities.

But then the favored majority have done not much better. On the whole their children have received a graded, bookish, lifeless education denying individuality and fostering instead a standardized learning environment which ignored the uniqueness of the individual. Now, education is registering some second thoughts about the entire system after decades of small efforts and a long period of upheaval. It makes sense, then, that as curriculums begin to reflect this commitment to educate *all* American children, the physical facilities and equipment must complement the resultant learning experiences.

This chapter ends with some first year examples of cross-disciplinary projects at the St. Paul Open School.

Ecology Project

This project involved air pollution in the industrial area around the St. Paul Open School.

Six students attending Joe Nathan's ecology class, noting that "It smells around here," decided to attempt to find out why, and what could be done about it. In the process they covered traditional subject matter disciplines of political science and government, speech, sociology, science, law and math (the comparative measurement of smell).

In a walk around the neighborhood, the class determined that the worst polluters were a paper manufacturer, a vinegar company, and a meat packing company. With this information they went to a college-student-financed, consumer action organization, which suggested research into anti-pollution laws, and a lawyer to aid them in any action they wished to take.

From the start, the students had tried to talk with the firms but repeated attempts had resulted in being put off for various reasons and finally the statement, "Don't call us, we'll call you." In December, the group filed complaints with the St. Paul Pollution Control Agency (PCA). Little happened.

The class then decided to circulate petitions against the offending firms. Besides the school community, they canvassed businesses and homes in the area affected by the smells, and learned why many small businessmen feared to support such a move openly (i.e., the barber who said the paper company executives would stop getting their hair cut there if he signed. . .). The students also testified at state hearings on guidelines for air pollution control in the state of Minnesota.

In January the PCA told the class it didn't have the money to do studies on the firms complained against. In early February, the class decided to tell a local newspaper reporter what it had learned and done; the PCA then told the reporter it *was* doing studies. As a result, the three firms and another meat packer were found in violation of St. Paul's anti-pollution laws and were ordered to submit implementation plans for cutting down on odors.

The story made front-page lead headlines at the point and the class learned dramatically the power of the press and publicity to help get something done.

Prehistoric Life, Indians, and a Trip to the Badlands

Mike Johnson had a class in prehistoric life for children 10 to 12 years old, which involved science and art; the group discussed doing other things besides reading and talking, and came up with building a dinosaur. Working in the art department, the class designed and constructed a papier-mache triceratops over a chicken wire frame. They had to figure out what materials they needed, in what quantity, and at what cost. About seven youngsters made up the core group, with seven others taking part occasionally.

At the same time, Joe Nathan was teaching Indian studies to a multi-aged group (7-18). From the suggestion of one student, the two classes decided to take a trip to the Badlands in South Dakota—an interesting geologic formation where many prehistoric fossils can be found, near two reservations of the Dakota (Sioux) nation. A side trip to the Pine Ridge (S.D.) Sioux reservation was included.

Twenty-eight students plus one teacher, one aid and one volunteer made the trip October 10th through 13th. Planning and making the trip involved many different subjects, such as home ec (planning and cooking meals), consumer studies (getting the best buys on food); experiments in human liberation and cross-age cooperation (in that all-aged children, from 7 to 18, and both sexes were active in all phases of the planning and doing—and, in fact, the younger children taught the older ones how to put up tents); geology (fossil studies, Badlands formation); sociology and history (Indian studies, past and present). As a side effect, the four day trip was a lesson in intercultural living, with five black, six Ojibway, and 17 white students, from a wide range of socio-economic backgrounds, taking part.

Extensive evaluation was made following the trip, and detailed suggestions written for future school trips.

Civil War Project

Four students who started a Civil War class with Joe Nathan at the beginning of the year drove in spring on a nine-day trip to Gettysburg, Pa. In addition to the traditional historical studies, the class members have used math and woodworking in constructing a papier-mache model of the Gettysburg battlefield; have planned routes for the trip while studying the geography of the area to be covered; have practiced practical English usage in the form of writing letters for information, accommodations, and seeking speaking engagements along the way; have consulted with students from the Badlands trip to get practical information on planning and traveling; and will have the experience of living, traveling and eating with one another toward a common purpose. They have not only figured out what their expenses will be, but have earned the money themselves through bake sales and five speaking engagements at colleges along the way. Students are 11, 16 and 17 years old.

An interesting aspect of the study of history in this class is that it has been done through many sources rather than a single textbook or two. Class members went to the Minnesota Historical Society to read old newspapers from the time of the Civil War and have read and discussed various accounts of battles and other incidents. Thus, they have learned in addition to the "facts" of the war, the "fact" that history is simply a composite of different people's views and versions of what happened in the past—some of higher quality than others.

The Golden Rectangle

The Greeks knew of the "golden rectangle" and used its proportions in much of their famed architecture; modern-day architects use its ratios, perhaps unconsciously; the perfect spiral found within it shows up in such natural forms as tree leaves, pine cones, acorns and the chambered nautilus. At the Open School, student Anne Lynch, who learned about the "golden rectangle," decided to construct one with the aide of math teacher Jeff Cottle and art teacher Pat Fitzgerald. The structure, which Ann built out of 4' by 1-1/3' plywood, represents the fact that the archtype of spirals begins with a rectangle with sides proportioned 1.6 to 1, which is scaled off into smaller and smaller equal rectangles.

Swimming Pool Count

During a two week period, several children went to the nearby YMCA swimming pool every day and counted how many children from the school used it. Two or three girls, 5 and 8 years old, then plotted a chart in the math department with the help of Terry Johnson, an aide. Younger children who helped with the counting learned to count accurately and to record numbers. Those who worked on the graph learned graphing and also discussed possible reasons why more children swam on some days than others, and attempted to discern if there was any pattern in swimming habits.

BIBLIOGRAPHY

Note: Several standard texts on school construction are stuffy in presentation and lack an understanding of modern learning theory and practices. The texts listed below are distincting not of this mold and are inexpensive.

American Association of School Administrators, *Schools for America.* Washington, D.C.: AASA, 1967. Much imaginative thought and excellent photography.

————, *Open-Space Schools.* Washington, D.C.: AASA, 1971. Key concepts, relationships, planning, and outstanding examples of open-space schools.

Council of Educational Facilities Planners has several splendid publications as well as filmstrips or slides of outstanding schools. Write for a current list to: 29 West Woodruff Ave., Columbus, Ohio 43210.

Educational Facilities Laboratory has many excellent, even extraordinary publications on facilities, e.g. early childhood, cafeteria, library, auditoriums, open-space buildings. Write for a complete list to: 377 Madison Ave., New York, N.Y.

Loeffler, Margaret H., *The Prepared Environment.* Oklahoma City: Trustees of the Casady School, 1967. Excellent diagrammatic and schematic layout sketches indicating space relationships and other points.

Chapter 10.   Evaluation on a Broad Basis

Limited Concept of Evaluation

Evaluation is one of the most underused and abused tools of education, even though education is concerned with what has been learned in a given situation and evaluation is the chief means for determining learning outcomes. It is commonplace that educational projects will be carefully planned and implemented, but that their final evaluative phases will turn out to be superficial rhetoric affixed to another paper report or study and doomed to collect dust in some file.

In the traditional subject centered school where major emphasis is upon mastery of content and on the transmission of the cultural heritage, evaluation is a means whereby the least capable students are eliminated. For example, of every 100 students entering the formal school program, not more than about five percent were regarded by nature or nurture as likely candidates for the rigors of higher education. Little interest has been demonstrated for the education of the remaining 95 percent dropped at different stages of the educational system. When evaluation is used as a selective process to determine who will pursue education past high school graduation, it can have dire consequences — particularly when this selective process takes place *before* the age of 12. In this situation, children whose parents are from the working class are, by and large, eliminated and only students from homes of professional people are permitted to pursue education beyond this magic age of 12. A child from a middle-class, professional background has a clear advantage in language alone over the child from a working-class one. Traditionally, the less gifted students without language facility have rarely been motivated to do what was considered possible by their teachers. Such students were not willing to work along lines approved by teachers to earn long-term goals; at best, these young people accepted learning tasks set by the schools with a minimum of rebellion.

Evaluation in problem solving is much more complicated and involved: Opportunities are provided for the full development of each student, enabling him to live effectively in a complex society and cope with its problems. Education within the problem solving concept has a role of helping a student to learn *how* to learn so that he can continue to learn independently and can evaluate his own achievements without domination of teachers or other school personnel. Within such a setting, the

223

schools need no longer look at the task of education as ending with high school or even with a college education. Instead, education becomes a continuous life process.

The educational program of the subject centered academic school was primarily committed to cognitive learning centering around memorization, organization, and systematizing of knowledge; it relied upon the student's ability to regurgitate this knowledge upon command. The philosophy attending the subject centered school was founded on the concepts of essentialism, authoritarianism, and materialism, and it insisted that there was a fixed curriculum content that all students must learn and retain. Evaluation within such a narrow framework was intended as a tool to determine how effectively each student had mastered the uniform content to a minimum degree. Those who had succeeded were promoted and those who failed to reach the anticipated standard would not pass onto the next grade.

For all purposes, as the numbers grew in American schools and the record-keeping multiplied, evaluation became the grading and classifying of students. It became a design to find those students who were constantly failing so that they could be eliminated, and the schools would no longer have to grapple with them or be bothered with their attendance and constant annoyance because these same students were often troublemakers who saw educational programs as relatively meaningless and uninteresting. Evaluation used in this way is limited.

Evaluation in Problem Solving

Instead of the negative use in the prevalent subject centered curriculum, evaluation has a much broader and far more useful place in education where it can serve a number of sound purposes:

1. As a method for acquiring and processing evidence needed to improve a student's learning and a teacher's facilitator role;
2. To aid in clarifying the significant goals and objectives of education and the processes which will be used in determining student development in the most effective ways;
3. As an ongoing system of quality control so that each step of the teaching–learning process can be viewed for progress and shortcomings and changes can be made before it is too late and students are eliminated;
4. As a tool in the educational practices to assess alternative procedures for achieving the set of educational ends originally projected by the problem solving group.

If — as in problem solving — the primary role of education is to produce changed behavior in every learner and to help him become increasingly proficient in the process of self-learning, then evaluation can largely determine the effectiveness of the behavioral change and the student's ability to work independently of teacher domination — planning his own educational endeavors, pursuing them systematically, and evaluating the consequences of his work. Important to this system of education is the formulation of educational goals and objectives. The teaching team is primarily responsible for thinking through possible goals and objectives which the group might pursue. Rather than finalize the goals they have selected, the teachers then involve students through cooperative planning.

In arriving at goals and objectives, teachers and curriculum workers are confronted with two types of decisions: what is possible and what is desirable. Research and experimentation in problem solving situations is somewhat limited; therefore, what is possible is primarily realized through the limited experiences of some people who have taught or administered a problem solving curriculum. But, much of what they achieved was done within the narrow setting of a subject centered atmosphere. Teachers and curriculum workers must lift their vision and look to broader and higher horizons in terms of what is possible in problem solving. The concept of what is desirable is even more baffling to the average curriculum worker and the average teacher because the possibilities — hinted in the Chapter 6 models — have not been fully realized in the majority of our schools.

Therefore, continuous research and experimentation are needed to determine both what is possible and what is desirable. Some of the possibilities are discernible in the taxomony of educational objectives by Bloom and Masia which cover cognitive and affective domains. A careful examination of these two fields will reveal that they have a much broader and more desirable potential than is actually being achieved in the schools.

The cognitive domain as envisioned in the taxomony of educational objectives covers a broad spectrum of educational achievements — far beyond the ones selected for schools having subject centered curriculums. In addition to the more elementary cognitive objectives, the problem solving curriculum emphasizes the importance of the higher levels of learning: the ability to make applications, analyze, generalize, synthesize, and evaluate. It further stresses the affective domain by its sensitivity to the fact that how a student *feels* about a situation may have a great deal more to do with how he behaves in a situation than what he knows about the situation, even though he is able to carry through at the higher levels of the cognitive domain. Most educators are coming to realize that what is

225

possible in education should be based upon the unique needs and characteristics of boys and girls as well as upon a teacher's style, ability, experience, and personality. Teachers do differ with respect to their respective capabilities — especially in their degree of self-confidence about particular objectives. But it is those teachers willing to work diligently at their tasks who can learn to implement new ways for improving their quality of teaching and, in turn, help students to improve their quality of learning. A teacher, once convinced of student needs and strengthened by necessary motivation, training, and experience *can* perform effectively in the cognitive and affective domains within a problem solving setting.

Another source which schools must utilize in determining educational objectives is the existing society and the kinds of demands which it makes upon students. Every individual who has studied the social order is aware that our society is changing very rapidly and that new advances in science and technology are constantly making existing information obsolete frequently before it even appears in printed form. The nature of careers is largely affected by this accelerated change, and any team of teachers unmindful of these kinds of demands facing their students will most likely plan educational objectives and experiences inappropriate for them. Changes in social structures, at government levels, in communications and transportation, through industrial development, and in international relations should have impact upon the kinds of objectives the schools are striving to achieve. Teachers must work as social scientists in selecting the more useful objectives to satisfy student needs, teacher capabilities, and social demands.

Teachers must also be sensitive to the special problems which students have had in relation to previous learning situations. Problem solving is a nongraded concept of education and an individualized concept of learning; therefore the unique needs, interests, capabilities, aspirations, and limitations of each student must be carefully evaluated. Then the desired objectives can be formulated, achieved, and discussed. As teachers and students go through the problem solving experiences, the former must perceive ways in which their students can move ahead and progress amid sound learning situations. Uniform learnings cannot be expected of students who are uniquely different in the ways they have been created and developed. Evaluation is the tool by which teachers can discover the needs with which students are confronted at each stage of the learning experience.

A principle task confronting teachers and schools in the future will be deciding insofar as it is possible, how students need to change and what

226

part the classroom can play in effecting the change. A subsequent task will be the evaluation of whether or not the students have actually changed in the desired way, what kinds of unanticipated outcomes were achieved, and which anticipated ones were not.

Evaluating the Total Student

While the process of evaluation in problem solving is complicated, demanding, and difficult of both teachers and pupils, it is also a far more rewarding experience for each. Learning what is manifested by modified behavior in the higher cognitive domain and in the affective domain is far more difficult to evaluate than simply the lower cognitive learnings primarily measured by pencil-and-paper tests. The problem solving team teacher becomes a creator of a learning environment, and the role has been beautifully described by Marie Rasey:

> The teacher, as she assumes the creator role, ceases to be an imparter of knowledge, if, indeed, she ever succeeded in doing it. Function becomes that of a stage manager, a scene shifter. She moves circumstances a little nearer, or lights an obscure corner. She does not try to put knowledge into him. She tries to lead him into areas which are rich and experience-laden. She trusts him to create his own knowing. She is not so much concerned with his habits as with his habitat, that state of nature in which a specie is at home. She does not attempt to feed him. She undertakes to make reasonable and highly inviting the ever-widening area of his awareness so that he can go in and out and find pasture.[1]

In this kind of learning, the evaluative process is vital; if the process is done well both teachers and students will be in a position to understand what the developed skills and outcomes mean to the group and its individual members, right from the beginning when goals and objectives are first discussed and shaped to the final stages when what was achieved is evaluated against what was projected.

Evaluation, then, is a continuous process affected by what each student does every day — particularly the decisions or choices he makes. The extent to which these decisions turn out to be correct for a student is primarily dependent upon how well teachers and students set class goals to enable the group's members to make projects and experiences learning ones. In this sense evaluation assumes some starting point (the original goals and objectives selected by the group) from which measurements can progress and some knowledge of direction in order to achieve success. Under these circumstances it is certainly more difficult to determine where students

[1] Marie Rasey, "Creativity and Its Psychological Implications," *Educational Leadership*, vol. 13 (February 1956) , p. 288.

are at a given point in time in relation to behavior, skills, knowledge, or attitudes; yet it is central to the problem solving learning experience that the stated goals and objectives be evaluated — if anything more than subject mastery is desired.

There are numerous techniques by which teachers and students can discover the starting point or the base line from which progress is to be measured. For example, there exist the familiar standardized and teacher-made achievement tests to determine the amount of skills each student has mastered. Other tests can help evaluate student work skills, human relations, critical thinking, social sensitivity, attitudes, appreciation, values, interests, and ideas. Teachers can learn much about individual students from school records. Students can add qualitative detail to these records; they might, for example, describe their behavior in a given situation or explain what they like most to do in their free time. They might also furnish evidence of their relationships with other people which can be put into their individual files.

Techniques, like a socigram or a social-distance scale, provide data about relationships among class members. Analyses of written work in terms of ideas, originality, expression, and mechanics can be placed in the files for later comparison. Samples of daily work can offer progressive clues to student progress and needs. Tape recordings of both individual and group sessions can indicate verbal skills and thinking processes.

Possibly the most useful information will come from student self-inventory and self-evaluation because they, above all, are keenly aware of their own strengths and weaknesses. They might help develop a checklist built around group and individual goals, filling them out as the group progresses. The students are quite proficient in determining what they can do well and what they do poorly; the point is that they need to self-evaluate regularly and progressively so that they become accustomed to reflecting on their ideas and actions. Group sessions — detailed in previous chapters — can bring out individual capabilities and potentialities, particularly if a student finds out these things himself or hears them verbalized by another group member. Then, what he knows can become *meaningful*.

Each of these techniques should be used with the firm understanding that its main value is to find some viable basis for evaluating each student's progress and achievements. No evaluative technique, however, will prove useful unless the team of teachers has developed good rapport with the students. Since students can be easily suspect of adult motives in a classroom situation and since no one will freely express himself until he is sure he can in confidence and without fear of ridicule, the most effective learning takes place when students have an actual participating role in setting goals, formulating ways and means for achieving them, and evaluating how many were in fact met.

Evaluation has to do with gathering evidence of growth: charts, profiles, records, and biographies. The degree to which some goals — reading, spelling, writing — are reached can be measured through skills tests. But evaluation is used here in a much broader sense, implying the discovery of personal meaning in the learning situation and in reflecting upon it. It has bearing upon what a student is doing, what he is thinking, how he feels, how he believes certain people react to him and his ideas, what other people say they think of him, and how they feel toward him. Such information comes from many sources: open forums, group sessions, committee discussions, and general social interaction during which ideas, opinions, and attitudes are either validated or discarded. It is not always possible to assess immediately the results of a learning experience; sometimes results are deferred for an extended period of time. Whether evaluation is immediate or deferred, it must not work to lessen a student's self-perception or make him feel less acceptable to others. If this happens, then something is wrong with the experience and with the criteria used to judge the experience. Effective evaluation — that which is useful to the group and its members — helps a student improve his self-image and concept of adequacy or can-ness. Without trying to tear him down, it will also show him ways in which he can improve.

Self-evaluation can be useful *only* if students can also see themselves as successful in some aspects of the work. No individual is willing to admit to inadequacy, even though he knows it exists. The risks are too great. Using the measurement of subjects as accomplishment leaves students in this position.

In problem solving students are free to evaluate all that they have tried to do — provided they participated in the defining of goals and objectives. If the preplanning was done cooperatively by teachers and students, they would have had the opportunity. As they continually appraise their own progress, students can look candidly at successes and failures. Questions like these can help them examine the step-by-step procedures they elected to take as well as analyze various roadblocks they encountered:

1. How might work have been improved on the project now underway?
2. Why has this unit of work not gone as well as planned or expected?

229

3. What could each participant have done to make the study more satisfying and rewarding for all the group members?
4. In what ways could the teaching team have worked more effectively with individuals, small groups, and large groups in helping students to iron out problems?
5. What could be done better the next time or throughout the remainder of solving the present problem?
6. What were the major obstacles in terms of achieving goals?
7. How would the group have to change its way of working in order to overcome these obstacles?

The student needs to keep the *total* problem solving process in mind as he evaluates. Its steps are briefly reviewed here:
1. Defining the problem and identifying its subproblems;
2. Selecting information with the intention of projecting particular hypotheses from the data, eventually narrowing it down to those most valid in the eyes of the group;
3. Collecting additional information and researching the feasibility of projected hypotheses with the understanding that if some fail to be valid in the opinion of the group, then other hypotheses must be sought and tested;
4. Drawing conclusions and generalizations relative to the applications of the problem and applying a solution to eliminate or at least minimize it;
5. Emphasizing learning outcomes which have been accomplished;
6. Evaluating not only the outcomes of the problem, but the processes through which they have moved.

While step 6 involves mostly evaluation, the other five draw heavily upon evaluative techniques. It is evident that evaluation is a key part of the total learning process and should not be separated from the other parts.

Abandoning the Obsolete

If the evaluative concept based on grading, marketing, and reporting — used in the past when a relatively small percentage of students would continue past the sixth, seventh, or eighth grades — is too narrow, why does it persist into the present day? Problems with this traditional system have certainly not gone unnoticed in the past. Educational literature abounds with criticisms of the system and countless attempts have been made to modify it. The A-B-C-D-F marking system is not quite as absurd as the percentage grade method used in the earlier part of this century. By no means have proponents of the percentage system, though, disappeared from the educational scene; there remain many who consider themselves able to distinguish within one percentage point the level of achievement of a given student at a particular time. Still, the percentage system has been largely replaced with the A-B-C-D-F system which is in wide use today. Some teachers, schools, and even school systems have tried to narrow the grade range from five letters to two — satisfactory and unsatisfactory — only to find that the latter fails to recognize outstanding student accomplishments as perceived by the teacher. To correct this a third letter is sometimes added: E for excellence. Still other educators have tried to modify the grade system in the hope of overcoming inadequacies by identifying a large array of behavioral, personality, and interaction comments. Under this adjustment, however, the resulting comments tend towards paragraphs rather than simple sentences and seem out of line with the abrupt letter grade. The end result of modifying attempts has been a great deal of lingering dissatisfaction on the part of student, teachers, administrators, and parents and more literature on why the system is inadequate, unclear, unfair, and unhumane.

Meanwhile, back at the school, the system remains in control. There are a number of reasons for its appeal:

1. Most people favor that which they already know over what they do not, and the human animal resists change in any form because it brings on a painful process as energy is expended to move from a state of inertia to one of action. Innovation is one thing, they reason, and change quite another. The system of letter grades is firmly entrenched in a large number of schools; it is exceedingly difficult to move forward in any unified manner towards breaking the inertia. As an added complication, the system is associated in people's minds with units of work which count toward high school graduation and college entrance at a later date.

2. People who have been successful in the present system of grading have an interest in seeing it continue. Administrators and teachers often feel relatively secure with it and they are supported, in turn, by leading citizens who serve on school boards and who grew used to the grading systems through their own educational experiences. Such persons look skeptically upon change.

3. Many people have the feeling that a simple letter grade provides a precise and concrete answer to what is being achieved — as though one pronouncement could report the complex learning process. It is by no means perfect, these people argue, but it is something.

231

4. Colleges and universities have come to rely on a prospective student's high school grading record as a key source in determining his qualifications for higher education. The fact that a student's grades may by no means reflect his learning experiences tends to disturb them, but — in the interest of time and numbers — the grades are a handy index.

5. Although many teachers harbor anxieties about the responsibility of marking accurately, they too resist change. Those who do aspire to change the system to one that is more accurate and helpful an evaluation of student progress are handicapped by administrative red tape and general human resistance to anything new.

6. Giving and receiving grades somehow is highly emotional and causes much anxiety, but evaluating individual student needs and progress in explicit terms is even worse. Teachers — like all human beings — work hard to avoid uncomfortable emotional aspects. They prefer, instead, the status-quo security of arbitrary letter grades which are perhaps protested but not challenged.

7. Even though they may have reservations about the system, school people in general have never been able to agree on a replacement; the lack of agreement has encouraged the system's widespread use. With the system entrenched, the argument is always advanced that change would upset a commonly used operation.

Each of these rationalizations opts for what is familiar and comfortable to the users rather than faces up to the much more central task of enabling students to learn. It is, on the whole, education by numbers and apathy.

Although change is hard to effect, innovative enterprises flourish. Great claims are continually being made about new patterns of school organization, unique teaching techniques, and radically different curriculum patterns. But such fads are weak in evaluation. A careful examination of curriculum projects reported in the past decade indicates that evaluation is possibly their weakest link.

Problem solving does not suffer from that weakness. A problem solving curriculum forces teachers and school systems to take a closer look at evaluation as a primary means for formulating and stating objectives in terms of changed behavior in the learner. In subject centered classrooms, teachers are still testing to find out what information they have taught to their students when they should be attempting to evaluate *what their students have learned to do*. But problem solving learning situations emphasize the latter. The concept does not mistake evaluation and measurement as one and the same. While it is true that evaluation depends upon measurement for facts, the process is much more comprehensive than measurement alone. Evaluation is concerned with the *quality* of data supplied by measurement, the adequacy and worthwhileness of behavioral changes, and the efficiency with which they can be implemented. In other words, changed behavior is not sufficient unless the change is toward desired goals. A youth may learn how to pick safes in order to steal the contents of a safe, but rarely would a teacher reward him with a high grade for this achievement.

Accenting Behavioral Goals

Problem solving–team teaching views evaluation in terms of student behavioral goals or objectives. It is impossible to determine what progress one is making or when he will arrive *unless* he knows where he is going. The evaluation pursued by each team or individual teacher should be closely related to the overall evaluation of the total educational enterprise in that particular school. It is only when the work done by one teacher is closely related to that done by another that real impact is felt by the student. Otherwise, few behavioral changes are likely to take place. Students should be encouraged to evaluate their own progress in light of original goals or objectives.

If curriculum and evaluation are to steadily improve, school personnel will need to develop competencies in these areas, particularly in treating evaluation more realistically. Frankly, teachers, school administrators, supervisors, and other educational personnel must become more proficient in the educative process before evaluation can be placed in a useful position beyond the records-keeping role. It is possible in a problem solving curriculum to develop a sufficiently pressure-free learning environment in which teams of teachers and groups of learners can experience open communication through self-evaluative and group-evaluative processes. Such a program can produce records and information necessary for the teacher, school, and school system. Hopefully, the teachers and the school would also be free of the tyranny of college entrance requirements in order to concentrate on the teaching–learning process. Just as hopefully, the traditional records-keeping, judgment-making image of the teacher can also disappear, as Fred Wilhelms has argued it should.

> Once more, it may be well to point out that one important purpose of the elaborate structure of evaluation . . . is simply to get the record-producing function "off the teacher's back." We believe that the instant that is achieved a teacher's energies can go directly to his true functions.

The world of the teacher and the world of the learner are intimately intermingled. In our proposal we are struggling to help that joint world take on a new character. Breaking the old shackles of test–measure–and–judge, we hope to open up genuine communication. We want to see teachers and learners planning together, testing together, deciding on next needs together. We want them able to talk about themselves as persons, with all their hopes and doubts and frustrations and aspirations. We want them able to explore possibilities, relish successes, evaluate failures together, and decide how to move on.

. . . The key to hard, constructive work, to throwing oneself boldly at the barely possible, lies in mutual understanding and acceptance of needs and purposes. It is *not* mere nice-Nellyism to estimate that a classroom, freed of the old loading of judgment-making, can become the kind of place where learners can mobilize their energies because they believe in their purposes.[2]

Dr. Wilhelms and his committee insist that they have gathered sufficient information to show that less time can be spent on simple records-keeping and that required time would be less than the clock-hours currently devoted to testing, grading, and records-keeping in most schools, particularly after teachers learn how to do the job.

But, if the slavish devotion to records could be corrected through reorganization and streamlining, the problem of the subject centered school remains. Curriculums within this traditional school are still founded upon mastery of content and evaluation under this orientation is a one-dimensional process. If goals of a course happen to focus on developing specific skills — such as shorthand or typing — then it is no problem to discover through a performance test whether or not students have achieved desired speed and accuracy. However, if the goal is mastery of a body of facts, a pencil-and-paper or achievement test is hardly an evaluation.

Fortunately, within a problem solving curriculum, subject mastery is not the focus. Concern is with the *total* development of the student — particularly development in his attitudes and understandings. They are likewise interested in his development as an individual and a social person. In the subject centered environment too much time is spent on covering the material to spend time on a student's personal and social traits or affective domain. Besides, it is much simpler to discover achievement in skills or areas of knowledge within a standardized scale than it is to evaluate all-around development. For every hour devoted in our schools to evaluation of the social and civic development of students within a subject centered curriculum, many more are given to examinations based upon subject-matter mastery.

---

[2] Fred T. Wilhelms, *Evaluation as Feedback and Guide.* Washington, D.C.: Association for Supervision and Curriculum Development, 1967, pp. 236-7.

In schools stressing a problem solving curriculum teachers are compelled to attempt this broader and more difficult kind of evaluation. They must set their goals to the challenging tasks of helping students achieve a more desirable social and vocational adjustment through guidance and they must look to developing well-rounded individuals through integrated learning experiences and group processes built upon democratic attitudes and actions. Under such circumstances, a teacher cannot avoid the implications of the goals he and the students have set out to evaluate. Since new purposes require fresh evaluative techniques, the problem solving team teacher is challenged by the nature of his assignment to develop procedures for the evaluation of changed behavior.

Good problem solving teachers cannot help but evaluate total learning because the impulse to seek improvement is an integral part of the ongoing work. But there are other motives. An experimental program usually is expected to justify itself in contrast with whatever program has preceded it in the school. The competent and experienced teacher will characteristically work hard to make the program succeed. Of course when expectations for a new program express themselves in a negative fashion and perhaps even result in a divided faculty, the program is in trouble.

Sources to be Explored

Evaluation has not always been done skillfully by educators, possibly because the process takes a form of self-analysis often uncomfortable. Consequently, the techniques for measuring the goals of problem solving classes — even in the skilled hands of experts — are still far from perfect. Problem solving teaching teams do not neglect conventional kinds of data found in school files, particularly scores from intelligence, aptitude, and achievement tests; grades; health records; listings of school activities; and even work records if the student has ever held a part-time job. These records are useful as means for knowing more about each individual at the beginning of a semester and for checking progress in some of the commonly accepted scales. For example, reading scores can be used as an index of academic progress in many problem solving programs. Teachers are likely to be interested in the use of individual test data as one means of evaluating student progress. Care must be exercised, however, that the testing program does not shift from the comprehensive goals of evaluating the individual's *complete* growth to the narrower one of providing an evaluation or measurement of only one part of the school program. If this happens, what is called problem solving is really much of the old subject centered curriculum.

Since problem solving team teachers generally get better results from their program than do other teachers the situation could become divisive because comparison can create hostility within the school staff unless the problem solving program and evaluative processes are psychologically owned by *all* the teachers. When all members of the staff begin to think of the problem solving program as theirs — even though they might not have actual classes of their own — it is then possible to control research based upon compassion without developing petty jealousy.

Another kind of caution is in order: Achievement tests may be useful as base line data about an individual, but it should be remembered that they yield limited data representing subject matter goals. The teacher should think in terms of new goals and methods, particularly in the evaluative area. It is especially essential that problem solving classes have leeway in selecting what methods are appropriate in a given situation. With such an emphasis, teachers are not too concerned per se with sequential detail mastery of subjects like American history, mathematics, literature, or science. Experience has demonstrated that, over a two- or three-year period, members of a problem solving curriculum are likely to learn even more in such fields than do those who are pursuing subject matter separately. But it is just as true that, at any given test point, the understanding and skills measured in achievement batteries in a problem solving class may not be as evident as in the case where subject matter has been emphasized. It would be both unwise and unfair to test the outcomes of the problem solving method by measuring it against the subject matter approach.

In a school system using problem solving, an extensive developmental record of each student in this kind of curriculum should be kept and passed on from kindergarten through the twelfth grade. Some of these books — often 30 or 40 pages — have space for semiannual posting of anecdotal information collected by the team teachers. The information contained in these records is so valuable that problem solving teachers must themselves learn how to develop them intelligently. The books are objective records of single instances or a closely related series of instances revealing characteristic behavior of each student — essentially, his story. Judgment or interpretation should be left to the reader of the records. Good anecdotal records in a problem solving situation will incorporate a number of valid criteria as a basis for development and use. Above all, the good record is specific, factual, and descriptive.

Problem solving team teachers can skillfully use the records in the evaluative process. The ratio of students to teacher in a problem solving class is much less than the traditional teaching load of five or six different

236

classes per day. The reduction in numbers reduces the record-keeping load as well. It is further desirable that the program have the same group of students for two or more years; at the end of the time, teachers are able to summarize many of the records for the next team.

Since evaluation in the problem solving process is broader and more an integral ongoing part of the program, many materials other than official and unofficial school records have value in assessing student needs and progress. Significant data can be drawn from the judgments of the students themselves and of those who coexist with them inside and outside of the classroom. The data is important when a program's purpose deals with change in human behavior as it does in problem solving studies. Two basic questions which evaluation procedures in problem solving are designed to answer are:

1. How are its students developing into more confident persons?
2. Are they changing their patterns of individual and group relationships in positive ways?

The students' own judgments and observations can shed light on these questions.

School files should contain samples of student work in art, music, and other areas as another resource. Autobiographies written at various stages of student development are kept also on file because they often reveal inside interests. Examples of creative writing are valuable. Responses by students to open-end questions aid the students in their own self-analyses. Most anything which can shed light on how students feel and how they are progressing in the school can help.

A problem solving team teacher's judgment also play a key role in the overall evaluation. It is his responsibility to place material regularly in the files, and his observations must approach objectivity as far as possible. He will add data from socigrams, social-distance scales, and other interaction instruments which have been used in the classroom at various intervals. Much significant information about individual students can come from these group interactions. It is possible, for example, to trace through these records how individual status within a group developed and changed, how a student's roles as leader and then as follower developed, and how the student is able to resolve conflict or changed social status. Problem solving teachers often add to the files a record of interviews held with the student himself and with his parents. Where personality adjustment tests or interest inventories are made, their results are also filed. Questionnaire results about study habits, hobbies, or jobs add further information along with student attendance records and participation in community and extra-curricular activities.

A third kind of information important to evaluation and the team teachers involves some measurement of how far each class group — large and small — has progressed toward the stated goals. There should be in the record some group judgments about what progress has or has not been made, and they can easily be culled from discussion sessions by the teaching team. Questions like these could be asked:

1. What have been the best features of our working together?
2. In what ways do you feel that you have benefited personally from studying this particular problem?
3. In what ways have we as a group perhaps become more efficient and unified?
4. Have we failed to achieve some objectives set earlier?
5. Do you feel the group has accomplished its major purposes?
6. How could we improve our ways of working together if we were beginning all over?
7. To what extent have the members of the group improved in cooperativeness, courtesy, enthusiasm, and responsibility-sharing?

A group must work hard at developing group evaluative judgment — a basic part of the group process. As it does, group members become skillful in the important business of reaching true consensus. Such discipline during the evaluative process helps to effect changes in the learners' behavior.

There are evaluative resources outside of the school. Parents, for example, can contribute information about their child or youth. The experienced teacher of a problem solving unit tries to keep a two-way communication between the school and the home. Many supplement the conventional marking card with letters giving meaningful and realistic personal insights into the students' achievements. Lack of stenographic help might be overcome by help from one of the shorthand classes. Such letters, however, should not degenerate into cliches or facile generalizations; they require real work. Here the team arrangement is especially useful. In a team of, say, three teachers, one can handle the letters while the other two can move ahead with the student groups and activities. Once the letters have been finished, the writer can join the team again. Some schools, limited in time but wishing to establish rapport with parents, have developed checklists covering specific items, supplemented by notations of group achievements and difficulties.

The most helpful of reporting devices in school–home relations — the personal conference between teacher and parent — is being used increasingly in elementary schools and in some high schools. Under the plan, students are released early that day so that conferences can take place, giving teachers and parents time to explore together the problem solving concept and program in terms of the total environmental pattern of the school and home. This kind of evaluation, though, is meaningful, particularly when the parent has participated in meetings, forums, and events stemming from the problem solving curriculum at his child's school.

This chapter has suggested some evaluative techniques for recording and reporting individual and group progress in problem solving classes. The drive to discover even more effective evaluative methods must continue. The educator — and particularly teacher — is directed to a 1969 Association for Supervision and Curriculum Development publication on improving problem solving teaching, learning, and evaluation. The publication, available from the Association, is a valuable index to techniques and devices.[3] In addition to many of the suggestions made in this chapter, the inventory has numerous attitude scales dealing with creative potentialities in the evaluative approach: interaction processes forming an integral part of an ongoing evaluation, rating scales presently in use, interest inventory scales of wide application and usage, various approaches to motivation relevant to evaluative progress, personal value inventory, measurements for readiness achievement, personality rating scales, approaches for determining the self-concepts of students as an evaluative aid, and student self-exploratory techniques.

Missing Links: Feelings and Emotions

The problem solving concept was shaped in part from perceptual psychology which takes into account in the education process the true affective domain of learning and which emphasizes helping people to *trust* their feelings and emotions instead of fearing them. Daniel Prescott in *Emotions and Educative Process,* published over 35 years ago, researched clearly these feelings and emotions which play so critical a part in the learner's progress and how — when ignored — they tend to block learning.

Feelings and emotions, in fact, are the primary determinants of what learning will eventually take place. Many research studies since Prescott's have supported his findings on the importance of feelings and emotions as an integral part of the total educative process. Carl Rogers, Abraham

---

[3] Wilcott H. Beatty, ed., *Improving Educational Assessment and an Inventory of Measures of Affective Behavior.* Washington, D.C.: Association for Supervision and Curriculum Development, 1969.

Maslov, Arthur Combs, and Earl Kelley in their respective writings have pointed out this centrality of the affective domain. In *Perceiving, Behaving, Becoming* they jointly argued the view. Others have contributed to and generally reinforced the concept — for example, Paul Young in *Motivation and Emotions* and Magda Arnold in *Emotions and Personality*. These writers have consistently pointed out the fact that when emotions and feelings are isolated from the total organismic structure, affective learning cannot take place in the classroom or anywhere else. In order for learning to take place, they have insisted, the teacher must be accepting of children and youths as well as understanding and open or transparent in his relationships with them. Somehow, in the American classroom, that point has been largely missed, even distorted to the narrow concern of fostering the intellectual behavior of children.

Problem solving emphasizes the importance of developing the self-concept as a means of motivating effective learning, and the affective domain is central in this emphasis. A self-image develops from the time an individual starts reflecting upon the things around him until he grows into a mature adult. Problem solving learning emphasizes that if an individual is to be loved, he must come to see himself as a lovable person in the view of others. It further points up the fact that if children and youths live with encouragement, they learn to be confident. If they live with tolerance, they learn to be patient. If they live with praise, they learn to be appreciative. If they live with acceptance, they learn to love. If they live with approval, they learn to like themselves. If they live with recognition, they learn that it is good to have a goal. If they live with sharing, they learn about generosity. If they learn to live with honesty and fairness, they learn what truth and justice are. If they learn to live with security, they learn to have faith. If they live with friendliness, they learn to live with some of us and also learn that the world, given problems, is a relatively decent place in which to live. These concepts engendered in problem solving learning situations fully incorporate the affective along with the lower and higher parts of the cognitive domain. Teachers and administrators must be continuously alert to *how individuals perceive themselves in the world because it is through this perception that students learn to behave — keeping the behavior consistent with the perception.*

Problem solving learning stresses another key part of the self-concept which grows along with perceiving oneself. Not only does an individual express appraisal of what he is like, but he is also perceiving what he could or should be like. If he has an excellent model in the form of father, mother, or teacher, then he will probably try to model his life after such an individual. This concept of self helps the individual to become adequate because he is learning to perceive what he should be and how he can achieve this goal. The perceived self and the concept of adequacy make up this self-concept. The way an individual sees himself and the way he thinks he should be in order to be adequate become one and the same eventually. When they combine, they provide the source of motivation for becoming what the individual perceives he should be. Because he has an awareness of the discrepancies between the perceived self and his picture of adequacy, he starts formulating goals to decrease the gap. He tries to realize these goals in whatever situation he encounters by taking action in the direction of the goals. His actions evoke responses from others, and the individual must then evaluate the meaning of these responses. If he evaluates these responses as consistent with the way he views himself, he can feel more adequate. Consistent responses like these enable him to become more like the concept of adequacy that he has perceived and the resulting behavioral change is *true learning*.

Essentially, a problem solving learning environment offers organization centers around which the concept of self and adequacy can develop through ample opportunities for breaking down the nature of self as it is concerned with the functioning organism. Although any number of organizational centers are possible, four centers around which the perceptual self and adequacy are most frequently and consistently clustered are mentioned here. Number one is an *opinion of worth* stemming from the experience of love, of being included, and of being accorded some priority. As children and youths realize that mother and father are loving as well as supervising individuals and as they are included by the parents in certain priorities, the young people, in turn, are realizing how they can further enhance their own feelings of worth through behavior more consistent with the behavior of parent or other idols whom they have learned to appreciate and love. As children and youths interact with parents and other individuals, they learn ways by which they can secure more love, be included in more things, and, in turn, receive more priorities. If the discrepancies are great, the indivdual may even become jealous of others and strive even harder for attention. The end result can be detrimental if an individual feels that — in order to secure added love, attention, and priorities — he must become obedient and conforming to the wishes of those from whom he is seeking love. This situation tends to curb creativity in the person and to limit the amount of originality that he is capable of exemplifying.

The second characteristic frequently exemplified in problem solving is the concept of *coping* — the ability to do something and the learning how to do it. For example, in building a picture of himself as a coping person, a youth would usually select a model from father, mother, sibling, or some other person — primarily someone who is capable in coping. The school, of course, works at the task of helping an individual become more proficient in doing things or in coping because this is the avenue of learning. As in the opinion-of-worth concept, trying to cope can lead to a detrimental effect. Everything, after all, has its risks. If the models or authorities tend to reward good behavior and withhold reward for bad behavior, the two areas can become confused in an individual's mind — causing him to develop a dependence on what others wish him to do. The school consistently makes this sort of mistake through the weapons of grades and standardized evaluation; these things can contribute to the confusion of worth and of coping, making it exceedingly hard for a student to strive continuously for advancement in order to improve his own worth. Advancement on these terms is made at high psychic cost.

The third approach through which problem solving learning helps a student to achieve self and a feeling of adequacy is through the avenue of *expression*. Every organism is so constructed that it must experience an effective tone. The tone can be pleasant or unpleasant. Much of the schools' efforts in the past dealing with expressive areas like music, art, or writing has had little to do with helping the student to express himself more effectively. Stereotyped, stale programs have too often destroyed the arts in the minds of children, even though they are avenues by which an individual can express himself. The student who cannot submit to the experience of literature, music, or painting in a fluid and vital sense has missed something in his development. Traditionally, the schools — and the homes in many instances — have guarded jealously against the idea of permitting students to express their feelings and emotions in any realistic way. They have made it appear that these expressions were undesirable and therefore best avoided.

A fourth organizational area in which problem solving can contribute to the student's concepts of self and adequacy is autonomy, a feeling stemming from the other three areas of worth, coping, and expression. He must be provided this opportunity for self-governance at each stage of his development. A feeling of autonomy encourages an individual to discover alternatives which might bring him greater feelings of satisfaction. He can, in turn, become more autonomous, more capable of making choices and of controlling his own future. Experimental situations giving him

242

independence and responsibilities in problem solving promote the process leading to autonomy.

Unlike the teacher-as-dominant-figure and fact-cluttered subject centered curriculum, problem solving aims mainly toward helping a student to mature. The mature person is one who feels worthy without having to defend his actions. He feels confident that he can cope with a situation he is likely to face; he can express himself, experience satisfaction, stay relatively free of tension anxiety, and feel that every situation provides genuine choices through which he can affect his own future. Such a person is not forced to discriminate between his perceived self and his adequate self because his own progress will decrease the gap between what can be and what is. Motivation for self-enhancement can then turn toward the things which will help him develop and function as a maturing individual.

The individual in a problem solving curriculum has more of a chance to be interested rather than be bored because he is dealing with relevant data and situations which are not inconsistent with the term of self-concept.

In this setting, how teachers view their students and how students see their own development become important factors, and both must seek answers through the evaluative avenue. The search is continuous throughout the problem solving experiences — from the earliest team–pupil planning, during projects and discussions, and to the final teacher–student and student self-evaluative sessions. It is sewn through the problem solving fabric rather than attached to an end. Solving the problem is only part of the learning experience for both teachers and students. Evaluating what they actually did, how goals and objectives were achieved, and what things they might have done differently or better is the other part. It is not unexpected amid such a learning environment of inquiry that the student learns as much about himself as about the problem. Such outcomes, seldom possible in the traditional school setting, argue for the possibilities of problem solving–team teaching.

BIBLIOGRAPHY

Ames, Gillespie and Streff, *Stop School Failure*. New York: Harper and Row, 1972.

Beatty, Walcott H. ed., *Improving Educational Assessment and an Inventory of Measures of Affective Behavior*. Washington, D.C.: Association for Supervision and Curriculum Development, 1969.

Blood, William and Donald Budd, *Educational Measurement and Evaluation*. Evanston: Harper and Row, 1972.

Bloom, Hasting and Madans, *Handbook on Formative and Summative Evaluation of Student Learning*. Washington, D.C.: Association for Supervision and Curriculum Development, 1969.

Combs, Arthur W., ed., *Perceiving, Behaving, Becoming*. Washington, D.C.: Association for Supervision and Curriculum Development, 1962.

Erickson, Carlton and David Curl, *Fundamentals of Teaching with Audiovisual Technology*. Riverside, N.J.: The Macmillan Company, 1972.

Inlow, Gail M., *The Emergent in Curriculum*. New York: John Wiley and Sons, 1973.

Neagley, Ross L. and N. Dean Evans, *Handbook for Effective Curriculum Development*. Englewood Cliffs, N.J.: Prentice-Hall, 1967.

Nora, Gertrude, *Individualized Instruction*. New York: John Wiley and Sons, 1972.

Popham, W. James, *Evaluating Instruction*. Englewood Cliffs, N.J.: Prentice-Hall, 1973.

Rosenthal, Robert and Paul B. Jacobson, "Teacher Expectations for the Disadvantaged," *Scientific American* 218: 19-23.

Rubin, Louis J., *Facts and Feelings in the Classroom*. New York: Walker and Company, 1972.

Segal, Rebecca, *A Motivation Program for Education*. Philadelphia: The Westminster Press, 1972.

Science Research Associates, Inc., *To Know is Basic, To Care is Important, To Serve is Vital*. Chicago: S.R.A., Inc. (IBM) , 1973.

Waskin, Yvonne and Louise Parrish, *Teacher-Pupil Planning*. New York: Pitman Publishing Corporation, 1967.

Wilhelms, Fred, ed., *Evaluation as Feedback and Guide*. Washington, D.C.: Association for Supervision and Curriculum Development, 1967.

Young, Paul, *Motivation and Emotions*. New York: John Wiley and Sons, 1961.

Afterword

Education is like the sitting duck, and a critic has to work hard to miss such a large target. Indeed, it has become commonplace at the lecture platform for critics inside and outside of education to string together a rhetorical litany cataloging the ills of education: its insensitivity to human needs, its neglect of minority interests, its drain on the taxpayers' sensitive pocketbooks, its neglect of its own professional personnel, its creation and nurturing of a monster known as the public school, and onward. Characteristically it ends on a troublesome note: what can be done?

In the case of the American School, the author maintains that criticism of a stale, mediocre curriculum is a valid criticism. It is hard to remember that beneath the public school's layers of administrative reports, dusty files, formal requests for this and that, wall-to-wall records, handy curriculum guides, staff gatherings, committee deliberations, and other bureaucratic activities that *there are students*. Although it has long been the rhetorical custom for educators and noneducators alike to proclaim that school exists for the education of students, in practice and in reality the student is a forgotten figure placed somewhere inside the school — generally assigned lessons, hopefully not giving trouble, and traditionally "being educated" as though the process involved the simple feeding of facts and ideas from the authoritarian figure at the front of the room to the class. Within this risky framework, there has always been a sort of wistful thinking that the student would also "learn." In any case, if he lasted it out, he would get a diploma as a sort of consolation prize.

But, while the school had graduated or dropped out its problem — i.e., the student — the student, now graduate, went out into the world and found that the subject centered curriculum he had endured for 12 years had little to do with the real world, and he had to begin another education course forged out of the far tougher tools of experience to learn how to cope with life situations.

This book has been concerned with how to replace the traditional subject centered curriculum in the American public schools with a more meaningful and relevant experience for its students. It has proposed as a new direction a curriculum based upon problem solving—team teaching. Since there is no single answer for any given problem, problem solving inquiry is offered here as an alternative to traditional public school education.

Change is an elusive process. Human beings do not easily surrender the ways they have done things in the past or the attitudes they have held. It is much easier to implement an innovative pilot program, struggle for a while, end it, write it up as mixed blessings, and resume what was being done before. This pattern is sadly proving true in the 70's as the great upheaval of the 60's is grinding down and tight budgets are dictating arbitrary cuts. *Real change,* though, is necessary if learning is to become the public school's focus and if the learner is to have an environment in which to seek and find. The chapters in this book have attempted to explain how the concept of problem solving can actually be implemented to help students develop into maturing individuals who will be able to cope with complex and frustrating life situations.

Innovation is just as much a sitting duck as education, and it is easy to dismiss a new way or direction without really examining its strengths and weaknesses. It would be easy to dismiss problem solving in a superficial flourish as simply warmed-over progressive education, a term which carries a bad connotation of kids running wild in a classroom. But problem solving, while it has many of the characteristics used in progressive education, does not make the same mistake which its forerunner did: that of opting out for what would make the child "happy," mistaking such catering for a healthy basis from which learning could take place. Clearly, in the case of progressive education, in many cases it did not.

It is also easy to insist that all teachers and other personnel should like problem solving–team teaching. Many educators would feel uncomfortable in a problem setting situation. In many cases they would feel threatened. They should remain in the setting they prefer.

It is easy, too, to advance the argument that, since a problem solving–team teaching curriculum is very demanding in terms of time, energy, and intelligence, the concept is not appropriate for the large numbers of students in our public school system.

But the last argument would say that students cannot learn for themselves and, therefore, need to be spoonfed by the subject centered method. No one would deny that a problem solving learning environment is a demanding one for everyone involved. Its practitioners work hard and need a wide range of skills and tools. The teaching role is one of facilitating or enabling rather than acting as an authoritarian voice from the front of the room. Teachers must establish good working rapport with their students and they must operate skillfully in both individual and group situations. Students must be active right from the initial planning stages to the final evaluative ones — making decisions, taking part in activities, researching, working within the framework of large and small groups, and seeing through their own individualized projects.

But in the case of problem solving, the rewards are worth the demands because our children will have the opportunity to learn for themselves under the skilled supervision of a teaching team which has been specially trained for inquiry learning experiences. What can be done in a good problem solving learning situation is often astounding — particularly in terms of inventiveness, time, and energy. Dr. Wayne Jennings, director of the St. Paul (Minn.) Open School and author of Chapter 9 of this book, has described the origin of an ecology project dealing with air pollution in the industrial area around the school.

Six students attending Joe Nathan's ecology class, noting that "It smells around here," decided to attempt to find out why and what might be done about it. In the process of their inquiry they covered traditional subject matter disciplines of political science and government, speech, sociology, science, law, and math (the comparative measurement of smell).

In a walk around the neighborhood, the class determined that the worst polluters were a paper manufacturer, a vinegar company, and a meat packing company. With this information they went to a college student-financed consumer action organization for guidance. The organization suggested research into anti-pollution laws and even suggested a lawyer to aid them in any action they might want to take.

From the start, the students had tried to talk with the firms, but repeated attempts had resulted in being put off for various reasons and finally they were told, "Don't call us, we'll call you." Clearly, they were being brushed off.

In December, the group filed complaints with the St. Paul Pollution Control Agency (PCA). Little happened.

The class then decided to circulate petitions against the offending firms. Besides the school community, the class canvassed businesses and homes in the area affected by the odors. They learned why many small businessmen feared to support such a move openly (i.e., the barber who said the paper company executives would stop getting their hair cut there if he signed . . .).

The students also testified at state hearings on guidelines for air pollution control in the state of Minnesota.

In January the PCA told the class that there was not sufficient money to do studies on the firms which were the main polluters. In early February, the class decided to tell a local newspaper reporter what it had learned and done. PCA then told the reporter that it *was* doing the studies. As a result, the three firms and a fourth were ordered to submit implementation plans for curtailing the odors.

Compare the ecology class and its actions with how the same subject of environmental protection would have been handled within the subject centered curriculum. The difference between the two situations is the reason for implementing a problem solving curriculum in many of the American public schools.

247